Futurethoughts

Futurethoughts

critical histories
of philosophy

edited by PETER OSBORNE

Published in 2024 by
CRMEP Books
Centre for Research in Modern European Philosophy
Penrhyn Road campus, Kingston University,
Kingston upon Thames, KT1 2EE, London, UK
www.kingston.ac.uk/crmep

ISBN 978-1-7391451-8-7 (pbk)
ISBN 978-1-7391451-9-4 (ebook)

Designed and typeset in Calluna by illuminati, Grosmont
Cover design by Lucy Morton at illuminati
Printed by Short Run Press Ltd (Exeter)

A catalogue record for this book is
available from the British Library

Contents

CRMEP Books

CRMEP Books is the imprint of the Centre for Research in Modern European Philosophy, Kingston University London. It currently publishes two series of open access electronic publications derived from research events organized by the Centre, which are also available in short-run paperback editions.

SERIES EDITOR Peter Osborne, Director, Centre for Research in Modern European Philosophy, Kingston University London

Books

VOLUME 1 *Capitalism: Concept, Idea, Image – Aspects of Marx's Capital Today*, ed. Peter Osborne, Éric Alliez and Eric-John Russell, 2019

VOLUME 2 *Thinking Art: Materialisms, Labours, Forms*, ed. Peter Osborne, 2020

VOLUME 3 *Vocations of the Political: Mario Tronti & Max Weber*, ed. Howard Caygill, 2021

VOLUME 4 *Afterlives: Transcendentals, Universals, Others*, ed. Peter Osborne, 2022

VOLUME 5 *Institution: Critical Histories of Law*, ed. Cooper Francis & Daniel Gottlieb, 2023

VOLUME 6 *Futurethoughts: Critical Histories of Philosophy*, ed. Peter Osborne, 2024

Pamphlets

The Gillian Rose Memorial Lectures
Generously supported by the Tom Vaswani Family Education Trust

PAMPHLET 1 Rebecca Comay, *Deadlines (literally)*, 2020

PAMPHLET 2 Donatella di Cesare, *It's Time for Philosophy to Return to the City*, 2022

PAMPHLET 3 Rowan Williams, *Solidarity: Necessary Fiction or Metaphysical Given?*, 2023

PAMPHLET 4 Samir Gandesha, *Identity Politics: Dialectics of Liberation or Paradox of Empowerment?*, 2024

www.kingston.ac.uk/crmep

Preface

PETER OSBORNE

It is commonplace to note that, unlike analytical philosophy,
modern European or so-called 'continental' philosophy operates
with a conception of philosophy as a practice that is in large
part constituted through its ongoing relations to its own history.
That is to say, post-Kantian philosophy in its Euro-American
or 'continental' trajectory is not only historical-philosophically
contextualist in its self-understanding of problems and concepts,
but it understands such reflexively incorporated contexts as
constitutive of philosophy itself – transformatively so – in a
strong and not merely secondary sense.

It is less commonplace, however, to include in this thought not
only broader, 'non-philosophical' social contexts (colonialism and
industrial capitalism), but also the disciplinary and other institutional mediations through which such contexts are categorially
filtered, as forms of knowledge, on their way to encountering
philosophical reflection. In this respect, philosophical thought
is both 'vertically' and 'horizontally' historical: vertically, in its
relations to past thought from the standpoint of a particular set
of expectations and hopes about the future (afterthoughts are
futurethoughts); horizontally, in its transversal relations to other

academic disciplines and forms of knowledge, through which philosophy acquires its 'food' for thought.

Reflection on this fact draws attention to philosophy as a transdisciplinary as well as a historical practice. From this standpoint the idea of a *critical* history of philosophy expands to include not only immanently philosophical characteristics – which makes all such history a political history of self-criticisms – but also philosophy's engagements at and beyond its own disciplinary limits.[1] These engagements initially primarily took place, in nineteenth-century European philosophy, in a serial and overlapping manner, via the relations of philosophy to *anthropology, political economy* and *sociology*, in turn.

The writings in this collection – organized according to the institutional genres of the presentations within CRMEP from which they derive – revisit some of these encounters of philosophy with its constitutive boundaries, expanding the trio of anthropology–economy–sociology to include, crucially, psychoanalysis: the critical, meta-theoretical counterpart to a liberal psychology that is increasingly being replaced by neurosciences that are at once technologically empiricist and narratively speculative.

The first section, introduced by Éric Alliez and Orazio Irrera (one of the editors of the series of Foucault's early lectures courses currently appearing in French), contains translated excerpts from Foucault's recently published 1954–55 lecture course, *La Question Anthropologique*, which were used as the basis for the workshops run by Éric Alliez at the Centre in November 2023. In his serial encounters with Hegel, Feuerbach, Marx, Heidegger and Nietzsche – in the shadow of the thought of Jean Hyppolite – the young Foucault came to see the line drawn between philosophy and non-philosophy, and the investigation

---

1. See Stella Sandford, 'What is Critical History of Philosophy?', forthcoming in *The Southern Journal of Philosophy*, special issue *On the History of Philosophy*.

of the latter by the former, as the place of philosophy itself. To accompany these excerpts, we present a translation of Foucault's obituary of Jean Hyppolite, in which Foucault summarizes the formative role played for his generation by Hyppolite's teaching and writings.

Part two presents recent public lectures by Stella Sandford and Howard Caygill. Sandford's on Lévi-Strauss's 'wild thought' inverts the young Foucault's approach and takes up the philosophy–anthropology relation from within anthropology itself, in structural anthropology's relations to the philosophical side of psychoanalysis. Caygill returns emergent environmentalist imaginaries of catastrophic climate change to the immediate post-war context of the imagination of nuclear annihilation. Each philosophizes out of the supposedly 'non-philosophical'.

Part three, 'Outtakes', presents essays by four CRMEP PhD candidates or recent alumni, derived from their doctoral research, which bear on the theme of the current volume. Daniel Gottlieb and Anna Argirò address issues about the temporal structure of historical experience to be found in the writings of Reinhart Koselleck and Hannah Arendt, respectively: Koselleck's ambiguous affirmation of historical multiplicity and Arendt's insistence on the novelty of the beginning immanent to the transmission of tradition. Morteza Samanpour and Louis Hartnoll take up historical issues that remain central to Critical Theory: how to incorporate, at a systematic theoretical level, the historical processes of colonialism into the categorial structure of Marx's mature critique of political economy; and how, precisely, to construe Adorno's nuanced dialectical critique of sociological categories, which performs a mutual 'philosophical critique of sociology' and 'sociological critique of philosophy', suspending each in the negativity of its relations to the other.

The final section presents the contributions to a CRMEP-convened panel marking the thirtieth anniversary of Jacques

Derrida's *Archive Fever*, a text that addresses historical experience and psychoanalysis together, through the concept of the archive, as a dense, tense historical-political drama, which continues to play itself out, in all of its contradictions, today. The question of the archive is the question of the future, Derrida argued. Afterthoughts are futurethoughts, we might say.

Acknowledgements

Stella Sandford's public lecture was delivered at the Swedish Psychoanalytical Association, Stockholm, 5 April 2024, as part of that week's programme of the CRMEP–Södertörn–Aarhus PhD Workshops collaboration. We would like to thank the Swedish Psychoanalytical Association for their hospitality. Howard Caygill's lecture was part of the CRMEP public lecture series at the Zaha Hadid Foundation (ZHF), Clerkenwell, London, 9 February 2023. We are grateful to Jane Pavitt, Head of Research and Learning at the foundation, for hosting that series. ZHF was also the venue for the panel 'Derrida's *Archive Fever* – 30 Years On', 15 February 2024, which forms the final section of this volume. Again, we thank Jane Pavitt for making that possible, and for the hospitality offered to us by the ZHF.

Piles of money for the few
Absolutely nothing for anyone else

WORKSHOPS

FOUCAULT AND THE QUESTION
OF ANTHROPOLOGY, 1954–55

INTRODUCTION

Foucault's *pas de deux* with Jean Hyppolite

ÉRIC ALLIEZ & ORAZIO IRRERA

The year is 1954. Michel Foucault delivers the lectures at the École Normale recently published as *La question anthropologique*, excerpts from which are translated below.[1] Foucault is no longer following in the wake of his ex-supervisor, Jean Hyppolite's Hegelian thought with its tensed 'relationship between *Phenomenology* and *Logic* ... between ontology and anthropology', as he had in his dissertation five years earlier.[2] Rather, with a Kantian bias, Foucault now turns to Alexandre Kojève's anthropological perspective on Hegel's *Phenomenology*, basing himself on a Feuerbachian reading of Hegel which draws on the 'philosophical meaning' *(sens philosophique)* of Marxism, 'precisely as a liquidation of that philosophy which was that of the entire bourgeoisie, at once humanism and anthropology'.[3] The unsurpassable tension between the transcendental logic of the conditions of possibility of knowledge and the movement of historicization, detected in

---

1. Michel Foucault, *La question anthropologique. Cours 1954–1955*, EHESS–Gallimard–Seuil, Paris, 2022. The passages translated in this section, below, were used as the basis for the Research Workshops run by Éric Alliez for PhD students at CRMEP, 22–24 November 2023.
2. Jean Hyppolite, *Logic and Existence*, trans. Leonard Lawlor and Amit Sen, SUNY Press, New York, 1997 (1953), p. 189. Michel Foucault, *La constitution d'un transcendantal historique dans la Phénoménologie de l'esprit de Hegel. Mémoire du diplôme d'études supérieures de philosophie*, Vrin, Paris, 2024 (1949).
3. Foucault, *La question anthropologique*, p. 119.

the *Phenomenology of Spirit*, is recoded here by the Kantian question 'What is Man?' (*Was ist der Mensch?*). The anthropological question concerning the empirical analysis of man's *finitude*, and therefore of human *nature*, thus began to take shape for Foucault, within Hyppolite's terms of 'Genesis and Structure', many years before it became the subject of his supplementary thesis, defended in May 1961, introducing his French translation of Kant's *Anthropology from the Pragmatic Point of View*.[4]

Foucault's treatment of the anthropological question was based on Heidegger's phenomenological interpretation of Kant in order to both re- and decentralize anthropology's relationship to Kant's *Critique* by affirming it as 'at once essential' and 'inessential'.[5] At the same time, Heidegger's Nietzsche of the 'completion of metaphysics' was nonetheless refused and rejected.[6] Far from being inscribed in metaphysics as its final exponent, Nietzsche is rather read as the *liquidator of* anthropology and humanism, announcing the 'death of man', in the famous phrase from *The Order of Things*, the prelude to which was none other than the commentary on Kantian anthropology. This was duly noted by Foucault's thesis jury in the person of its chairman, Henri Gouhier: 'His master is more Nietzsche than Heidegger... Criticism falls into anthropology and Nietzsche pulls it out.'[7] The very last line of Foucault's *Introduction to Kant's Anthropology* reads: 'The trajectory of the question *Was ist der Mensch?* in the field of

---

4. Michel Foucault, *Introduction to Kant's Anthropology*, trans. Roberto Nigro and Kate Briggs, Semiotext(e), Los Angeles CA, 2008.
5. Ibid., p. 120. The French translation of Heidegger's 1929 *Kant and the Problem of Metaphysics*, which aimed to place Kantian philosophy within the horizon of a 'fundamental ontology', posited as the truth of the Copernican revolution, was published in 1953. Martin Heidegger, *Kant et le problème de la métaphysique*, trans. Walter Biemel and Alphonse de Waelhens, Gallimard, Paris, 1953.
6. See the texts by Heidegger quoted by Foucault at the very end of the 1954 course, under the heading 'Nietzsche's Philosophy as Completion' in the last section devoted to the interpretation of Heidegger. *La question anthropologique*, p. 212.
7. Didier Eribon, *Michel Foucault*, Champs-Flammarion, Paris, 2011, p. 188.

philosophy reaches its end in the response which both challenges and disarms it: *der Übermensch*.[8]

Nevertheless, in 1954 Kantian anthropology did not yet have for Foucault, as it did in 1961, the function of ensuring the transition between the questions raised by the three *Critiques* ('What can I know?', 'What must I do?', 'What is there to hope for?') and those of human finitude marked by the 'relationship of freedom and truth'.[9] On the contrary, 'despite the text of the *Logic* on Anthropology', which refers to these same three questions, anthropology in Kant occupied a marginal place, 'until, for Feuerbach, [anthropology] became the original dimension of philosophical experience'.[10] Kant's anthropology is rather the reason for another transition, that between the philosophy of the Enlightenment and the nineteenth-century reflection on man that took place in Feuerbach and, before him, in Hegel.[11]

Foucault's analysis of Hegel in *The Question of Anthropology* focuses on the 'two anthropologies' of the *Encyclopaedia of Philosophical Sciences*: that of the first subsection of Subjective Spirit, titled 'Anthropology', and that of Subjective Spirit as a whole, which includes, in addition to 'Anthropology' itself, the two subsections devoted to 'Phenomenology' and 'Psychology'. More precisely, by focusing on the transition from soul to consciousness, from the immediate sensation of self to the habit of being oneself, the aim is to show the movement through which we go beyond abstract reflection on the forms of understanding and the *a priori* conditions of knowledge to grasp the concrete

8. Foucault, *Introduction to Kant's Anthropology*, p. 124. Foucault's statement in his interview with G. Barbedette and A. Scala comes to mind: 'I began by reading Hegel, then Marx, and I began to read Heidegger in 1951 or 1952; and in 1953 or 1952, I don't remember, I read Nietzsche. I still have here the notes I took on Heidegger when I was reading him ... and they are far more important than those I took on Hegel or Marx. My entire philosophical development was determined by my reading of Heidegger. But I recognize that Nietzsche won out.' 'Le retour de la morale' (1984), in Michel Foucault, *Dits et écrits*, Volume IV: *1980–1988*, Gallimard, Paris, 1994, p. 703.
9. Foucault, *Introduction to Kant's Anthropology*, p. 106.
10. Foucault, *La question anthropologique*, p. 55.
11. Ibid.

character of the self and of nature. This amounts *to doing away with criticism by giving it a foundation in man himself.* This makes Hegel the first anthropologist *philosophos.*

Bending the reading of Hegel in the direction of an *anthropological becoming of critique* consisted in 'accomplishing and founding, on the basis of a philosophy of nature, the subjectivity of the subject in what is most immediately natural – in order to surpass it in the objective spirit of morality and law, and then in the free spirit'.[12] In the economy of the course, this return to Hegelian anthropology plays a dual role: as a redefinition of the relationship between freedom and man's sensible nature, which transcendental philosophy had failed to articulate; and as the announcement of Feuerbachian anthropology, centred on the essence of being – on the essence of the human being, of man as a sentient being, or of man joined to nature, but reluctant to accept the mediation of absolute knowledge in which the mind manages to recognize both its freedom and its necessity.

The issues at stake in this anthropological reading of Hegel proposed by Foucault must, however, be seen in a broader context marked by the work of Hyppolite and Jules Vuillemin. Vuillemin, in *L'Héritage kantien et la révolution copernicienne*, published in 1954, had from the outset identified the Hegelian critique of the freedom/nature-sensibility antinomy (already pointed out by Hyppolite) dividing Kant's thought and his transcendental philosophy as what made it possible to discover, beneath the supposed unity of the latter, 'a real duality' that Kant had tried to conceal:

> By making the object revolve around the subject instead of the subject revolving around the object, [transcendental philosophy] found a way to make the transition from certainty to truth, from the I to the World, and thus seemed to complete the efforts that thought had accumulated since Descartes in favour of subjectivity.[13]

---

12. Ibid., pp. 69–70.
13. Jules Vuillemin, *L'Héritage kantien et la révolution copernicienne. Fichte, Cohen, Heidegger*, PUF, Paris, 1954, p. 1.

What Hegel had pointed out, namely that nature (and, above all, human nature) obeys its own laws, which are opposed to the laws that freedom autonomously gives itself, independently of and in opposition to man's sensitive nature, marked the whole difficulty of transcendental philosophy. Hence the Kantian effort to conceal or resolve it by a whole series of conceptual shifts from one to the other in a 'moral vision of the world' centred on the postulates of *practical reason*, which, according to Vuillemin, accompanied the anthropological drifts of post-Kantianism in Fichte, Cohen and Heidegger. This was exactly what was at stake in Foucault's anthropological question, which, refusing to seek the foundation of anthropology in the universal structures of consciousness, made him choose another path: an anthropological reading of Hegel, which addressed the sensible concreteness of human existence and life.

It is the role that Vuillemin gives to Hegel at the beginning of his book which marks the point of departure for Foucault. For Hegel, this was to lead to the recognition of man by man, neutralizing the opposition of master and slave by introducing mediation into the relationship and turning it into 'a spiritual relationship'. It was in this way that in a collection of articles between 1936 and 1952, published together in 1955 in the volume *Studies on Hegel and Marx,* Hyppolite emphasized the ambition of Hegel's philosophy, 'which aims to be *a thought of human life* [*une pensée de la vie humaine*]'.[14] With this problematic of 'human life' a dialogue was established with the humanist philosophy of the young Marx, who had read and commented on Feuerbach, before posing anew the historical question of alienation and the concrete essence of man. We can understand why, beyond the

---

14. Jean Hyppolite, *Studies on Marx and Hegel,* trans. John O'Neill, Heinemann, London, 1969, p. 4. Published in 1938, this first article, 'The Concept of Life and Consciousness of Life in Hegel's Jena Philosophy', concludes with the dialectic of master and slave: 'The consciousness that comes to know fear and enforced service in this way moves from the state of immediacy to a mediated condition which is the foundation of a spiritual relationship' (p. 17).

very brief analysis devoted to Hegelian anthropology (a mere two pages!), it was with Feuerbach that anthropology 'became the original dimension of philosophical experience'.[15] In addition to the important article by Vuillemin published in 1952, on which he relies,[16] Foucault is dependent on Althusser, who was soon engaged in translating Feuerbach's manuscripts.

Feuerbachian anthropology is presented as one of the 'return paths of Hegelianism', with the resumption of the theme of sensible certainty which Feuerbach, in his reading of Hegel, displaces from the plane of the spirit and the concept to that of the essence of a human nature. This naturalist radicalization of anthropology assigns to the human essence the status of an *originary*: the human essence as an ahistorical origin situated before all history, but to which we must return in order to realize it by suppressing history, the latter being only 'an exile in which [this essence of Man] is alienated'.[17] Alienated in religion, where it appears as separate from man and projected in the image of divine omnipotence, the critique had to take the form of a fundamental atheism supposed to eliminate the alienation of the human essence. Conceived à la Hegel as a movement of exteriorization (*Entäusserung*) of the Idea, or à la Feuerbach as the projection of the human essence outside its origin in the guise of a divinity alien to it, alienation is always thought in relation to an *ideal* origin and not in its *real* instance, in the immanence of history and a given society.

This is why Marx was the first to make a real break with the anthropologism of Hegel and Feuerbach, since 'it is from history that Marx will demand an account of alienation'[18] to discover that alienation is the fact of labour that annihilates the producer

15. Foucault, *La question anthropologique*, p. 55.
16. J. Vuillemin, 'La signification de l'humanisme athée chez Feuerbach et l'idée de nature', in Jean Wahl, ed., *Le Diurne et le nocturne, dans la nature, dans l'art, et dans l'acte*, Éditions de la Baconnière, Neuchâtel, 1952, pp. 11–46.
17. Foucault, *La question anthropologique*, p. 70.
18. Ibid., p. 115.

in the object produced. This itself refers to the 'real and immediate condition of man's life' in the social organization of capitalism: 'not ... ideal interiorization, but ... real exteriorization'.[19]
Here Foucault confronts the Hyppolitian theme of 'human life'
and the set of relations that socially and materially determine
alienation. It was in these terms that Hyppolite posed the
question of the opposition between Hegelian philosophy and
'human reality' in the young Marx, and, by the same token,
placed it in the context of a 'phenomenological philosophy [that]
ends up renouncing philosophy itself – as a rigorous science –
[and] becomes an anthropology, a humanism'.[20] According to
Hyppolite, this is what would influence the young Marx's efforts
to 'make the Hegelian Idea pass into the reality of things' and
to transform speculative idealism into a philosophy of action
capable of eliminating real alienation, thus reconciling philosophy and life 'in the human subject' through the consciousness
(la prise de conscience) of the proletariat.[21]

So humanism can only take the form of anthropology. The
crucial point, then, is that Foucault opposes this anthropological
and humanist Marxism with *another Marxism*, one that breaks
completely with the one that serves Hyppolite's demonstration.
It is a Marxism that aims to undo Marx's *constitutive and failing*
relationship to Hegel put forward by Hyppolite, translating
Hegel's *Phenomenology* 'after Marx' (dressed up as a 'beautiful
soul', *une belle âme*).[22] For Foucault, this 'serious' Marxism is the
key to contesting and overturning the 'humanist' confidence
in a young Marx, philosopher, still far away from the scientistic
pretensions of *Capital*, in order to adopt a perspective which,

19. Ibid., p. 118.
20. Jean Hyppolite, 'Marx and Philosophy' (1946), in *Studies on Marx and Hegel*, p. 95;
'On the Logic of Hegel', in ibid., p. 175.
21. Hyppolite, 'Marx and Philosophy', pp. 93, 124.
22. Cf. Jean Hyppolite, 'Alienation and Objectification: Commentary on G. Lukacs' *The
Young Hegel*' (1951), in *Studies on Marx and Hegel*, pp. 70–92. We know the fate of this
'beautiful soul' in Deleuze's *Difference and Repetition*, a 'beautiful soul' avoided by Marx
and Nietzsche.

at the same time, defeats the primacy of subjectivity or of any human essence, and puts man back into his social and historical determinations.

However, the fact remains that this anti-humanist path, deeply nourished by exchanges with Althusser, was still far from having the status it would acquire with the publication of *Pour Marx* and *Lire le Capital* in 1965, immediately preceding Foucault's *Les Mots et les choses* the following year. Antihumanism, Foucault explained in 1966, had become 'a political work, in so far as all the regimes of the East and West pass off their bad merchandise under the flag of humanism'.[23]

In the 1954 course, the decisive break with humanist anthropology was made less with Marx, and with Marx of maturity, as in Althusser, than with Nietzsche. It was to be Nietzsche's thought that would bifurcate the philosophical postulate of antihumanism in 'the discovery that man and truth belong to each other only in the form of freedom'.[24] Or, to put it another way, in a more critical mode: 'the truth of man is liberated with truth itself' on 'the line of flight [*la ligne de fuite*] of the philosophical path that proposes to liberate man *and* truth; that is to say, to liberate both truth from its human determinations and freedom from the objective forms of truth.'[25]

Thus, the anthropological critique that had engaged Hegel's philosophy right up to (and beyond) Marx would be re-engaged by a subsequent radicalization of the dissociation between man's freedom and the truth of his nature (or essence). The Dionysian philosopher will become 'the extreme risk taken by philosophy' in 'repeated contact with non-philosophy' which, in Foucault's

---

23. Michel Foucault, 'Entretien avec Madeleine Chapsal', *La Quinzaine littéraire*, May 1966, in *Dits et écrits*, Volume I: *1954–1975*, Gallimard, Paris, 1994, pp. 541–6.
24. Foucault, *La question anthropologique*, p. 119.
25. Ibid., p. 176.

words, brought Hyppolite's Hegel 'to the other side of his own limits'.[26]

In the light of a Dionysian nature, neither 'the naturalistic reduction of man nor the foundation of truth in the objective forms of nature' makes sense. The Dionysian is first and foremost a return to nature, and a most courageous return, for 'it means confronting the absolute danger of a truth that dissolves and a freedom that escapes itself', just as 'it means denying nature as natural truth, in the very movement that seeks its truth to rely on a paradoxical instance of denaturalization, opposed to the naturalization of the sciences of objectivity. In this return to nature it is a question of 'going beyond it by placing ourselves at the very limits of its possibility'. This is the most obscure and apparently elusive of the links of philosophical kinship that, through Nietzsche, link Foucault to Bataille, Canguilhem, Deleuze. To return to nature is also to 'free man from the beast', by discovering that it is not freedom that separates man from the beast but an experience *of* madness that pushes existentialism 'to the very limits of its anthropological possibility' in a Dionysian freedom that affirms the *ontological liberation* of the human being that we are. Dionysus' return to nature will constitute what Foucault calls 'the effort towards the truth of nature [which] destroys nature and its truth', an effort that overlaps with 'the divinatory and sacrilegious act of Oedipus: he can only gain access to the truth of nature by walking *against* nature'. We know that this physiological and Dionysian materialism would be challenged by Foucault in his readings of Sophoclean tragedy in the early 1970s, in opposition to the symbolic materialism of Lacan and Althusser.[27]

---

26. Michel Foucault, 'The Order of Discourse' (1970), in Robert Young, ed., *Untying the Text: A Post-Structuralist Reader*, Routledge & Kegan Paul, London, 1981, pp. 48–77; pp. 74–5.
27. Foucault, *La question anthropologique*, pp. 176–8. See also Michel Foucault, *Leçons sur la volonté de savoir. Cours au Collège de France, 1970–71; Le savoir d'Œdipe,*

Nevertheless, Dionysus' return to nature and against nature is also 'a return to the world, a return to the appearance of the world in the light of being, beyond the negation of the truth of the world'. This dissociation between nature and truth, as well as the absence of any foundation, is not a reference to the Heideggerian figure of the oblivion of being, but on the contrary to a joyful and affirmative acceptance of its destruction, since through Dionysus life *eternally* returns from its perpetual apparent dissolution in 'the drift of man' (*la dérive de l'homme*).

If Dionysian laughter makes the philosophical face of humanism wince, it is because it restores to this shattered and adrift man the feeling that he is, as Nietzsche writes in §295 of *Beyond Good and Evil*, 'newer than before, unblocked, penetrated and surprised as if by a thawing wind, perhaps more uncertain, more delicate, more fragile, more broken, but full of hopes that as yet have no name, full of new desires and currents, countercurrents and bad new desires'.[28]

To emerge from humanism through this Dionysian return to nature proposed by Nietzsche means accepting both the dissociation of the subject or of man (through dreams, madness, sexuality, etc.) and the play of his masks. Caught in the middle of these currents and countercurrents driven by the multiplicity of desires, we do not abandon ourselves to the flows, but remain vigilant in the historical and corporeal immanence of Being itself, in its conflicts and violence. This is the specific dimension of the Eternal Return, where laughter *also* repeats the Dionysian courage that restores this man in pieces to the luminous space of his dispersion, where the play of masks and appearances is given, admittedly, on a void that serves as their support, but always in the immanence of language and discourse, where Foucault will

EHESS–Seuil–Gallimard, Paris, 2011, pp. 177–92, 223–51; Foucault, 'La vérité et les formes juridiques' (1973), second lecture, in *Dits et écrits*, vol. II (1970–1975), pp. 553–70.
  28. Foucault, *La question anthropologique*, p. 192, citing Nietzsche.

soon see a 'need for history' that will accompany, in a different way, both his archaeological and his genealogical methods. Indeed, Foucault refuses to ontologize this difference into a becoming without history corresponding to a 'fantastic cosmology of life', at the risk of turning Nietzsche into a 'Bergson in disorder, a Bergson in flagrante delicto of immorality and delirium'.[29] It is not by this 'aesthetic' route, in a sense followed by Deleuze, that Foucault thinks we can break with Hyppolite.

In the gap that perpetually widens in the very actuality of becoming, in the real (wirklich) becoming of the drift of man's masks, a difference always opens up that is not only that between the past and the future, but also that which situates this actuality at a distance from the present itself, where the affirmative courage of the thought deployed by Dionysus joins Being both in its dispersion and in its violent conflictuality. This is what Foucault would soon call the diagnostic instance that, following Nietzsche, would redefine the philosophical enterprise free of any anthropological mortgage.

Foucault's diagnosis of ourselves and our actuality extends from the description of the cultural constraints of the archive and of discourse to the analysis of the 'forces [that] have played and are still playing a part for us being here'. It would constitute one of the crucial operators in the inclusion of archaeology in genealogy. Diagnosis was to be redefined as a gesture 'that bears on the very body of the present' and makes the present the theatre 'of what is there in us in our bodies'.[30] It would be a matter of picking up where Foucault left off in 1954, with his return to the nature of Dionysus, in order to grasp in the fragmented physiology of man and culture the 'multiple origins' that unfold

29. Ibid., pp. 188–9.
30. BNF, Fonds Foucault, reference NAF 28730, Box 65, 'Nietzsche. Cours donné au Centre universitaire expérimental de Vincennes (1969–1970)', to be published under the direction of Orazio Irrera in 2024 in the series Cours et travaux de Michel Foucault avant le Collège de France.

as instincts, valuations and contradictory elements in struggle with one another.

In the famous 1971 text 'Nietzsche, Genealogy, History', Foucault's diagnosis will indicate even more clearly the different use that he makes of Nietzsche in relation to Deleuze. Foucault preferred the genealogist's 'need for history' to the ontology of becoming, of its forces and the diagrams that can reproduce them, by drawing a horizon of intelligibility within which philosophy itself would be forced to lodge if it wanted to 'diagnose the body's illnesses, its states of weakness and energy, its cracks and resist-ances in order to judge what a philosophical discourse is'.[31]

It was through this itinerary, which goes back to 1954 and the reversal of tragedy that the return to the nature of Dionysus made it possible to grasp, that Foucault could return to Hyp-polite's thought in his 1969 homage and argue that his work 'has always been, from the outset, to name and make visible – in a discourse that is both philosophical and historical – the point at which the tragedy of life takes on sense in a *logos*'.[32] For Foucault, this meant breaking with both ontological/anthropological Hegel and a Marxist humanism with phenomenological-existential features. It was thus a Nietzsche who was quite alien to the philosophical sensibilities of his master (including when he wanted to believe that 'Hegel anticipates Nietzsche' in disquali-fying 'humanist reflection' as 'a fall into the "human all-too human"')[33] who provided Foucault with a completely different solution to the problems posed by Hyppolite in terms of 'philo-sophical thought'. For Hyppolite, actuality and the tragedy of life constituted the two elements that both undermined any phil-osophy that sought to close itself off as a system, and delimited

31. Michel Foucault, 'Nietzsche, Genealogy, History', in *Language, Counter-Memory, Practice: Selected Essays and Interviews*, ed. D.F. Bouchard, Cornell University Press, Ithaca NY, 1977, pp. 139–64; pp. 144–5.
32. Michel Foucault, 'Jean Hyppolite, 1907–1968', below, p. 67.
33. Hyppolite, *Logic and Existence*, p. 186.

the area of tension between philosophy and non-philosophy, where the full significance of the sense that must be attributed to the notion of actuality is played out.

It should not be forgotten that since his translation of the *Phenomenology of Spirit*, Hyppolite had been translating the Hegelian *wirklich* as 'actual', so that, as Foucault recalls in his homage, his idea of 'philosophical thought' corresponds to 'that which in any system – however complete it may seem – overflows it, exceeds it and places it in a relationship of both exchange and default with philosophy itself ... [it is] its incompleteness ... that by which, however far it continues, it remains behind compared to philosophy'. By 'philosophical thought', Foucault continues, Hyppolite

> also meant that moment, so difficult to grasp, covered up from the outset, when philosophical discourse makes up its mind, snatches itself from its silence, and distances itself from what from then on will appear as non-philosophy: philosophical thought is then less the obscure and prior determination of a system than the sudden and ceaselessly renewed sharing by which it is established ... this twisting and redoubling, this escape from and re-seizure of itself, by which philosophical discourse says what it is, pronounces its justification, and, moving away from its immediate form, manifests what can found it and set its own limits.[34]

Actuality indicates the moment when philosophy is made (*se fait*), becomes effective and real in its relationship to non-philosophy, which is always both *instituting and destituting*.

For Hyppolite, this same doubling is at the heart of Hegel's philosophy, which marks

> the moment when philosophical discourse has posed for itself, and within itself, the problem of its beginning and its end: the moment when philosophical thought sets itself the inexhaustible task of expressing the total field of non-philosophy, and undertakes to succeed, in all sovereignty, in enunciating its own end... With

---

34. Foucault, 'Jean Hyppolite, 1907–1968', p. 64.

> Hegel, philosophy, which at least since Descartes had an ineffaceable relationship with non-philosophy, became not only aware of this relationship, but the effective discourse of this relationship: the serious implementation of the interplay of philosophy and non-philosophy.[35]

It is thus in more than one sense in the wake of his former master that Foucault poses the question of the relationship of philosophical discourse to its actuality as the movement by which philosophy is incessantly called upon to begin, and begin again, without ever being able to find in its discourse its realization, its effectuation, its fulfilment or its completion. Yet, unlike Hyppolite, Foucault does not raise the question of the actuality of philosophy, or its intrinsic link to non-philosophy, either in relation to Hegel, Marx or science (whether through Fichte or in relation to information theory), or in relation to Bergson or the tension between logic and existence.

It was the thought of Nietzsche which, for Foucault, would constitute the threshold of discontinuity or the 'new mutation' of a philosophical discourse that breaks with 'philosophical finitude' and with its anthropological recovery, but which, in Hyppolite, was still able to appeal to the philosophical humanism of the young Marx, or rediscover in *Capital* the ontological-historical figure of a 'real humanism'. It would thus be up to Nietzsche's Dionysus, whose 'figures' Foucault deploys in his 1954 lecture, to assert the endgame of (post-)Hegelian anthropology by (to use the Deleuzian metaphor) making a monstrous child, with Hyppolite. For, in the end that comes at the beginning, and that makes this 1954 lecture a beginning, it is Nietzsche's Dionysian becoming and his critique of truth that explain Foucault's project against a Hegel *anthropologos*.

TRANSLATED BY ERIC-JOHN RUSSELL

---

35. Ibid., pp. 68–9.

1

Anthropology as the realization of critique: Hegel and Feuerbach

MICHEL FOUCAULT

Framed within this general search 'for the point of departure for critique', we find great 'anthropological advances' which have the meaning, or at least the aim, of going beyond critique by realizing it within an anthropology.[1] In other words, to abolish critique by giving it a foundation in man,[2] himself:

α suppressing it as an abstract reflection, developing in the form of the understanding, on the *a priori* conditions of knowledge.

β finding it in a real discovery of man, in the movement of his free rationality, as:
   — an original and concrete subject of knowledge,
   — a real labourer in the work of objectivity,
   — an effective and living content in the knowledge it takes of the world.

This is the project we find realized:

— in Hegel: to accomplish and found, on the basis of a philosophy of nature, the subjectivity of the subject in its most

---

1. This text is an excerpt from Michel Foucault, *La question anthropologique. Cours 1954–1955*, EHESS–Gallimard–Seuil, Paris, 2022, Part I, C, II and Part II, A and B, pp. 69–70, 83–9.
2. Although it is jarring, we have translated *l'homme* as 'man', in its general sense as humanity, to retain the usage of the day, despite its false universality.

immediately natural form – in order to go beyond it in the
objective spirit of morality and law, and then in the free spirit;
— in Feuerbach: to undertake the truth of man as self-
knowledge/real self-fulfilment. Anthropology realizes critique
in the sense that it recalls the consciousness of man from the
exile in which it is alienated, in order to render it adequate to
its natural existence;
— in Wilhelm Dilthey: to undertake critical thinking as a
historical destiny, that is to say:
  α enclose the limits of knowledge within the horizon of a
     Weltanschauung [world-view];
  β make man announce his own truth on the basis of each of
     the *Weltanschauungen*, and their succession;
  γ finally, to constitute philosophy as a systematics of the
     history of *Weltanschauungen*.

Man will no longer be able to gain access to truth except from
the given concrete face of *Weltanschauungen*; and, conversely,
he will only have access to truth from his truth, in so far as it is
the actual work that projects and carves out the profile of his
Weltanschauung. [...]

A. Hegelian anthropology[3]

There are two anthropologies [in Hegel]: [on the one hand] the
particular section that bears this title and, on the other hand,
the whole movement of subjective spirit.[4]

---

3. Materials from the following section, including citations copied from the 'Anthropology' section of Augusto Vera's French translation of Hegel's *Philosophy of Mind*, can
be found in the Fonds Foucault of the BNF, Box 37, in a folder entitled 'Anthropologie de
Hegel'.
4. Hegel's *Philosophy of Mind* (the third part of the *Encyclopaedia of the Philosophical
Sciences*, following the *Science of Logic* and the *Philosophy of Nature*) comprises three
main sections: 'Subjective Spirit', 'Objective Spirit' and 'Absolute Spirit'. 'Subjective Spirit'
contains within it a separate subsection entitled 'Anthropology' (§§388–422), which is
presented as a study of the soul. G.W.F. Hegel, *Philosophy of Mind*, trans. W. Wallace and
A.V. Miller, Clarendon Press, Oxford, 2007.

In fact: [in] the first section, anthropology designates the immediate and natural form of subjective spirit, but the whole section on subjective spirit is characterized by:

1. the fact that spirit immediately relates to itself (whereas it relates to the world in objective spirit);
2. the fact that its being is to exist with itself, therefore in an immediate freedom that ignores the necessity of *Dasein* [being-there];
3. the fact that it thus develops in its pure ideality, hence in the form of knowledge: knowledge is thus self-determined.

It is precisely these features that characterize this anthropological perspective, which is defined in its unity with critique. And it is in this dialectic of subjective spirit that Hegel realizes, undertakes and surpasses critique.

The particular problems of anthropology in the narrow sense:

1. What is the soul? It is the immediate presence of spirit in nature (see citation[5]). Hence:
— The problem of immateriality does not arise, because:
   α it assumes that spirit is a thing;
   β it forgets that life is already the objective form of suppressed matter.
— The problem of the soul and body does not arise: it would arise if it were a question of the relationship between two particular things; but it is in fact a question of the particular and the universal.
The soul is the immediate universality of the body.
The body, this is the other being.

---

5. See Hegel, *Philosophy of Mind*, p. 29, where Hegel defines the soul as the spirit which 'is the universal immateriality of nature, its simple ideal life. Soul is the *substance*, the absolute foundation of all the particularizing and individualizing of spirit, so that it is in the soul that *spirit* finds all the stuff of its determinations'; translation amended.

Hence the relation of separation and unity between the soul
and body.

The soul can therefore be defined as the awakening of spirit, but
conversely the soul is only possible in so far as spirit is already
awake in nature. *The soul is the awakening of this threshold* [*veille*].
It is the unity and freedom of the morning.

2. This explains the profound unity of the soul with the natural
determinations that seem to identify and imprison it, but where
it is already its first negativity and its first freedom:
— qualities
— alterations
— *Empfindung* [sensation].

3. But this recognized unity allows for the emergence of feeling,
of *Fühlung* as the interiority of sensation:
— dreaming as an immediate form of feeling:
   • its content all taken from the world,
   • but as an immediately subjective form of this world,
   • the world that has become my world.
In this way, the dream can become meaningful. It is the world
expressed in the first person, the *idios kosmos* [world of its own]
of Heraclitus.[6]
— Madness[7] is the moment of fixation of the dream as a subjective moment within the element of objective consciousness.
   Hence the specific dialectic of madness:
   α Alienation from oneself within oneself; silting within the
      interiority of subjectivity; and at the same time attachment
      to natural and immediate being.
   Hence access through body and soul.

6. This is a reference to Heraclitus' aphorism, as cited by Plutarch: 'Heraclitus says that
people awake enjoy one world in common, but of those who are fallen asleep each roams
about in a world of his own.' Plutarch, 'Superstition' (1962), in *Plutarch's Moralia in Fifteen
Volumes*, vol. II, trans. Frank Cole Babbitt, Harvard University Press, Cambridge MA and
London, 2007, p. 463 §166.
7. Again, Foucault is here simply following the outline of Hegel's 'Anthropology'.

β But consciousness retains the external form of objectivity;
there is dissociation between the soul and consciousness:
a splitting of the personality. The objectivity of consciousness works within the subjective content of the soul.
γ The work of rationality as therapeutic.
NB. It is an absolute possibility, like crime in relation to the law.

4. Habit,[8] as *Gewohnheit*, establishes a home for itself in its own
subjectivity:
— without the expression of dreams,
— nor the rupture of madness.

It is the work of consciousness that recognizes itself in the
realm of the soul: it is the unity of sleep and wakefulness, of the
silence of character and the disturbance of madness.[9]

To have habit is, for consciousness, to be at home in one's
soul.

B. The anthropology of Feuerbach

Introduction

For him, as for Hegel, it is a question of 'realizing' critique; that
is to say, of carrying out its content at the level of an anthropology, and thereby of abolishing it as an *a priori* determination of
the forms of knowledge, since anthropology must:

— be precisely a concrete determination;
— develop a broader content of experience than mere knowledge.

For Feuerbach, anthropology is the critical development of the
concrete essence, the *wirkliches Wesen* of man.

---

8. Hegel, *Philosophy of Mind*, §§409–410.
9. 'Habit' is the final determination of the natural and sentient soul, which includes,
by synthesizing them in the calm unity of a 'home', among other things: 'races' (§393
– 'natural qualities'), sleep and wakefulness (§399 – 'natural alterations') and madness
(§408 – 'self-feeling'). Ibid.

But how can the development and exploitation of the concrete domain of a particular essence have the meaning and scope of a critique?

On two conditions:

1. The first is that this essence constitutes the concrete *a priori*, not only of all possible knowledge, but of all real experience. Anthropology must therefore present itself as a return to concrete immediacy, a rediscovery of the most primitive forms in which man inhabits his own truth.

Philosophy must then above all be a prayer for a better way of seeing, for a newer light, loser to the morning: 'What logic is, that I learned at a German University; but what optics is – the art of seeing – that I learned first in a German village' (*Fragments Concerning My Philosophical Development*).[10]

Hence the need to abandon the positions of a speculative philosophy that only finds man's concrete home in the element of absolute knowing.

α Hence the need to overthrow speculative philosophy: 'what is original, first in reality, is what is derived, subordinated in philosophy; and, conversely, what is last in reality is what is first in philosophy' (*Die Unsterblichkeitsfrage vom Standpunkt der Anthropologie*);[11]

β and consequently to abandon Hegelianism, which is 'the *absolute reality* [*Wirklichkeit*] of the idea of philosophy' (*Towards a Critique of Hegel's Philosophy*),[12] in favour of a philosophy that will unite 'what is closest and what is furthest away, the

---

10. Ludwig Feuerbach, '1836–1841, Bruckberg', in *The Fiery Brook: Selected Writings*, Verso, London and New York, 2012, p. 284.

11. Ludwig Feuerbach, 'Die Unsterblichkeitsfrage vom Standpunkt der Anthropologie (1846/1866)', in *Sämtliche Werke*, Volume 1: *Gedanken über Tod und Unsterblichkeit*, frommann-holzboog Verlag, Stuttgart, 1960, pp. 93–162.

12. Feuerbach, 'Towards a Critique of Hegel's Philosophy', in *The Fiery Brook*, p. 56; translation amended.

abstract and the concrete, the speculative and the empirical,
philosophy with *Leben* [life]' (*Letter to Karl Riedel*).[13]
Philosophy will therefore be the end of philosophy, but not for
the Hegelian rationale that it would become absolute knowing,
but for the reason that it is a return to the immediate, a
rediscovery by man of his most familiar homeland: '*No* religion!
– that is my religion; *No* philosophy! – that is my philosophy.'
(*Fragments Concerning My Philosophical Development*)[14]
    For such a philosophy, 'its greatest triumph consists in
the fact that it does not appear to have the character of
philosophy for all those dull and scholastically warped minds
that see the *essence* of philosophy in what is only the *semblance*
[*Schein*] of it.' (*The Essence of Christianity*, 'Preface to the
Second Edition'.)[15]
    Philosophy, as the uncovering [of the] concrete essence of
experience, is therefore philosophical non-being for speculative
philosophy. And yet it is nothing other than the concrete
existence of philosophy.

2. In fact, what is the philosophizing subject of this philosophy?
It is not the Hegelian philosopher, a determined individuality
taken to be absolute (which is why Hegelianism is nothing
other than the attempt to 'restore a lost and defunct Christianity through philosophy' [*Principles of the Philosophy of the
Future*]),[16] but rather humanity in general as it is constantly
embodied in determined individuals. Johann Wolfgang von

---

13. 'That it always connects the high with the apparently common, the most distant
with the closest, the abstract with the concrete, the speculative with the empirical,
philosophy with life.' Ludwig Feuerbach, 'Brief an C. Riedel [1839]', in *Sämtliche Werke*,
Volume 2: *Philosophische Kritiken und Grundsätze*, frommann-holzboog Verlag, Stuttgart,
1959, p. 398.
14. Feuerbach, '1836–1841, Bruckberg', p. 296.
15. Ludwig Feuerbach, 'Preface to the Second Edition of the *Essence of Christianity*', in
The Fiery Brook, p. 254.
16. Ludwig Feuerbach, 'Principles of the Philosophy of the Future', in *The Fiery Brook*,
p. 206.

Goethe (to Friedrich von Schiller): 'only all men taken together live the human'.[17]

And the sign that one is a philosopher is that one is not a professional philosopher, because philosophy is not the business of a specific function, but about the whole essence of man: 'the true philosopher is universal man' (*The Essence of Christianity*, 'Preface to the Second Edition').[18]

But if the philosopher is universal man, any realization of philosophy as the uncovering [of the] concrete essence of experience must, at the same time, be man's realization of his own essence. Or, rather, philosophy as the realization of critique must be nothing other than the expression of critique as the realization of man.

And this is why the new philosophy is linked to the emergence of a new man; it is basically nothing more than the reflexive demand of the new man: 'Anything else is a philosophy that falls into a common epoch with earlier philosophies; anything else is a philosophy that belongs to an entirely new period of humanity; anything else is a philosophy that owes its existence only to a philosophical need (Fichte/Kant); anything else a philosophy that corresponds to a need of humanity; anything else a philosophy that is immediately the history of humanity' (*The Necessity of a Reform of Philosophy*).[19]

So the realization of critique as anthropology has the following conditions:

— that critique unfolds in the domain of the most original and
    immediate experience;

---

17. Cited by Feuerbach in 'Towards a Critique of Hegel's Philosophy', p. 56; translation amended to accord with Foucault's notes and the French translations employed therein.
18. Feuerbach, 'Preface to the Second Edition of the *Essence of Christianity*', p. 262.
19. Ludwig Feuerbach, 'The Necessity of a Reform of Philosophy', in *The Fiery Brook*, p. 145; translation amended to accord with Foucault's notes and the French translations employed therein.

— that anthropology, as an analysis of the concrete essence of man, is only the other side of a critical realization of man by himself.

If this is the meaning of Feuerbach's philosophy, it is not legitimate to look for its essential dimensions in sensualism, naturalism or materialism, which only involve abstract analysis and speculative critique.

TRANSLATED BY ERIC-JOHN RUSSELL

2

Real man and alienated man: Marx

MICHEL FOUCAULT

Introduction[1]

This problem of real and alienated man [opens up] the space
for reflection in which three questions [become] intertwined in
themselves:
— What is the meaning of critique?
— How can man respond to his own essence?
— Should philosophy be the end of philosophy?
Each of these questions – and all of them together – is the very
problem of history, and of action in history:
— What meaning should be given to the wars, conflicts and
  contradictions of our time?
— Under what conditions and through what historical transfor-
  mation can man regain possession of himself (Revolution)?
— What can the historical moment of revolution mean – the end
  of history or the beginning of a new history?
These questions are the same as those asked earlier:

---

1. This text is an excerpt from Michel Foucault, *La question anthropologique. Cours
1954–1955*, EHESS–Gallimard–Seuil, Paris, 2022, Part II, C, pp. 108–19.

α These are not double-sided questions, the philosophical and historical, the ideal and the political.

β These are one and the same question:
— the philosophical meaning of critique is a real contradiction;
— man's philosophical responsibility for his own essence is revolution;
— the [end] of philosophy is the decisive moment in history.

That a philosophical investigation of conceptual meaning has become a real problem of historical development is a radical change in the philosophical horizon, giving new life to a whole new manner of investigation. This is now the problematic horizon of Marxism as a whole:
— at once the general problem of problems,
— but also the problem whose weight can be found in each particular problem.

But there is more. This theme that philosophical investigation is one and the same with a real problem can be said in various ways:
— by adopting Kantian vocabulary: what is the real meaning of critique?
— by adopting Feuerbach's vocabulary: how is man really and concretely responsible for his own essence?
— by adopting Hegel's vocabulary: what is the historical meaning of the end of philosophy?

So the problem of alienated man and real man, whether we take it as a speculative, ideal and anxious investigation of alienated man about himself in the reflective form of philosophy, or whether we take it as a reflection on the discovery of the real meaning of the problems and discovery of the concrete content of philosophical investigation – in either case, we have this tripartition of problems.

And we discover that this investigation is linked to the question of Marxism as philosophy.

I. What is critique?

1. Critique and the critique of man

a. The two meanings we usually give to the word 'critique':
— Moral, political and psychological critique: always based
   on a [postulate] of nature (Christian critique of a fallen
   nature, humanist critique of a forgotten nature). Critique
   is always a path of return, even if the return is promised as
   transfiguration.
— Philosophical critique as the determination of the *a priori*
   conditions of knowledge: that from which nature can be
   thought, that from which we have access to being. Critique is
   then a promise, even if the promise is the metaphysical mirage
   of being.

b. But these two meanings of [critique] were not always as
different as they are for us:
— Kant fancied himself an *Aufklärer* (to unpack the philosophical
   meaning of *Aufklärung*),[2]
— but above all, his work, far from invalidating this superficial
   relationship, only deepened it by turning it on its head when
   he discovered that the question of man was at the root of his
   critique.
As a result, critique takes on a new meaning:
— On the one hand, critique can only be carried out and completed by reflection upon man.
— But, on the other hand, man cannot be taken against the
   background of nature, since nature is called into question by
   critique itself.
It is therefore criticized man who must form the basis of
critique.

---

2. Reference to Kant's essay 'Was ist Aufklärung?' ('What is Enlightenment?'), published
in the *Berlinische Monatsschrift* in December 1784.

Thereafter, for the nineteenth century, a task opens up which is the philosophical path to Marxism: to complete and carry out critique in a critique of man in so far as he is the foundation of critique.

2. The French Revolution and the critique of man

Now this movement, in its abstract formulation, is the very movement of political reform; that is to say, the movement by which

— from a critique of institutions, linked to a critique of morality, we came to define in the city or in the *res publica* the conditions of possibility of virtue, of morality, of equality;

— but [nonetheless] in the liquidation of the Revolution, it was realized that the private man or the property owner is not the citizen. So the completion and fulfilment of the Revolution must begin at the level of a critique of *man*.

It is the criticized man or the renewed man who must be the foundation of the Revolution. This demand [was] born directly out of Thermidorian reaction.[3] See Hegel (article on 'Natural Law', Jena period):[4] the Revolution failed because there aren't only citizens, but also property owners.

Hence all these forms of thought that seek to complete the Revolution in the dual sense of trying to both fulfil and liquidate it.

3. The critique and reform of consciousness

This whole period, which is both the period of philosophical critique and the period of political reaction – one reinforcing

---

3. This formulation refers to the period between the fall of Robespierre (July 1794) and the royalist insurrection repressed by Bonaparte (October 1795). It corresponds to the abandonment of the 'Terror', the establishment of a 'bourgeois republic' and the rejection of revolutionary 'radicalism'.

4. Hegel's essay 'Natural Law' was written in 1802–03 for the *Kritisches Journal der Philosophie*, founded with Friedrich Wilhelm Joseph von Schelling, during the so-called 'Jena period', from 1801 to 1807, when Hegel began his academic career as *Privatdozent* at the University of Jena. Jean Hyppolite, who published an *Introduction to Hegel's Philosophy of History* (Marcel Rivière, Paris, 1948), devotes the fourth chapter of his book to this essay.

the other – culminates in a critical philosophy from which Karl
Marx will draw, in which the themes of the eighteenth century
meet the fundamental features of German philosophy.

a. the theme that there is a concrete, immediate and total
essence of man, as defined by Feuerbach:
— as presence of man in his sensitive unity with the world.
   You don't learn what man is at a German university, but in a
   village;
— as community of the individual with others: man is *Gemeinmensch* [social].[5]
In short, as sensuousness and as love: both as a natural being
and spiritual community.

b. The theme that this concrete existence is concealed by an
abstract essence, the essence that defines man's actual existence:
— as suprasensible essence in religion;
— as individual and egoistic essence in desire.
Hence the supernatural becoming of man and the inhuman
becoming of nature, in religion/desire.

c. Hence the idea that critique must be the critique of religion
and desire, or, rather, of religious consciousness and desiring
consciousness:
α Of the desiring consciousness: that is, forgetting its concrete
   relation to the other in love,
   — on the one hand, [man] alters his own essence;
   — and, on the other hand, instead of fulfilling what is most
      human in nature, he turns it into the most inhuman.

---

5. 'It is also clear from these arguments how grossly Feuerbach is deceiving himself
when (*Wigand's Vierteljahrsschrift*, 1845, Band 2) by virtue of the qualification "common
man" [*Gemeinmensch*] he declares himself a communist, transforms the latter into a
predicate of "Man", and thinks that it is thus possible to change the word "communist",
which in the real world means the follower of a definite revolutionary party, into a mere
category.' Karl Marx and Friedrich Engels, *The German Ideology* (1845), in *Marx and Engels
Collected Works*, vol. 5, Progress Publishers, London, 1975, p. 57.

Feuerbach: male/female relations as a condition of
philosophy.[6]
Marx: the text on man and woman.[7]

β Religious consciousness:
David Friedrich Strauss: *The Life of Jesus* (1835); two theses:
Jesus had no historical reality; he is only a moment in the
development of humanity, which alone is the complete
God.[8]
Feuerbach: 'the essence of nature *differentiated from nature*;
that is, as a human essence, the essence of man *differentiated from man*; *that is*, as non-human essence – this is the
non-human essence – such is the essence of God, and the
essence of religion [...]; such is the miracle of all miracles
(*Lectures on the Essence of Religion*).[9]
Marx: religion is not only the forgetting of man's essence; it is
a way of maintaining this forgetting, a way of maintaining
lost nature.

d. But all this is presented as a critique of the forms of consciousness; that is, a critique characterized by the fact that:
— it is exercised on the basis of what it criticizes: it is by questioning the meaning of religion, etc.;
— it can only be thought of as the liberation of an essence, or a
nature that is already there, not as a construction;

---

6. 'Follow the senses! Where the senses take over, religion and philosophy come to an
end. And you have as a consequence the plain, shining truth... Follow the senses! You
are masculine through and through... But as masculine, you relate yourself essentially,
necessarily, to another "I" or being – to a woman.' Ludwig Feuerbach, '*The Essence of
Christianity* in Relation to *The Ego and Its Own*', in *The Philosophical Forum*, vol. 8, no.
2–4, 1976, pp. 85–6. On the relation of male and female, see pp. 85–7.
7. Marx's work on the basis of the male/female sexual division of labour can be found
in *The German Ideology* (Part 1 'Feuerbach', pp. 42–3). Foucault had copied extracts from
it onto an index card entitled 'Division travail' (Box 37, folio 430).
8. Published in 1835, *Das Leben Jesu* by David Friedrich Strauss presents a Jesus
deprived of all divinity. The scandal caused by the book led to Strauss's dismissal as
philosophy tutor at the Protestant seminary of Tübingen.
9. Ludwig Feuerbach, *Lectures on the Essence of Religion*, trans. Ralph Manheim, Harper
& Row, New York, 1976, pp. 320–21; translation amended to accord with Foucault's notes
and the French translations employed therein.

— it only takes place through a consciousness, as a reform of the understanding, an exercise of consciousness on itself.

This is why critique can be no more than the critique of religion; or, further, it can be said to be anthropology; that is, both the postulate and the claim of an essence of man which, by forgetting itself, can be recalled to its original presence and restored in its natural rights (see Marx's text on critique).[10]

But if critique understood as such is only ever carried out as an operation of consciousness, if, to this extent, it remains as ideal and speculative as the Kantian critique of knowledge, if, finally, it only addresses total and real man in the form of the essence of real and total man, at least it appeals to a notion which, when questioned in its foundation, will ensure that critique sublates itself and constitutes a problem for philosophy.

α The forgetting of essence, its fantastic corruption in religion, its egoistic reification in desire are made possible because human essence is able to:

— project itself outside itself (in imagination, or desire);
— take on an aspect and form where it no longer recognizes itself;
— and thus finally enter into a relationship with itself in which what it is is erased: real man sacrifices himself to God; real man debases himself in sexuality.

β But this movement uncovered by critique goes beyond critique and reveals more than the postulate of critique would allow.

Indeed, critique possesses only the negative concept of the forgetting of self (in the form of Rousseau's forgetting of consciousness, Kantian forgetting of the finitude of knowledge), but does not possess the positive concept of the projection beyond

---

10. On the Marxist critique of religion, there are at least two notes in Foucault's reading files (Box 37, folios 397 and 421), based on *Critique de la philosophie du droit de Hegel* (1927) and *L'Idéologie allemande*, t. II (1932).

the self and the presentation of the self in the unrecognizable, disguised and estranged form of the other.

This movement of alienation unlocks the positive content of critique, or rather discovers that critique was secretly dealing with positive content, which it reflected only in the negative form of finitude, but whose positive and real movement, in the form of alienation, can be brought to light.

Critique becomes positive critique by taking alienation seriously. Alienation is the critical deepening of finitude, the positive meaning of finite consciousness.

But this path to the positive is at the same time a path to the real: for if consciousness can ideally overcome its finitude and thus negate its negation, the movement by which it no longer recognizes itself outside itself is not its own internal movement; it is a more fundamental movement, the movement of real man.

The concept of alienation fulfils critique, transforming it into a critique of real man. But [it] sublates it, and denies it: for only reality can criticize reality, only material forces can struggle against material forces.

This transition from critical movement to the analysis of alienation corresponds to the transition from the struggle of the bourgeoisie for liberties to the struggle of the proletariat for liberation.

II. What is alienation?

This concept of alienation was common in critical thinking, but it has been taken up again and developed further.

1. Alienation in Hegel

It entails:

— The concept of positivity (religion and law): history is alienation, in so far as it is the absolute standpoint of positivity.

— The concept of labour, as the concept of self-realization in matter or in life (the object, bondage). In this sense, all actual production is alienation.

— The illusion of consciousness: mistaking the object for the subject and the subject for the object – when life gives itself as matter or consciousness, it gives itself as life.

— Objectivity (in general): nature in general, etc. The entirety of the *Phenomenology of Spirit* is the odyssey of this: the Idea is objective only in the form of alienation.[11]

But practically, with Hegel:

α   It is the last form of alienation that commands all others: it is because the Idea or consciousness can alienate itself that objectivity is possible, that consciousness deceives itself, that the product of labour escapes its producer, and that finally history carries the weight of positivity.

β   As man's essential and fundamental destiny, alienation can only be overcome if it is grasped as such and enunciated in its truth: this is *Erinnerung* [recollection].

And by *Erinnerung* is meant internalization and recollection; that is to say

— the suppression of objectivity (*Entäusserung* = exteriorization);

— that of history through recollection, repetition.

In the ahistorical repetition of consciousness, objectivity loses its form of exteriority: phenomenology is thus the destiny of spirit overcome.

The interpretations of Henri Lefebvre and Jean Hyppolite point in this direction, and it is essentially this alienation to which Marx's early writings adhere.[12]

---

11. In 1949 Foucault devoted his first philosophy dissertation, under the supervision of Jean Hyppolite, to Hegel and his *Phenomenology of Spirit*, but he focused his analysis on the formulation of a 'historical transcendental'. Michel Foucault, *La constitution d'un transcendantal historique dans la Phénoménologie de l'esprit de Hegel. Mémoire du diplôme d'études supérieures de philosophie*, Vrin, Paris, 2024.

12. It was in Henri Lefebvre's *Le Matérialisme dialectique* (Félix Alcan, Paris, 1939)

2. Alienation in Marx

Marxist reflection is:

— On the one hand, the reversal of the Hegelian movement which finds in the becoming-objective the foundation of historical positivity. It is from history that Marx will demand an account of alienation.

— On the other hand, this reversal is the very dissolution of the notion of alienation, or at least its apparent disappearance.

a. Analysis of the conditions of alienation:

First question: what is alienated?

α It is not history, or the Idea; it is not even the essence of man. See the page 'Real man'[13] (critique against Feuerbach; the English cellar).[14]

β What is alienated is real man. But what does it mean that real man has become alienated from himself, that reality has become alienated from reality? What can alienation mean when it has been deprived of the metaphysical heaven of essence.

Second question: perhaps alienation is not the fact of becoming a stranger to oneself [?]

b. Alienation is the obscuring of economic relations, the constitution of a determinism over which man has no control.

---

that Foucault found Lefebvre's main analysis of the Hegelian meaning of alienation. Jean Hyppolite, *Genesis and Structure of Hegel's 'Phenomenology of Spirit'*, Northwest University Press, Evanston IL, 1979. One can only be amazed to discover in this lecture, as if in passing, a thesis (alienation is a pre-Marxist concept) which would be at the heart of Althusser's famous *For Marx*, a good decade later. Box 37 contains a folder entitled 'Marx. Écrits de jeunesse', containing ten or so folios: reading notes on 'Debates on the Law on Thefts of Wood', 'The Jewish Question', etc.

13. The sheet entitled 'L'homme réel' is in Box 37 (folio 399), with a quotation from Marx and Engels, *The German Ideology*.

14. This is an allusion to a passage from *The Holy Family* (1845): 'Since, *the* "Truth", like history, is an ethereal subject separate from the material mass, it addresses itself not to the empirical man but to the "*innermost depths of the soul*"; in order to be "*truly apprehended*" it does not act on his *vulgar body*, which may live deep down in an English cellar or at the top of a French block of flats; it "stretches" "from end to end" through his idealistic intestines.' Karl Marx and Frederick Engels, 'The Holy Family, or Critique of Critical Criticism', in Marx and Engels *Collected Works*, Volume 4: *1844–1845*, Progress Publishers, London, 1975, p. 80.

See the Robinsonade of Vol. I of *Capital*.[15]

How does this obscuring, this opacity, arise?

Alienation is labour as the destruction of the producer in the object produced, its negation therein (see early writings on alienation):[16]

α the product infinitely exceeds the life of the worker;

β working conditions are the death of the worker;

γ labour as creation only benefits the other.

Labour as a divine and creative act, labour as the presence of God in man, has become the death of man: it is man who is responsible for alienation. This is the crucial step: in Hegelian or neo-Hegelian philosophy, alienation is in God, in nature, in the object. Now, it is in man. Alienation is no longer the fact that man escapes from himself into a world that is alien to him. It is now that man becomes a stranger to himself in and through man himself. His exile is hidden within his innermost world.

Hence, in place of the Feuerbachian theme [of a] 'return to the immediate, intersubjective essence', there is the theme of 'denouncing alienation in the very place where man feels most at home, among other men'.

Marx establishes a philosophical critique of the immediate, the lesson of which has not yet been learned.

c. [However,] if alienation is not a forgetting or a loss of the human essence, but a world of human relations, what comprises this relationship?

---

15. This formulation is used to describe a 'thought experiment', popular with economists, which consists of imagining oneself living on a deserted island in order to describe a simplified economic model. The 'critique of the Robinsonades' can be found in *Capital, Volume I* (1867) and *A Contribution to the Critique of Political Economy* (1859); see also the 1857 Introduction to the manuscripts of 1857–58, known as the *Grundrisse*.

16. As Althusser established, Marx's early writings make much use of the concept of alienation to describe the sordid exploitation of the worker in the age of industrial capitalism. See in particular his 'Economic and Philosophical Manuscripts of 1844', in *Marx and Engels Collected Works*, vol. 3, pp. 229–349, Progress Publishers, London, 1975.

— It is a relation characterised by exchange. But then alienation is *abstraction*. There is more to it than that, however:
for through abstraction that which is inalienable can be
exchanged (see card).[17]

— It is a relation characterised by the commodity (see card).[18]
The commodity is considered to have: its own value (fetishism); its own laws (economism).[19]

— It is a relation characterized by the rupture between (collective) working conditions and the (private) forms of acquisition.
See Marx's[20] dialectic of value.[21]

— It is a relation characterised by surplus value.

At that point, alienation is exploitation.

α Labour produces all value.

β The worker therefore does not sell his labour, but his
labour-time.

γ The wage represents the *average social labour-time* necessary
for society to reproduce the worker.

δ And this time is necessarily less than the labour of the worker.
The history of exchange and the exploitation of labour shows
that man is not alienated, that man remains whole: only the
product of his labour is translated into the abstraction of the
commodity, and his labour-time is exchanged for socially average
labour-time.

Neither man nor labour as human activity is alienated. Only
the products of labour and labour-time. Alienation is nothing
other than a conflict between *product* and *time*.

---

17. Foucault had written several pages on 'Abstraction in Marx' (Box 37, folios 255–256).
18. One can list around a hundred reading notes written by Foucault on Marx. They
can be found in Boxes 10, 37 and 43.
19. *In the margins*: 'objectification'.
20. *In the margins*: 'individualization and depersonalization'.
21. An index card exists under this name (Box 37, folios 410–411), without any
precise bibliographic reference, which presents this dialectic in two phases: 1. 'highly
individualized product of labour'; 2. break-up of primitive societies, development of
exchange and loss of 'individual labour' in an 'indistinct mass'.

3. Alienation and the end of philosophy

a. Alienation as the destiny within which philosophical critique
[was exercised], as the milieu of philosophical reflection, has
disappeared, leaving room only for an alienation that is the totality of the working conditions of a given society.

By making it the most immediate reality of man, Marx
condemned alienation to be the concept of reality closest to man.

Hegelian and Feuerbachian reflection could present philosophy as the way back from alienation, or the effort to expend
oneself on earth ... In so far as it was objectification and exteriorization, alienation had to be overcome by the reflexive path of
philosophy.

b. But Marxist alienation, as a real and immediate condition
of man's life, can only be overcome by [the] path of uprooting,
detachment, not from an ideal interiority, but from a real
exteriority.

But isn't the end of alienation the end of philosophy? Is
revolution the inversion of philosophy?

From this point of view, the Marxist philosophy of alienation
would be no more than a moment – between philosophical
critique and historical revolution – in the major discovery that:
— the alienation of philosophers is the opposite of real
    alienation;
— the end of real alienation is the end of philosophy;
— and, consequently, alienation as thought by philosophy is only
    a sign, a historical phenomenon of real alienation.

c. This takes us very far, and raises the problem of the possibility
of a Marxist philosophy:
— All Marxist philosophy has always presented itself as human-
    ism (Marx himself).
— But all humanism is a claim to a human essence, a reminder
    of man to himself, an awakening: therefore there is no

humanism except in the form of an anthropology, which is itself only the reflexive space whereby the concept of aliena-tion acquires its dimensions.

In other words, a Marxist philosophy, or a Marxist humanism, can only be based in a concept of alienation that Marxism has dissociated and rejected.

A Marxism that wants to think of itself as philosophy, at the level of its own concepts, cannot be serious: *Marxism is the end of its own philosophical concepts. The seriousness of Marxism is to be the tomb of Marxist philosophy.*[22]

But Marxism nonetheless has philosophical meaning, precisely as the liquidation of that philosophy which was the philosophy of the entire bourgeoisie, at once humanism and anthropology: which thinks that man and truth belong to each other, by the rights of a forgotten essence which it is still the duty of phil-osophy to reawaken and of humanism to carry out. Marxism is the end of all philosophies of man; it is philosophically the end of all humanisms. To give Marxism its weight is not to render it the heir to all humanist insipidities, all anthropological platitudes, in which man and truth are linked together from the elementary forms of natural existence to the most spiritual achievements of the human essence. Marxism must be taken [as] the first, clearest and most profound of those experiences that man has been making obscurely for more than a century, which is the end of a philosophy, the end of an art, the end of a truth – the discovery that man and truth belong to each other only in the form of freedom.

TRANSLATED BY ERIC-JOHN RUSSELL

---

22. *In the margins*: 'Marxism is neither a philosophy nor the end of philosophy: it is the most compelling summons to philosophize differently.'

3

Dionysus: Nietzsche

MICHEL FOUCAULT

I. Nature

Philosophical reflection on psychology or biology does not necessarily mean a naturalistic reduction of man, nor the foundation
of truth in the objective forms of nature.[1]

α The set of relationships which constitute the natural horizon.
  — sets neither the forms for the determination of freedom
    nor the conditions of possibility of truth,
  — but limits the space in which man can reopen himself to
    truth, and render himself disposed towards his freedom.

The presence of this natural horizon does not enclose philosophical reflection within the framework of the objectivity
of an anthropology, but merely sketches the landscape and
the line of flight of the philosophical development which
sets out to liberate man *and* truth; that is, to liberate both
truth from its human determinations and freedom from the
objective forms of truth. Paradoxical for classical naturalism,
Nietzschean nature: 1. is the element that dissolves objectivity
and determinism; 2. denounces and unmasks the belonging
of man to truth, and of truth to man; 3. reveals that the

---

1. This text is an excerpt from Michel Foucault, *La question anthropologique. Cours
1954–1955*, EHESS–Gallimard–Seuil, Paris, 2022, Part III, C, I–II, pp. 176–94.

relationship of their non-relation, the connection of their non-connection, is freedom.

β Hence the paradoxical character of nature in Nietzsche – nature as a theme and term of philosophical existence.

— The return to nature as an authentic form of existence is not a return to immediate determinations, but access to the very limits of truth, an opening onto the most impossible forms of freedom. 'I talk about a "return to nature" too, although it is not really a going-back as much as a *coming-towards* – towards a high, free, even terrible nature and naturalness, the sort of nature that plays, that *can* play, with great tasks [...] Napoleon was a piece of "return to nature", as I understand it' (*Twilight of the Idols*).[2]

— So much so that this return is the very opposite of a return. It is a repetition that must never be [given the meaning of] a reiteration, nor even of a discovery of the originary. '*Not* "return to nature" – for there has never yet been a natural humanity. [...] man reaches nature only after a long struggle – he never "returns"' (*The Will to Power*).[3]

— The return to nature is not even the mythical and reversed chronology of an ideal conformity, which would be for all men the standard of their truth. For conformity is meaningless if it is not based on a kinship of origin or on a system, implicit at least, of references. For man to return to nature, nature must concern him, refer to him, as a house does to its inhabitants. Now: 'Do you want to live "in accordance with nature"? Imagine something like nature ... indifferent without measure ... fertile and barren and uncertain at the same time, think of indifference itself as power – how *could* you live according to this indifference?' (*Beyond Good and Evil*).[4]

2. Friedrich Nietzsche, *The Anti-Christ, Ecce Homo, Twilight of the Idols, and Other Writings*, Cambridge University Press, Cambridge, 2005, p. 221.
3. Friedrich Nietzsche, *The Will to Power*, Vintage Books, New York, 1968, p. 73.
4. Friedrich Nietzsche, *Beyond Good and Evil*, Cambridge University Press, Cambridge

— To return to nature is to face the absolute danger of a truth that dissolves itself and a freedom that escapes itself – or, more precisely, it is, on the path towards the truth of nature, the discovery that this path is the dissolution of the truth of nature. This gives the return to nature a threefold meaning:
— To return to nature is to deny nature as natural truth, in the very movement that seeks its truth.
— To return to nature is to go beyond nature by placing oneself at the very limits of its possibility.
— To return to nature means emancipating man from beast, by discovering that it is not freedom which separates man from beast.

The return to nature is to liberate truth by the grace and favour of truth; it is to liberate freedom by the grace and favour of freedom.

It is because of this, and not because of some chronological resonance, that the Nietzschean return to nature is the absolute form of repetition.

This form of repetition, in which the effort to reach the truth of nature destroys nature and its truth, is the divinatory and sacrilegious act of Oedipus: he can only gain access to the truth of nature by going against nature (first page of the text).[5]

But this is the beginning of a struggle to the death between man and nature: the death of man and the annihilation of nature appear, from the dawn of Greek antiquity, as the conditions for the emancipation of truth and freedom. '[T]he

2002, p. 10; translation amended to accord with Foucault's notes and the French translations employed therein.
5. Foucault makes a reference here to chapter 9 of *The Birth of Tragedy*: 'Oedipus, murderer of his father, husband of his mother, Oedipus the solver of the Sphinx's riddle! [...] the riddle-solving Oedipus who woos his mother immediately leads us to interpret this as meaning that some enormous offence against nature (such as incest in this case) must first have occurred to supply the cause whenever prophetic and magical energies break the spell of present and future, the rigid law of individuation, and indeed the actual magic of nature. How else could nature be forced to reveal its secrets, other than by victorious resistance to her, i.e. by some unnatural event?' Friedrich Nietzsche, *The Birth of Tragedy, and Other Writings*, Cambridge University Press, Cambridge, 1999, pp. 47–8.

myth seems to whisper to us [that] whoever plunges nature into the abyss of destruction by what he knows must in turn experience the dissolution of nature' (*The Birth of Tragedy*).[6]

In contrast to the Rousseauian return to nature, as a return to a lost homeland, Nietzsche's return is a confrontation – beyond death, beyond the security of familiar landscapes – with foreign lands. The return to the Forgotten is also the repetition of the unknown, the iteration of the Stranger: 'Whither does this mighty longing draw us, this longing that is worth more to us than any pleasure? Why just in this direction, thither where all the suns of humanity have hitherto *gone down*? Will it perhaps be said of us one day that we too, steering westward, hoped to reach an unknown India – but that it was our fate to be wrecked against infinity? Or, my brothers. Or?' (*Daybreak*).[7]

In so far as it is thus repetition, this return to beast, this return to nature, is what can be most profound, even deeper than this search for foundations that had been established by early critical thought.

Daybreak, 446 [features]:

— 'deep thinkers – those who go down into the depths of a thing [*gründlich*]';
— 'thorough thinkers [*abgründlich*], who thoroughly explore the grounds of a thing';
— 'finally, those who stick their heads into the swamp: which ought not to be a sign either of depth or of thoroughness! They are the dear shallow diggers [*Untergrund*]'.[8]

This *Untergrund*, this bottom [*bas-fond*] of the swamp, is nature as it is present in Nietzsche's thought. It is thus

---

6. Nietzsche, *The Birth of Tragedy*, p. 48.
7. Friedrich Nietzsche, *Daybreak: Thoughts on the Prejudices of Morality*, Cambridge University Press, Cambridge, 1997, p. 575; translation amended.
8. Ibid., p. 188; translation amended to accord with Foucault's notes and the French translations employed therein.

neither pre-critical nature nor the nature whose possibility critical thought is questioning; it is the background of every foundation, deeper than the foundation of critique, just as the foundation of critique was itself deeper than metaphysical depth.

And if one says that critique was a metaphysics of metaphysics, we can say that nature for Nietzsche, or rather the repetition of nature, uncovers the horizon of a metaphysics of critique.

In contrast to all the anthropologies of the nineteenth century which, at the foundation of critique, only ever posited a pre-critical metaphysics of man or a naturalism of man, Nietzsche, by deepening the meaning of nature and going beyond nature as such, discovers the whole horizon of a metaphysics that gives critique an absolutely new meaning, and makes it possible to criticize man, values and the world.

II. The metaphysics of truth

This metaphysics of truth begins with the sentence to which we arrived on our journey through the psychological nature of man: 'To be destroyed by absolute knowing could be part of the foundation of existence' (*Beyond Good and Evil*).[9]

1. [To perish by knowledge]

What does this text mean? It is diversified by Nietzsche at difference levels of reflection and interpreted:
— As an inverse relation between knowledge and being: knowledge was defined as distance from being: 'The more knowable a thing, the farther from being, and the closer to a mere concept' (*The Will to Power*).[10]

---

9. Nietzsche, *Beyond Good and Evil*, p. 37; translation amended to accord with Foucault's notes and the French translations employed therein.
10. Cited from Karl Jaspers, *Nietzsche: An Introduction to the Understanding of His*

— As a definition of knowledge as the will of non-being: knowledge is forgetting and flight from the horror and sacredness of being: 'It is pleasant to *contemplate* things, but terrible to *be* them' (*Early Notebooks, 1873–1876*).[11]

— As a refusal to think of the world as a universe; that is, as a totality of being closed in on itself, closed in its type of rationality, objectivity and necessity: 'Let us beware of thinking that the world is a living being ... that the universe is a machine... Let us beware of saying that there are laws in nature... When will all these shadows of god no longer darken us?' (*The Gay Science*).[12] The world as universe, as the real body of the knowable, is not the manifestation of being; it is its obliteration and veil.

— As a refusal to think of being in terms of an infinite understanding or sensibility which, while guaranteeing ontological weight, would give it its absolute character as knowable being: 'a suffering and all-seeing God, a "total sensorium" and "cosmic spirit" would be the greatest objection to being' (*The Will to Power*).[13]

— Finally, as the discovery that thought is not the measure of being, and that if there is a kinship between thought and being, it does not imply necessity and tautology. One needs to circumvent the lesson of Parmenides and realize that we do not think being, but rather non-being: 'That thinking is a measure of actuality – that what cannot be thought, *is* not – is a rude *non plus ultra* of a moralistic trustfulness (in an essential truth-principle at the bottom of things), in itself a mad assumption,

Philosophical Activity, Regnery/Gateway, South Bend IN, 1979, p. 294.

11. Friedrich Nietzsche, *Writings from the Early Notebooks*, Cambridge University Press, Cambridge, 2009, p. 195.

12. Friedrich Nietzsche, *The Gay Science*, Cambridge University Press, Cambridge, 2001, pp. 109–10.

13. Nietzsche, *The Will to Power*, p. 377.

which experience contradicts every moment. We are altogether unable to think anything at all just as it *is*' (*The Will to Power*).[14] The life of being is therefore impossible in the element of absolute knowing (hence the critiques of Hegel): this can only ever be the death of being; but in a more profound manner, access to being as an approach of philosophy can only have meaning through perpetual contestation, an incessant overcoming of oneself. 'Knowledge has the value of refuting "absolute knowledge"' (*Inédits. 1881–1886*).[15]

In other words, in order to become the truth of being, truth must discover itself as the non-truth of truth, and progress along the path of this truth of non-truth.

2. The interpretation of meaning and the enigma of being

What is the path by which truth, by surpassing itself as truth, can open itself up to being?

This movement begins the day knowledge takes itself seriously as interpretation, as hermeneutics, as philology.

Knowledge is akin to consciousness: it is the interpretation of a text; in other words, it is that by which a meaning emerges as the intelligible unity of elements that are thereby revealed to be signs and figures. And just as reason was only the language and the forgetting of language, so rational knowledge will only be interpretation, and also the forgetting of this original status of interpretation.

Knowledge and consciousness are not based on each other, but both belong to this genre which encompasses them and characterizes both:

— by the fact that the essence which constitutes meaningful unity derives from the phenomenon and manifestation:

---

14. Nietzsche, *The Will to Power*, p. 240.
15. Cited from Jaspers, *Nietzsche* – this specific quotation was not found in the English. We thus retain here the French editors' reference as Karl Jaspers, *Nietzsche. Introduction à sa philosophie*, trans. Henri Niel, Gallimard, Paris, 1950, p. 175.

'There is no event in itself. What happens is a group of phenomena *selected* and synthesized by an interpreting being' (*Writings from the Late Notebooks*).[16]
— by the fact that this presence of essence is always, however, perspective, and that it is presented through pattern, or rather according to a system of projections by which the dimensions of the information serve as referent figures for referent dimensions: '"Comprehending everything" – that would mean abolishing all perspectival relations, that would mean comprehending nothing, mistaking the meaning of knowledge' (ibid.).[17]

In other words, the unity of meaningful essence is the condition of the multiplicity of manifest meanings. Hence a whole movement of interpretation in search for itself, which is both the achievement of knowledge and the march of knowledge into self-knowledge:

α Remove the prejudice that there can be an absolute form of meaning and a complete manifestation of truth: 'The same text allows of countless interpretations: there is no "correct" interpretation' (ibid.).[18] 'The basic presupposition that there is a correct interpretation at all – or rather *one* single correct one – seems to me to be experimentally false... There is no single beautifying interpretation' (letter to Fuchs).[19]

β To make oneself master of all actual interpretations proposed, to traverse the perspectives and meanings, not in order to arrange them in a geometrics [*géométral*] of essence, nor in order to totalize them within *Geist* [spirit], but in order to show how the meaning of meaning is to be the non-meaning of essence: alteration, forgetting, concealing, obliteration

16. Friedrich Nietzsche, *Writings from the Late Notebooks*, p. 63.
17. Ibid.; translation amended to accord with Foucault's notes and the French translations employed therein.
18. Ibid.; translation amended to accord with Foucault's notes and the French translations employed therein.
19. Cited from Jaspers, *Nietzsche*, p. 289.

– that in which essence is hidden. The march of meaning is not even towards truth, it has no effective relation to truth in itself: 'The world with which we are concerned is false … it is "in flux" … as a falsehood always changing but never getting near the truth' (*The Will to Power*);[20] 'We must love and cultivate error, for it is the matrix of knowledge' (*Inédits. 1881–1886*).[21]

γ   But this brings to the fore the negative relief of what is concealed and covered by meaning. Meaning, traversed and revealed in its meaninglessness, negatively indicates that of which it is the meaning: it indicates the *text*. As interpretation, meaning covers and disguises the text, and imposes a return to the text, where the text comes only to mean itself. 'It requires a great deal of understanding to apply to nature the same kind of rigorous art of elucidation that philologists have now fashioned for all books: with the intention of comprehending what the text intends to say but without sensing, indeed presupposing, a *second* meaning' (*Human, All Too Human*).[22]

Meaning as a possible reading of the text becomes meaning as the indigenous word of the text: there are several interpretations, there is only one word.

δ   But this meaning as *word* [*parole*], as an abyssal proliferation of meanings and interpretations, is obscure and opaque to any effort at reading: 'to be able to read off a text as a text without interposing an interpretation is the last-developed form of "inner experience", perhaps one that is hardly possible' (*The Will to Power*).[23]

In fact, this word is the most fundamental, the original movement by which being designates itself: 'at our foundation, "at the very bottom", there is clearly something that will

---

20. Nietzsche, *The Will to Power*, p. 330.
21. Cited from Jaspers, *Nietzsche*, pp. 198–9.
22. Nietzsche, *Human, All Too Human*, p. 15.
23. Nietzsche, *The Will to Power*, p. 266.

not learn, a brick wall of spiritual *fatality*... In any cardinal problem, an immutable "that is me" speaks up... In time, certain solutions are found to problems that inspire *our* strong beliefs in particular; perhaps they will start to be called "convictions". Later – they come to be seen as only footsteps to self-knowledge, signposts to the problems that we *are*, – or, more accurately, to the great stupidity that we are, to our spiritual *fatality*, to that thing "at the very bottom" that *will not learn*' (*Beyond Good and Evil*).[24]

Interpretation has been transformed into an enigma, and the possibilities of meaning ultimately refer only to the fatality of being. The fatality of being and the enigma of the world set the positive and nocturnal background to all negatively clear interpretations of truth. In their mutual negation, interpretations both conceal and reveal the impenetrable affirmation of being: 'plurality of interpretations a sign of strength. Not to desire to deprive the world of its disturbing and enigmatic character!' (*The Will to Power*).[25]

But then, is the most cardinal word of being nothing more than the negation of truth?

3. Overcoming truth

Is this designation of being through negation of meaning the same as the abolition of truth? What meaning should be given to the often-repeated assertion that 'everything is false'?

If it is to carry its full weight, this assertion must not be taken as the conclusion and last word of philosophy, but as the principle which turns philosophical investigation itself on its head. In unpublished works around *The Wanderer*:

---

24. Nietzsche, *Beyond Good and Evil*, pp. 123–4; translation amended to accord with Foucault's notes and the French translations employed therein.
25. Nietzsche, *The Will to Power*, p. 326.

— after Descartes, the question 'How is error possible?' has determined the field of enquiry of philosophy;

— now, the question becomes: 'How is any kind of truth possible at all if knowledge is founded upon non-truth?' (*Écrits et Esquisses. 1869–1872*).[26]

1. Of course, the possibility of truth as the knowledge of knowledge or the genesis of error is impossible:

— first, because self-knowledge is [as much] perspective as knowledge tout court: 'the human spirit cannot avoid seeing itself under its perspectival forms, and *solely* in these' (*The Gay Science*).[27]

— secondly, because the genesis of error can only take place against the absolute background of truth.

The type of truth to which we have access is therefore neither gnoseological nor transcendental: for both presuppose that truth is the condition of error, whereas 'error [is] the condition of truth – error of the most profound kind' (*Unpublished Fragments, 1881–1886*).[28]

2. If, then, truth is not to be thought of as a condition of error, error must be reconsidered as a condition of itself in the disappearing horizon of the transcendental: 'Error is not eliminated by being seen for what it is' (ibid.).[29]

How can this be taken seriously? What does it mean to take seriously the fact that knowledge of error does not transcend error? It means:

---

26. Cited from Jaspers, *Nietzsche*, p. 197; translation amended to accord with Foucault's notes and the French translations employed therein.
27. Nietzsche, *The Gay Science*, p. 239; translation amended to accord with Foucault's notes and the French translations employed therein.
28. Cited from Jaspers, *Nietzsche*, p. 198; translation amended to accord with Foucault's notes and the French translations employed therein. See also Friedrich Nietzsche, *Unpublished Fragments (Winter Spring 1885–Spring 1886)*, vol. 16, trans. Adrian Del Caro, Stanford University Press, Stanford CA, 2019, p. 157.
29. Cited from Jaspers, *Nietzsche*, p. 198.

— that 'we do not have the truth': consciousness that is already
infinitely more profound than sceptical consciousness, since
the latter presupposes error against a background of truth,
and correlatively thinks of ignorance in the form of truth
(*Unpublished Fragments from the Period of 'Dawn'*);[30]
— that truth can only be illuminated in the instantaneous form
of its suppression; truth is only the lightening which evokes
its own darkness: 'Truth kills – it even kills itself (in so far as
it realizes that error is its foundation)' (*On Truth and Lies in a
Nonmoral Sense*).[31] 'Considered as an unconditional duty, truth
is the annihilation of the world' (ibid.).[32]
— that truth as a position of meaning is what is most and least
conditioned.

α What is the most conditioned, in the sense that it rests
only on its contradiction; it is the lightening that is only
possible in the dark, the instantaneous spark that springs
from steel: 'Things themselves do not really exist; they are
merely the flash and the flying sparks of drawn swords;
they are the glimmer of victory in the war of opposed
qualities' (*Unpublished Fragments, 1873–1876*).[33]

β What is most unconditioned, most abandoned to itself,
most originally given over to freedom: 'To give meaning –
this task always remain absolutely unconditional, assuming
there is no meaning yet' (*The Will to Power*).[34]

---

30. Friedrich Nietzsche, *Unpublished Fragments from the Period of 'Dawn' (Winter
1879/80–Spring 1881)*, vol. 13, trans. J.M. Baker Jr and Christiane Hertel, Stanford
University Press, Stanford CA, 2023.
31. Friedrich Nietzsche, 'On Truth and Lies in a Nonmoral Sense', in *Philosophy and
Truth: Selections from Nietzsche's Notebooks of the early 1870's*, Humanities Press, Atlantic
Highlands NJ, 1979, p. 92.
32. Ibid.; translation amended to accord with Foucault's notes and the French
translations employed therein.
33. Cited from Jaspers, *Nietzsche*, p. 209; translation amended to accord with
Foucault's notes and the French translations employed therein.
34. Nietzsche, *The Will to Power*, p. 327; translation amended to accord with Foucault's
notes and the French translations employed therein.

Truth is the conditioned unconditioned, that whose absolute
position is one and the same thing as absolute contradiction.
And this is why the knowledge of error does not transcend error
since, as knowledge, it is nothing other than error, nothing other
than its truth as knowledge.

3. But then thought – no longer under the form of science or
knowledge of truth, but in the form of philosophical reflection, regressive with regard to the error of truth – returns to
the point of its origin; that is to say, to the knowledge of the
fact that it ignores its own origin, that its origin is darkness.
Thought 'makes its appearance within me – whence and how? I
don't know... The source of thought remains hidden; it is highly
probable that it is only the symptom of a far more encompassing
state' (*Unpublished Fragments, 1882/1883–1888*).[35]

α This darkness, the origin of thought, the position and destruction of truth, this is the will, in the complex sense that:
   — as a fundamental act of freedom, it is the beginning of the
     unconditioned beginning of truth;
   — and as a creative will, it is the destruction of this will to
     truth, which is the will to a given, offered, open truth:
     '"Will to truth" – *as the impotence of the will to create*' (*The
     Will to Power*).[36]
   Truth is both the will and the decay of the will, its primary
   courage but also its self-denial and cowardice, its youth and
   daybreak, but also its drowsy evenings.
β But this is why we see the possibility of overcoming truth; or,
   rather, since it always remains true that we do not have the
   truth nor do we think we are truth, the task opens up, as an
   absolute possibility; that is to say, as a duty of freedom, for

35. Cited from Jaspers, *Nietzsche*, p. 290.
36. Nietzsche, *The Will to Power*, p. 317.

the being of truth and thought – without resting on a truth of thought or taking refuge in the thought of truth.

The being of truth and thought is nothing other than discovering that this darkness which thought thinks at its origin, this night which the lightening of truth evokes in an instant, is the height of the world, its true light. The night of truth is the sunlight of being.

This midday [*midi*] is the will tearing itself away from the will to truth, from the cowardice and laziness of a will that prefers to linger beyond appearances on what may be stable, permanent, consistent. This midday of being and thought is the will freeing itself from all will to truth, and courageously resuming itself as the will to the ever-dissolving truth, to becoming, to illusion, as will to appearance.

γ In this way, thought and being come together at last in this nearby homeland of appearance, which is the night of truth but which was once the sun of the earth and Greek beauty.

'Oh, those Greeks! They knew how to *live*: what is needed for that is to stop bravely at the surface, the fold, the skin; to worship appearance, to believe in shapes, tones, words – in the whole Olympus of appearance! Those Greeks were superficial – *out of profundity!*' (*The Gay Science*).[37]

In the colour and light of becoming and appearance, being finally and now thinks – thought, finally and now, is.

δ So if there is an overcoming of truth, it is the most familiar, in the closest of errors, in the most instantaneous of illusions. Attachment to truth will be attachment and fidelity to the nearest land.

'[R]emain faithful to the earth' (*Thus Spoke Zarathustra*).[38]

---

37. Nietzsche, *The Gay Science*, pp. 8–9.
38. Nietzsche, *Thus Spoke Zarathustra*, p. 6.

'We must again become *good neighbours to the closest things*' (*Human, All Too Human*).[39]
But this familiarity is not proximity to existence, a return to concrete forms of determinate being. On the contrary, the familiarity of appearance is linked to the solitude of being. The labour of holding on to the merciless and inescapable light of appearance (to appearance as the overcoming of truth) is incessantly punctuated: by nostalgia for nocturnal truths; by concern for stable truths; by the desire to be linked to the world through ties that are more solid and less disorienting than that of diffuse illumination.

4. Dionysus

This whole movement of overcoming truth is expressed at the same time:
— by the familiarity of thought in the homeland of appearance;
— by the solitude of being lost in its own illumination;
— by the proliferation of this light through which appearance appears, in such a way that appearance gives itself to light and within light, but also in such a way that light is lost, as pure transparency, in the warmth and cries of colours.
The *disappearance* of truth reveals that *appearance* is only fully given if it *shines* within the light of being. Or again: it is when being gives itself as illumination, yet as the pure transparency of light, that truth disappears and appearance immediately appears.
This movement is the very essence of the *Dionysian*.

a. In the classical interpretation, Dionysian has two meanings:
— As opposed to Apollonian: the opposition of order and disorder, kosmos and hubris, destructive and individualistic pessimism to city-building optimism.
  Greek tragedy would be the moment of this balance, expressed and at the same time protected by the chorus.

---

39. Nietzsche, *Human, All Too Human*, p. 309.

— In opposition to the Crucified, it would be the opposition of life and death, of the Will to Power and *ressentiment*, of the exultant joy of the strong against the grovelling, democratic morality of the slaves.

In this second meaning, the Dionysian would be the synthesis of the Dionysian (first sense) and the Apollonian.

The Dionysian would be the aesthetic concept that would make it possible to think of 'life bursting forth in the myriad of beings' that 'no longer plunges into immobile stillness', that 'does not tend to annihilate itself, but to flourish' (Charles Andler).[40]

The Dionysian is the positive reversal of Arthur Schopenhauer's pessimism. Dionysus would be the will to life.

An interpretation with consequences:

— to turn the philosophy of truth into a metaphysics of the will, which would itself be no more than a kind of fantastic cosmology of life; Nietzsche would be no more than a disordered Bergson, Bergson in flagrante delicto of immorality and delirium.

— to present Nietzsche as a philosopher of becoming, triumphing over the philosophies of being, a philosopher of the moment rejecting all philosophies of the eternal – which condemns the *Übermensch* and the Eternal Return to nothing more than the mythological paradoxes of a thinking that escapes its own meaning.

b. In fact, the analysis of the Dionysian must be seen in a completely different light.

1. The Dionysian is drunkenness, as opposed to the dream, which is Apollonian. However:

— if the dream is the apotheosis of appearance, that is to say, the whole of being in the order of appearance,

---

40. Charles Andler, *Nietzsche. Sa vie et sa pensée*, vol. VI, *La Dernière Philosophie de Nietzsche. Le Renouvellement de toutes les valeurs*, 10th edn, Gallimard, Paris, 1931, p. 357.

— drunkenness is the destruction of appearance, the inverse of
the dream, its fall into disorder, into darkness, into non-being.
Dionysus is the disappearing of appearance, the non-being of
what gives itself over to being in the form of truth. And this is
why, when he advances in the form of personhood, it is in the
form of the theatre, on stage, in the appearance that is not given
as truth, but as appearance. Greek theatre – the confrontation
and compromise between Dionysus and Apollo, of drunkenness
and dream, of delirium and sleep – is the infinitely fragile surface
of appearance that covers over only its non-being, returns only to
it, and indicates as its destiny and *pathos* its own disappearance,
which is precisely what Platonic philosophy accomplishes.

But if Dionysus, in his tragic confrontation with Apollo,
made philosophy possible as the metaphysics of the *true idea*, as
opposed to the *deceptive sensation of appearance*, philosophy was
wrong about Dionysus, and misled Dionysus. It had forgotten
the delirium of its intoxication for the 'bones and rattling' of
metaphysics:[41] it has neglected the saving grace of Dionysus.

2. Indeed, if appearance loses itself in its own enigma, where it
abandons all the trappings of its truth, it is saved from this truth
and enigma by this very loss. This is the myth of Ariadne:
— the Apollonian Theseus, in order to slay the Minotaur which
threatens mankind, to kill the darkness which kills the light,
loses himself in the labyrinth. But he is saved by Ariadne, not
by her truth, nor by the truth he was seeking, but by what is
most opposed to that truth, by what is darkest: by his desire.[42]

'A labyrinthine man never seeks the truth but always only
his Ariadne, what he also wants to tell us' (*Unpublished Fragments, 1881–1886*).[43]

---

41. Nietzsche, *The Gay Science*, p. 237. Here, within aphorism 372, Nietzsche asserts
that nothing remained of Spinoza but the sound of bones rattling.
42. *In the margins*: 'Annihilation of truth in desire'.
43. Cited from Jaspers, *Nietzsche*, p. 226; translation amended.

— But, by the same token, Ariadne and the thread of desire throughout the labyrinth are Theseus' salvation only in so far as they are his loss. If the man who seeks truth is saved from truth by that which is most contrary to truth, he loses his own truth in the process. If the labyrinth is the night of appearance that has lost its truth, Ariadne, who leads man back to the light, can only show Theseus one thing: that in the labyrinth he has lost his own light and has become darkness: "'Ariadne", says Dionysus, "you are a labyrinth. Theseus has become lost in you, he has no more thread. What does it profit him not to be devoured by the Minotaur? What now consumes him is worse than the Minotaur." Ariadne answers: "That is my last love to Theseus: I destroy him'" (*Inédits. 1882/1883–1888*).[44]

— But Ariadne, the loss of man whom man himself, in the panic of his desire, abandon and forgets, Ariadne, the discovery that man loses himself in his truth when he saves himself from the truth he seeks at the bottom of the labyrinth of enigmas; Ariadne offers herself to Dionysus and loses herself in him; 'Ariadne: "I am your labyrinth"' (*Poésies*).[45]

The myth of Dionysus, Ariadne and Theseus is therefore, in this sense, the resumption of the overcoming of truth, but it is at the same time the discovery that in losing truth, man loses himself, and that if he surpasses truth, to find himself both in the familiarity of appearance and in solitude, it is no longer in the essential form of the authentic man, but in the form of the superseded man, in the Dionysian delirium.

3. But who is Dionysus? This brings us back to the question: what becomes the face of man, when truth has disappeared into the appearance of the appearance[46] that shines through the light of being?

---

44. Ibid.
45. Ibid.
46. To understand this enigmatic expression, we can go back to an unpublished

α Within the Platonic metaphysics of the Idea and the other
world, the Crucified (or again: the essence of the Christian
man) appeared in his sacrifice as 'a curse on life, an invitation
to detach oneself from life' (*The Will to Power*).[47] And the
holiness of the sacrifice was merely a 'path to a holy existence'
(ibid.). In other words, the Platonic sacrifice of appearance to
truth summoned Christian sacrifice on the path to a purer
access to oneself.

Whereas in the Dionysian appearance, which is played out
in the light of being, the sacrifice of the god does not refer to
the other world. If it is a promise of resurrection, it is down
here below, on earth. Man who has lost himself in the Dionysian loss of truth will find himself again, but freed from his
own truth, in inescapable suffering: 'being is counted as *holy
enough* to justify even a monstrous amount of suffering' (ibid.).

The loss of man in Dionysus is his divinity, in the form of
tragedy, whereas Christian divinity is the desperate holding on
to a truth without appearance or being. 'The tragic man affirms
even the harshest suffering: he is sufficiently strong, rich, and
divine. The Christian denies even the happiest lot on earth. The
god on the cross is a curse on life, an invitation to detach oneself
from life; Dionysus cut to pieces is a promise of life: it will be
eternally reborn and return again from destruction' (ibid.).[48]

β This is why Christian man will always accuse God in the
vocabulary of *ressentiment*, will always practise the denigration

---

development from 1955–56 (Box 65, folder 1): 'The weighing of the world [...] the dawn:
the morning before the morning, neither night nor day: neither appearance nor the
dissolution of all appearance, but the appearing of appearance, which appearance
hides in its jealousy (*Eifersucht*). In this clarity, which is not yet diurnal, which is not yet
appearance, the world is: decipherable, thinkable, finite, offered to pleasure, arranged
by dreams, open in its secrets; something human and good.' The 'weighing of the world'
refers to the 'Three Evils' passage in *Thus Spoke Zarathustra*: 'In a dream, in the last
dream of morning I stood today on a foothill – beyond the world, holding a scale, and
I *weighed* the world. But the dawn came too early, and glowed me awake, this jealous
one!' Nietzsche, *Thus Spoke Zarathustra*, p. 149.
    47. Nietzsche, *The Will to Power*, p. 543, translation amended to accord with Foucault's
notes and the French translations employed therein.
    48. Ibid.

of values and practice revenge, whereas Dionysus, who finds himself in the painful dispersion of his body and appearance, affirms, blesses and sanctifies this world which has been his suffering and his death – and which has only been his own death in so far as it has been the death of the truth of this world.

This is why contemplation must end in 'a *theodicy,* that is, by saying an absolute yes to the world, but for the same reasons it was once said no' (ibid.).[49]

Dionysus, then, is the return of the world, the return to the appearance of the world in the light of being beyond the negation of the truth of the world.

γ Dionysus is the philosopher god, as opposed to the Christian God, the calculating God: 'Even the fact that Dionysus is a philosopher and that, consequently, even gods philosophize, seems to me like something new and not without its dangers, something that might arouse mistrust precisely among philosophers' (*Beyond Good and Evil*).[50]

— The Christian God calculates, he does not philosophize: and it is when he calculates that the world is made, a world that is above all divine truth.

— Dionysus philosophizes; in other words, he is the very movement that destroys the truth of the world. As Dionysus philosophizes, the world unravels.

δ And at the same time, Dionysus, unlike the Christian God, does not tinker with hearts and minds; nor does he restore man to the truth. On the contrary, if he is a 'born pied piper of consciences' (ibid.),[51] it is to drive man away from truth. The joy of his springtime is the thawing, the wandering of man. At his touch, we feel 'newer than before, broken open, blown

49. Ibid., p. 527; translation amended to accord with Foucault's notes and the French translations employed therein.
50. Nietzsche, *Beyond Good and Evil*, p. 176.
51. Ibid., p. 175.

on, and sounded out by a thawing wind, perhaps less certain, more gentle, fragile and broken, but full of hopes that do not have names yet, full of new wills and currents, full of bad new wills and countercurrents...' (ibid.).[52]

Dionysus is the man thrown ahead of himself, outside his truth, man pushed to the limits of his possibilities which contradict, deny and destroy the rest of his truth: 'for me, humans are pleasant, brave, inventive animals that have no equal on earth, they find their way around any labyrinth. I am very fond of them: I think about how I can help them advance and make them stronger, more evil and more profound than they are' (ibid.).[53]

Dionysus is the overcoming of man at the moment when, in the overcoming of truth, appearance appears in the light of being. Dionysus engulfs man, just as the light of being dissipates truth in the play and cry of colours in the sun. Dionysus is the revelation that man has no truth at the midday of being [*midi de l'être*]. In other words, being cannot be questioned either from the truth of man or even by man taken in his truth; metaphysics can only provide one and the same thing with the overcoming of man himself: 'with the name Dionysus, becoming is actively apprehended and subjectively experienced as the raging lust of the creator who, at the same time, knows the fury of the destroyer' (*Unpublished Fragments, 1882/1883–1888*).[54]

ε   And so, in this destruction of truth in the light of being, man, 'the last disciple and initiate of the god Dionysus' (*Beyond Good and Evil*),[55] rediscovers, in the dislocation of *his* truth, the great Greek tradition of tragedy, of masked man as prey to the

52. Ibid.; translation amended to accord with Foucault's notes and the French translations employed therein.
53. Ibid., pp. 176–7.
54. Cited from Jaspers, *Nietzsche*, p. 377.
55. Nietzsche, *Beyond Good and Evil*, p. 176.

god, of that reckless line where the edge of freedom separates art and madness.

— 'Let us pray to the mask as to our last deity and saviour' (*Unpublished Fragments, 1882/1883–1888*).[56]
— 'we need all exuberant, floating, dancing, mocking, childish, and blissful art lest we lose *that freedom over things* that our ideal demands of us... How then could we possibly do without art and with the fool?' (*The Gay Science*).[57]
— 'the Harlequin and God are neighbours' (*The Will to Power*);[58] 'I do not choose to be a saint, ... but rather a clown. ... Perhaps I am a clown. ... But still ... the truth speaks through me' (ibid.).[59]
— According to Franz Overbeck, the insane Nietzsche found in Turin called himself the 'jester of the new eternities'.[60]

With new promise, we return here to the initial theme of the philosopher as acrobat and tightrope walker, and the theme of philosophy as a long tragedy (*Beyond Good and Evil*).[61]

Just as we saw earlier how philosophy, as a critique of the truth of appearance, was both the truth and the error of tragedy, we can now understand why tragedy is the truth of philosophy. The Platonic forgetting of the Greek meaning of tragedy is now allayed by the rediscovery of the absolutely tragic meaning of philosophy.

---

56. Cited from Jaspers, *Nietzsche*, p. 406.
57. Nietzsche, *The Gay Science*, pp. 104–5.
58. Cited from Jaspers, *Nietzsche*, p. 407.
59. Ibid., p. 408.
60. As reported by Carl Albrecht Bernoulli, *Franz Overbeck und Friedrich Nietzsche. Eine Freundschaft*, E. Diederichs, Jena, 1908, p. 234; cited from Jaspers *Nietzsche*, p. 408.
61. 'Not to mention the absurd spectacle of moral indignation, which is an unmistakable sign that a philosopher has lost his philosophical sense of humor. The philosopher's martyrdom, his "self-sacrifice for the truth," brings to light the agitator and actor in him; and since we have only ever regarded him with artistic curiosity, it is easy to understand the dangerous wish to see many of these philosophers in their degeneration for once (degenerated into "martyrs" or loud-mouths on their stage or soap-box). It's just that, with this sort of wish we have to be clear about *what* we will be seeing: – only a satyr-play, only a satirical epilogue, only the continuing proof that the long, real tragedy *has come to an end* (assuming that every philosophy was originally a long tragedy –).' Nietzsche, *Beyond Good and Evil*, p. 25.

But this philosophical repetition of tragedy brings new promises.

— In its Greek form, it was the expression of the mythic power of a people: as a myth of the 'worst of all possible worlds', it illuminated, like the dissonance of Wagnerian music, 'a region where dissonance and the terrible image of the world fade away in chords of delight'. In this way, it called to life 'the entire world of appearances' (*The Birth of Tragedy*).[62]

— In its present form, philosophy, restored to the tragic form of its origins, is also the festival of appearance, in the very disappearing of appearance. But this play of appearance is not accomplished in the movement of life, as was the case for the Greek Dionysus; it is now exalted in the light of being. This is why, if the Dionysian tragedy in its Greek dawning was of mythical order, in its philosophical repetition, it is of metaphysical order: myth is the Dionysian movement of appearance that exalts itself in its suffering and death within the movement of life; metaphysics is the Dionysian movement of appearance that overcomes itself as truth, but appears in its appearance in the light of being.

The playground of myth is covered and taken over by the playground of metaphysics. The break with Richard Wagner was the discovery that the essence of the Dionysian could not be taken up as myth, but only as metaphysics, that it was not the promise of a new life, but of new eternities.

TRANSLATED BY ERIC-JOHN RUSSELL

---

62. Nietzsche, *The Birth of Tragedy*, p. 115.

4

Jean Hyppolite, 1907–1968

MICHEL FOUCAULT

Those of us who were in *khâgne*[1] in the aftermath of the war will remember Mr Hyppolite's lectures on the *Phenomenology of Spirit*: in that voice, which never stopped repeating itself as if it were meditating within its own movement, we did not just hear the voice of a teacher, we heard something of the voice of Hegel, and perhaps even the voice of philosophy itself. I don't think we could have forgotten the strength of this presence, or the closeness that he patiently invoked.

The memory of this discovery allows me to speak on behalf of those who shared it with me and who have certainly made better use of it.

Historian of philosophy, that was not how he defined himself. More readily, more accurately, he spoke of a history of philosophical thought. In this difference laid undoubtedly the singularity and the scope of his undertaking.

Philosophical thought: Mr Hyppolite meant by this what in any system – however complete it may appear – overflows it, exceeds it, and places it in a relationship of both exchange and default with philosophy itself. Philosophical thought was not, for

---

1. A two-year selective academic programme in the French undergraduate system with a specialization in literature and the humanities.

him, the first intuition of a system, its informal intimacy; it was its incompleteness, the debt that it could never pay, the blank that none of its propositions could ever cover; that by which, however far it goes on, remains behind compared to philosophy. By philosophical thought, he also meant that moment so difficult to grasp, covered over from the outset, when philosophical discourse makes up its mind, breaks out of its silence, and distances itself from what from then on will appear as non-philosophy: philosophical thought is then less the obscure and prior determination of a system than the sudden and ceaselessly renewed division [*partage*] through which it is established. By philosophical thought, I believe that Mr Hyppolite finally meant this twisting and redoubling, this outcome and recapturing of oneself, by which philosophical discourse says what it is, pronounces its justification, and, shifting from its immediate form, manifests what can found it and set its own limits.

Thus conceived, philosophical thought maintains the philosopher's discourse in the instance of an indefinite vibration, and makes it resonate beyond all death; it guarantees the excess of philosophy over any philosophy, a light that was already standing ahead of any discourse, a blade that still shines once it has gone to sleep.

By taking philosophical thought as his theme, Mr Hyppolite surely meant that philosophy is never actualized or present in any discourse or text; that in truth philosophy does not exist; that it rather hollows out all philosophies by its perpetual absence, that it inscribes in them the lack where they ceaselessly chase, continue, disappear, succeed one another, and remain for the historian in a suspense where it has to be taken up again.

So what does it mean to analyse philosophical thought then? Mr Hyppolite did not want to describe the movement of these ideas – scientific, political, moral – which little by little and in scattered order have penetrated philosophy, settled there, and taken on a new systematicity. He wanted to describe the way in which all philosophies take back into themselves an immediacy that they have already ceased to be; the way in which they aim for an absolute that they never reach; the way in which they set limits that they always transgress. It was a question of playing philosophies in this light and shadow, where their distance from philosophy both manifests itself and conceals.

The problem that Mr Hyppolite never ceased to address was perhaps this: what is this limitation specific to philosophical discourse which leaves it, or rather makes it appear, as the word of philosophy itself? In a word: *what is philosophical finitude?*

And if it is true that, since Kant, philosophical discourse has been the discourse of finitude rather than the discourse of the absolute, perhaps we could say that Mr Hyppolite's work – the point of his originality and his decision – was to double the question; to this philosophical discourse that spoke of the finitude of Man, the limits of knowledge or the determinations of freedom, he asked for an account of the finitude that is proper to it. A philosophical question posed to the limits of philosophy.

A natural consequence of this question, rather than first choice: to carry out an historical analysis of works – of their beginning and of their perpetual new beginning, of their always incomplete end. Isn't history the privileged place where philosophical finitude can appear?

But history did not consist for Mr Hyppolite in seeking out the singularities or determinations that may have marked the birth of a work; nor did it consist in showing how such a monument bore witness to the era that saw it come into being, to those who conceived it or the civilizations that imposed their values on it. More precisely still, to speak of a philosophical work was not to describe an object, to encircle it, to enclose it within its contours, but rather to open it up, to identify its ruptures, its gaps, its blanks, to establish it in its irruption and its suspense, to unfold it in that lack or that unsaid through which philosophy itself speaks. From there, his position as historian was not outside but within the space of the philosophy he was talking about and the systematic erasure of his own subjectivity.

Mr Hyppolite was fond of quoting Hegel on the modesty of the philosopher who loses all singularity. Anyone who has heard Mr Hyppolite will remember the serious modesty of his speech; anyone who has read him will be familiar with his ample writing which is never torn apart by the indiscretion of a first person. This was a modesty that was neither neutral nor relentlessly against himself, but that enabled him to make what he said resound with the multiplied breadth of a voice that was not his own; and in his texts, which unfolded continuously from quotation to commentary and from reference to analysis, with almost no need for inverted commas, philosophy continued to write itself. The prose of thought, more muted, more insistent than anything men have ever thought.

On several occasions, Mr Hyppolite returned to this point of Bergsonian philosophy, the analysis of memory. I may be wrong in supposing that he saw in it more than a truth, a model for the history of thought: it is that, for him, the present of thought was not ontologically separated from its past, and the historian's attention had only to form the sharp point, present and free, of a past that had lost nothing of its being. And just as according to Bergson the present happens to recapture its shadow by a kind of torsion upon itself, for Mr Hyppolite – the historian that he himself was – the historian marks the point of inflexion from which philosophy can and must recapture the shadow that cuts it up at every moment, but nevertheless binds it to its invincible continuity.

It was from within philosophy that Mr Hyppolite questioned the different philosophies. And he questioned them in their always elusive, but never undone, relationship to philosophy. He wanted to grasp them at the point where they begin, and at that other point where they finish and delimit themselves as a coherent system. He wanted to capture in a work the relationship, never quite established, never quite mastered, between an experience and a rigour, an immediacy and a form, the tension between the barely perceptible day of a beginning and the exactitude of an architecture.

Mr Hyppolite liked to compare his own undertaking with two of the great works of his contemporaries, both of which he praised in his inaugural lecture at the Collège de France.[2] That of Merleau-Ponty's research into the original articulation of meaning and existence; and that of Mr Guéroult's axiomatic analysis of philosophical coherences and structures. Between these two reference points, Mr Hyppolite's work has always been, from the outset, to name and reveal – in a discourse that is both philosophical and historical – the point at which the tragedy of life takes on meaning in a Logos, where the genesis of a thought becomes the structure of a system, where existence itself is articulated in a Logic. Between a phenomenology of prediscursive experience – in the manner of Merleau-Ponty – and an epistemology of philosophical systems – as it appears in Mr Guéroult – the work of Mr Hyppolite can be read as a phenomenology of philosophical rigour, or as an epistemology of philosophically reflected existence.

What relationship does philosophy have to that which is not itself, and yet without which it could not be? To answer this question, Mr Hyppolite rejected two familiar attitudes: the one

2. Jean Hyppolite, 'Leçon inaugurale au Collège de France', 19 December 1963, in *Figures de la pensée philosophique*, vol. II, coll. Épiméthée, PUF, Paris, 1971, pp. 1003–28.

that considers that philosophy has to reflect on external objects,
be they science or everyday life, religion or law, desire or death;
the other that considers that philosophy must interrogate all
these various naïveties, discover the meanings hidden in them,
question their mute positiveness and ask them to account for
what can ground them. For him, philosophy is neither reflexive
nor foundational in relation to what is not itself; but it must
grasp both the interiority that makes it already silently inhabit
everything that is not itself (it is already there in the activity of
the mathematician as in the innocence of the beautiful soul)
and the exteriority that makes it never necessarily implied by
a science or a practice. It is this relationship of interiority and
exteriority, of proximity and distance, that philosophy must take
back into itself.

From this starting point, we can understand, I think, certain
characteristic features of Mr Hyppolite's work.

I am thinking first of his relationship with Hegel. For him
Hegel marked the moment when philosophical discourse posed
for itself, and within itself, the problem of its beginning and
its end: the moment when philosophical thought set itself the
inexhaustible task of expressing the total field of non-philosophy,
and undertook to succeed, with complete sovereignty, in enun-
ciating its own end. Hegel was, for Mr Hyppolite, the moment
when Western philosophy took up the task of expressing being
in a logic, planned to discover the meanings of existence in a
phenomenology, and attempted to reflect itself as the completion
and end of philosophy. Hegelian philosophy marked in this
manner the moment when philosophy became, within its own
discourse, the holder of the problem of its beginning and its end:
the moment when, taking itself, as it were, to the extreme of its
own limits, it became the question of the immediate and the
absolute – of that immediate from which it does not free itself,
even though it mediates it, and of the absolute which it can only

achieve at the cost of its own disappearance. With Hegel, philosophy which, since Descartes at least, had been in an inefface-
able relationship, with non-philosophy, became not only aware
of this relationship, but the actual discourse of this relationship:
the serious implementation of the interplay of philosophy and
non-philosophy. While others saw in Hegelian thought the withdrawal of philosophy into itself, and the moment when it moves
on to the narrative of its own history, Mr Hyppolite recognized
in it the moment when it crosses its own limits to become the
philosophy of non-philosophy, or perhaps the non-philosophy of
philosophy itself.

But this theme which haunted his studies on Hegel went far
beyond them and carried his interest further. The relationship
between philosophy and non-philosophy he saw carried out in
Marx – both fulfilment and reversal, in his view, of Hegelian
philosophy, critique of all philosophy, in its idealism, assignment
to the world to become philosophy, and to philosophy to become
the world. He was also to recognize it more and more, over the
last years, in the relationship to science. He returned in this way
to the concerns of his youth and the diploma he had written on
the mathematical method and Descartes' philosophical path. It
also brought him closer to the work of two men for whom he
shared the same admiration and undivided loyalty, the ones who
are for us the two great philosophers of physical and biological
rationality.

These then became the fields of his reflection: Fichte, on the
one hand, and the possibility of holding a philosophical discourse on science that was entirely rigorous and demonstrative;[3]
and, on the other hand, the theory of information that makes
it possible to discover, in the depths of the natural processes

---

3. Jean Hyppolite, 'L'idée fichtéenne de la doctrine de la science et le projet husserlien'
(1959), in *Figures de la pensée philosophiques*, vol. I, coll. Épiméthée, PUF, Paris, 1971, pp.
21–31.

and exchanges of the living, the structure of the message.[4] With
Fichte, he posed the problem of knowing whether it is possible to
hold a scientific discourse on science, and whether, starting from
purely formal thought, it is possible to reach the actual content
of knowledge. And, conversely, information theory posed him
the following problem: what status should be given, in sciences
such as biology or genetics, to texts that have not been spoken by
anyone or written by any hand?

Around these questions, many themes were organized, many
lines of research were opened up: in relation to Freud,[5] analysis
of the effect, in desire, of the formal instance of denial; in relation to Mallarmé,[6] reflection on the interplay, in a work, of the
necessary and the improbable; in relation to Lapoujade,[7] analysis
of the mode according to which painting can be painted in the
naked and original form of its elements.

There is no mistaking it: all the problems that we – his
students of the past or his students of yesterday – have to face,
all these problems, it was he who established them for us; it was
he who chanted them in words that were strong, deep, without
ceasing to be familiar; it was he who formulated them in this
text, *Logic and Existence*, which is one of the great books of our
time.[8] In the aftermath of the war, he taught us to think about
the relationship between violence and discourse; yesterday
he taught us to think about the relationship between logic
and existence; just now he suggested that we think about the

4. 'Information et communication' (1967), in ibid., pp. 928–71.
5. 'Commentaire parlée sur la *Verneinung* de Freud' (presentation at the Freudian
Technique Seminar of 10 February 1954, held by Jacques Lacan at the Faculty Clinic of
the Hôpital Sainte-Anne, and devoted to Freud's technical writings for 1953–54; first
published in *La Psychanalyse* 1, 1956, pp. 29–40; reprinted in ibid., pp. 385–96; trans. John
Forrester as 'A Spoken Commentary on Freud's *Verneinung*', Appendix to Jacques Lacan,
The Seminar of Jacques Lacan B:ook 1, Freud's Papers on Technique, 1953–54, Cambridge
University Press, Cambridge, 1988, pp. 289–97.
6. 'Le Coup de dés' de Stéphane Mallarmé et le message' (1958), in ibid., vol. II, pp.
877–84.
7. 'Preface to "Mécanismes de la fascination" de Lapoujade' (1955), in ibid., pp. 831–6.
8. Jean Hyppolite, *Logic and Existence*, trans. Leoanard Lawlor and Amit Sen, SUNY
Press, Albany NY, 1997 (1953).

relationship between the content of knowledge and formal necessity. He taught us in the end that philosophical thought is an incessant practice; that it is a certain way of putting non-philosophy into practice, but always remaining as close to it as possible, where it is tied up with existence. With him, we must constantly remind ourselves that if 'grey are all theories ... green alone life's golden tree'.[9]

TRANSLATED BY JUDITH BASTIE

First published in *Revue de métaphysique et de morale*, vol. 74, no. 2, April–June 1969, pp. 131–6, this tribute to Jean Hyppolite was delivered at the École Normale Supérieure on 19 January 1969.

---

9. Goethe, *Faust*, Part 1 (1808), iv, 509–14, trans. Bayard Taylor. These lines of Mephistopheles in Goethe's *Faust* are quoted by Hegel at the end of the Preface to his *Philosophy of Right* (25 June 1820).

LECTURES

5

Wild thought:
Lévi-Strauss, Freud and Metzger

STELLA SANDFORD

In *La pensée sauvage* (1962), recently newly translated into English as *Wild Thought*, in a discussion of the classification of natural products and the medical purposes for which they are employed, Claude Lévi-Strauss includes the report from a 1936 text about the use by Yakut Siberian peoples of the woodpecker's beak as a remedy against toothache. The context is an argument against the idea that so-called 'primitive' thought is driven to know things only in so far as they are useful, neglecting the 'appetite for objective knowledge forms' that, on the contrary, Lévi-Strauss saw everywhere. The particular example cited, like all of those that accompany it, is evidence of a 'form of knowledge [so] systematically developed that [it] cannot be a function of mere practical usefulness'.[1] These systems suggest, rather, that things are not known to the extent that they prove useful, but are found to be useful or interesting because they are known. Accordingly, the objection that 'such a science can hardly be effective on the practical plane' misses the point that its primary objective is not practical; it fails to see that such a science (note that he explicitly calls it a 'science')

---

1. Claude Lévi-Strauss, *Wild Thought*, trans. Jeffrey Mehlman and John Leavitt, University of Chicago Press, Chicago IL, 2021, p. 10.

meets intellectual requirements before, or instead of, satisfying needs. The real question is not knowing whether contact with a woodpecker's beak cures toothache, but whether it is possible, from a certain point of view, to make the woodpecker's beak and the human tooth 'go together' (the therapeutic formula from this congruence constituting only one of its hypothetical applications, among others) and whether it is possible to introduce an initial order into the universe through such groupings of things and beings – classifying, of whatever kind, possessing a virtue in itself in comparison to the absence of classifying.[2]

This lecture explores whether it is possible, from a certain point of view, to make Lévi-Strauss's *Wild Thought* and Freud's *The Interpretation of Dreams* 'go together', in an attempt to understand what Lévi-Strauss means by 'wild thought' and whether and how it manifests itself in each one of us.[3] I will suggest that both Lévi-Strauss and Freud point us towards a transcendental, but open and contingent, multi-dimensional logical structure in 'wild' human thought, which allows both to discern sense in apparent nonsense. But I will also suggest that both need to be supplemented with Hélène Metzger's notion of 'spontaneous thought' to prevent this idea of wild thought appearing (counter-intuitively, perhaps) static, to bring this idea of wild thought properly to life and to indicate its role in philosophy – in the history of philosophy and in philosophy's future.

---

2. Ibid., pp. 11–12

3. Of course, Lévi-Strauss and Freud already 'go together', and Lacan, via Saussure, is the most famous mediator of that relationship. In his own remarks on the influence of Freud on his thought, Lévi-Strauss identifies one major lesson, indeed one major lesson from *The Interpretation of Dreams* specifically: that 'even phenomena of the most irrational appearance can be subjected to rational analysis' (Claude Lévi-Strauss and Didier Eribon, *Conversations with Claude Lévi-Strauss* (1988), trans. Paula Wissing, University of Chicago Press, Chicago IL, 1991, p. 107). Earlier, in *Tristes Tropiques*, he said a little more: 'Psychoanalytic theories taught me that the static oppositions around which we were advised to construct our philosophical essays and later our teaching – the rational and the irrational, the intellectual and the emotional, the logical and the pre-logical – amounted to no more than a gratuitous intellectual game... Freud's work showed me that the oppositions did not really exist in this form, since it is precisely the most apparently emotional behaviour, the least rational procedures and so-called prelogical manifestations which are at the same time the most meaningful.' Claude Lévi-Strauss, *Tristes Tropiques* (1955), trans. John and Doreen Weightman, Penguin, Harmondsworth, 1976, p. 67.

Lévi-Strauss: the logic of sensation

What does Lévi-Strauss mean by 'wild thought'? On the one
hand, and although it is contrasted with Western scientific
thought, 'wild thought' (or 'thought in the wild state') is not 'the
thought of a primitive or archaic [non-Western] humanity' but
a universal form of thought 'always present and alive among us'.
On the other hand, however, Lévi-Strauss does seem to identify
wild thought with what he calls the 'science of the concrete',
or the 'logic of sensation' – another 'distinct mode of scientific
thought' – that he finds exemplified in the symbolic systems
of what he sometimes calls the 'indigenous thought' of various
peoples. Is 'wild thought', then, the universal substratum of
all thought? Or is it manifested in a 'logic of sensation' that
stands as a critical rejoinder to the presumed universality of the
restricted logic of Western scientific thought? Is it universal and
necessary or culturally specific and historical?

We can broach these questions via Kant's concept of the
transcendental. In chapter 1 of his *Structural Anthropology*, a
paper dating from 1949, Lévi-Strauss suggests that the transdisciplinary concept of 'structure' functions transcendentally in
his work as the mediator between the universal and the cultural-
historical: Lévi-Strauss writes:

> If as we believe to be the case, the unconscious activity of the mind
> [*l'esprit*] consists in imposing forms upon content, and if these forms
> are fundamentally the same for all minds – ancient and modern,
> primitive and civilised (as the study of symbolic function, expressed
> in language, so strikingly indicates) – it is necessary and sufficient
> to grasp the unconscious structure underlying each institution and
> each custom, in order to obtain a principle of interpretation valid
> for other institutions and other customs, provided of course that the
> analysis is carried far enough.[4]

4. Claude Lévi-Strauss, 'Introduction: History and Anthropology', in *Structural
Anthropology* (1958), trans. Claire Jacobson and Brooke Grundfest Schoepf, Basic Books,
New York, 1963, p. 21.

To arrive at the unconscious structure, ethnological method
and historical method must converge. Analysis of the synchronic
structure requires an understanding of 'institutions in the
process of transformation', which alone makes it possible 'to
abstract the structure which underlies the many manifestations
and remains permanent through a succession of events'.[5] Slightly
earlier, in 1946, Lévi-Strauss criticized Durkheim and the general
neo-Kantianism of French sociology for not being Kantian
enough. For Durkheim fails to see, according to Lévi-Strauss,
'when an a priori form is inescapably required' and precisely
because Durkheim did not have the option of 'calling upon the
activity of the unconscious mind'.[6]

It is no doubt passages such as this that led Paul Ricoeur
to claim that the 'unconscious' in Lévi-Strauss's work is more
Kantian (that is, categorial and combinative) than Freudian, 'but
only as regards its organization, since we are here concerned
with a categorial system without reference to a thinking subject',
or a 'Kantianism without a transcendental subject'.[7] In *The Raw
and The Cooked* (1964), projecting the possibility that the study
of mythology might prove that 'the apparent arbitrariness of
the mind, its supposedly spontaneous flow of inspiration, and
its seemingly uncontrolled inventiveness imply the existence
of laws operating at a deeper level', Lévi-Strauss admits that in
having allowed himself 'to be guided by the search for constraining structures of the mind, I am proceeding in the manner of
Kantian philosophy, although along different lines leading to
different conclusions'.[8] Instead of assuming universal forms of
human understanding, the ethnologist, he says, 'prefers to study

5. Ibid.
6. Lévi-Strauss, 'French Sociology', in Georges Gurvitch, ed., *Twentieth Century
Sociology*, The Philosophical Library, New York, 1946, p. 518.
7. Paul Ricoeur, 'Structure and Hermeneutics', trans. Kathleen McLaughlin, in *The
Conflict of Interpretations: Essays in Hermeneutics* (1969), Northwestern University Press,
Evanston IL, 1974, pp. 33, 52.
8. Claude Lévi-Strauss, *The Raw and The Cooked: Introduction to a Science of Mythology*
(1964), Pimlico Books, London, 1994, p. 10.

empirically collective forms of understanding, whose properties have been solidified, as it were, and are revealed to him in countless representations systems', although the hope remains that these systems will be able to be translated into the terms of the ethnologist's own system to reveal 'a pattern of basic and universal laws'.[9] That is, there are diverse forms of understanding and therefore knowledge (systems of representations), but underlying them universal forms of thought.

Referring directly to Ricoeur's characterization of his approach, Lévi-Strauss embraces it as the inevitable philosophical consequence of the ethnographical approach. This seeks, he writes, 'the conditions in which systems of truths become mutually convertible and therefore simultaneously acceptable to several different subjects' – meaning, the subjects of several different concrete representational systems. As such, the 'pattern of those conditions takes on the character of an autonomous object, independent of any subject'. Indeed, it may be possible to disregard the thinking subject completely and to proceed as if 'the thinking process were taking place in the myths, in their reflection upon themselves and their interrelation'.[10]

This is not just a 'Kantianism without a transcendental subject'; it is a Kantianism that completely overturns Kant's methodological procedure (it begins with an empirical enquiry) or that revokes the fundamental Kantian distinction between the transcendental and the empirical. It reverses the Copernican turn that put the Western scientific subject at the centre of the epistemological universe, recasting what Kant presumes to be the universal form of understanding as a particular representational system, imagining Kant – and perhaps all philosophers in general – as a kind of auto-ethnologist studying 'the conditions in which his own thought operates, or the science peculiar to his

9. Ibid., p. 11.
10. Ibid., pp. 11, 12.

society and his period'.[11] This means that the *a priori* requirement that is affirmed in Lévi-Strauss's critique of Durkheim is little more than the requirement to take the existence of something for granted, rather than (as Durkheim does) seeking to explain its genesis.[12] It refers therefore to a generalized transcendental form of argument, rather than to any transcendental structures per se.[13]

Further, in Lévi-Strauss's *Wild Thought* it becomes clearer that, if the idea of 'unconscious structures' evokes a Kantian conception of the transcendental, it does so primarily critically. The core of one aspect of this critical approach is indicated in Lévi-Strauss's free use of the idea of logic, and the attempt to map the 'science of the concrete' (the title of the first chapter). What is taken for granted in *Wild Thought* is the actuality of what Lévi-Strauss calls 'the logic of sensation' or, and significantly in the plural, 'concrete

---

11. Ibid., pp. 10–11. Gayatri Spivak later made the same point with more political-critical intent. Spivak identifies the 'raw man' of Kant's *Critique of the Power of Judgment* – the Savoyard peasant incapable of the feeling of the sublime – with the 'native informant' or 'the primitive' more generally, 'a name for that mark of expulsion from the name of Man'. Gayatri Chakravorty Spivak, *A Critique of Postcolonial Reason: Toward a History of the Vanishing Present*, Harvard University Press, Cambridge MA, 1999, p. 6. The 'raw man' is human by nature but not by culture. The subject of the sublime is the human beyond nature. Because the 'primitive' or 'native informant' cannot be the subject of the sublime, 'the subject as such in Kant is geopolitically differentiated'. Spivak, *A Critique of Postcolonial Reason*, pp. 26–7.

12. In relation to Durkheim specifically this is the requirement to take symbolic thought for granted as a condition of possibility for society, as opposed to the attempt to see how symbolic thought grows out of or has its origins in society (social organization). Lévi-Strauss, 'French Sociology', p. 518. Lévi-Strauss makes the same point about Durkheim in *Totemism*, trans. Rodney Needham, Merlin Press, London, 1962, p. 96.

13. When, in an interview with Didier Eribon, Lévi-Strauss describes his books *Totemism* and *Wild Thought* as 'critiques in the Kantian sense' – 'I needed to free anthropology from certain illusions that obscured the study of religion in preliterate societies', he says (*Conversations with Claude Lévi-Strauss*, p. 71) – a more significant relation to Kant's philosophy may appear to be indicated. Comparing the logic of totemic classifications to a kaleidoscope, where the arrangement of the bits and pieces is the result of 'an encounter between contingent events ... and a law', Lévi-Strauss insists that the relations within the provisional model of intelligibility thus projected 'have no content other than the arrangement itself, for which there is no corresponding object in the observer's experience' (*Wild Thought*, pp. 42–3). The 'totemic illusion', as he calls it, is the ethnographical assumption that there is a unitary phenomenon called 'totemism', various examples of which the ethnologist experiences. But the totemic illusion is not a dialectical or transcendental illusion; it is an ethnological error. As he writes in *Wild Thought*, 'the error of classical ethnologists was to want to reify this [totemic] form, to tie it to a determined content' (*Wild Thought*, p. 86; see also p. 152). It is precisely an error, and not a transcendental illusion, because it does not survive Lévi-Strauss's analysis.

logics'.[14] In *The Raw and the Cooked* this is also called 'a kind of logic in tangible qualities'.[15] This critical transformation of the Kantian conception of the transcendental – if that is indeed what it is – challenges, as Claude Imbert says, the classical notion of logic, or at least 'the Greek featuring of logic', and thereby the 'predicative and conceptual stance of classical epistemology', subjected to 'the categories of a propositional grammar'.[16]

Why does the logic of sensation do this? It does this because it is an intellectual – and indeed Lévi-Strauss would say scientific – achievement of the 'speculative organisation and exploration of the sensory world in [concrete] sensory terms',[17] where the logical intersection or association between terms in a ground-level, classificatory schema is based not on abstraction from sensory experience but on the empirical, sensorial grasping of differences and similarities. Logical relation is in a sense 'perceptible to the senses' because 'a certain dose of content'[18] is incorporated into logical form. For example (though it is not clear if this is a made-up example in chapter 1 of *Wild Thought*), if tobacco smoke is 'the intersection of two groups – one also including grilled meat and bread ... the other including cheese, beer, and honey', this is because of the sensed association between their odours.[19] This is a logic 'whose laws are limited to transposing the properties of the real'.[20] As Claude Imbert puts it, the logic of sensation is one in which 'the qualitative structure of sensibility ... encode[s] a symbolic organisation ... where human sensibility emerges as articulated systems of differences, with degrees of intensity, and preferences'. The logical operator in this case, then,

14. Lévi-Strauss, *Wild Thought*, pp. 15, 43, 75.
15. Lévi-Strauss, *The Raw and The Cooked*, p. 1.
16. Claude Imbert, 'On Anthropological Knowledge', in Boris Wiseman, ed., *The Cambridge Companion to Lévi-Strauss*, Cambridge University Press, Cambridge, 2009, pp. 123, 122.
17. Lévi-Strauss, *Wild Thought*, pp. 19–20.
18. Ibid., pp. 19, 41.
19. Ibid., p. 15.
20. Ibid., p. xix.

is 'a scale of qualitative differences which implies opposition and intensity, and allows the unlimited insertion of further differences and oppositions'.[21] No structure organizes the empirical contents of sense *a priori*; the contents organize the structure. The logic of sensation deserves the name 'logic', Lévi-Strauss says, to the extent that the relations that it establishes are necessary relations. For Kant it would be impossible to ground such necessity on empirical, sensed similarities and differences. But the logic of sensation is not troubled by this because it is a logic of 'an *a posteriori* necessity', as Lévi-Strauss says in *Wild Thought*.[22] In this context the transcendental is to be thought then, if at all, as concrete, sensuous *a posteriori* necessity, derived from a particular cultural or ethnographic context.[23]

The totemic operator

Arguably, *Wild Thought* suggests that ethnography discovers the logics of sensation in trying to understand their higher-level manifestations and particularly in their elaboration in what is called 'totemism', a term that Lévi-Strauss continues to employ though 'sceptical ... as to the reality of what it denotes'.[24] The 'totemic illusion' of ethnography is the result of an abstraction of parts of a semantic field from the system of which they form an integral part.[25] This stems from the presumption that the relationship between totem animal, for example, and clan is

---

21. Imbert, 'On Anthropological Knowledge', pp. 122, 124.
22. Lévi-Strauss, *Wild Thought*, p. 41.
23. Lévi-Strauss writes (ibid., p. 15) that chemistry 'confirms the evidence of the senses' because the group 'cheese, beer and honey', for example, contains diacetyl; 'wild cherry, cinnamon, vanilla and sherry form a group that is not only sensorial but also intelligible, because they all contain aldehyde', and so on. But consistency demands that the sensorial group is itself already intelligible qua sensorial – the sensorial/intelligible distinction is inappropriate in a logic of sense. The *a posteriori* necessity derives from a particular cultural or ethnographic context because the relevant groups comprise elements with a specific place or places in a specific system of differences – the smell of tobacco does not mean the same in all contexts, even if (which in itself is doubtful) it smells the same in all contexts.
24. Lévi-Strauss, *Totemism*, p. 15.
25. Ibid., p. 18.

Clan A	::	Animal X
≠		≠
Clan B	::	Animal Y
≠		≠
Clan C	::	Animal Z

FIGURE 1 Clan A and Clan B do not resemble each other because they are clans; Animal X and Animal Y do not resemble each other because they are animals. Clan A does not resemble Animal X. The differences between Clan A and Clan B resemble the differences between Animal X and Animal Y.

based on the subject's relation to that animal as object (for example, food object, good to eat) or based on its identification with one feature of the animal, for example its strength or cunning.[26] The totemic illusion is the presumption of a one-to-one relation (of utility or resemblance, for example; but it may also be arbitrary) between animal and clan, or the relation between one group of people and one animal species. Lévi-Strauss proposes, as is well known, that the basic totemic relationship is, rather, a relationship between two systems: 'one based on distinction between [social] groups, the other on distinction between species, in such a fashion that a plurality of groups on the one hand, and a plurality of species on the other, are placed directly in correlation and opposition'.[27]

The correlation/opposition is based on the postulated homology between differential features between clan A and clan B and between species X and species Y (FIGURE 1).[28] This does not mean that clan A and clan B resemble each other because they are clans, and species X and species Y resemble each other because they are animals, so that their respective resemblances allow the clans and animals to be matched up: '*it is not the resemblances,*

26. Imbert ('On Anthropological Knowledge', pp. 119, 132) describes this kind of presumption as entrapment within a Kantian approach, privileging the problem of the relation between subject and object when this is 'a fleeting philosophical problem inseparable from a propositional stance frozen in transcendentalism', though it is not clear what 'transcendentalism' means here.

27. Lévi-Strauss, *Totemism*, p. 20.

28. Ibid., p. 13.

but the differences, that resemble each other'. There are animals
that differ from each other and there are people who differ from
each other, 'and the resemblance is between these two systems
of differences'.[29] Although this may at first seem to suggest that
the various systems of differences are in principle separate and
independent of each other, in fact the 'internal' differences are
only known as such through relations between systems.

The basic totemic relationship sketched above is, to be sure,
an anthropological abstraction, but such are the methodological
constraints. Totemism is, though, only one example of the more
general problem of classification, or one aspect of much more
– indeed possibly infinitely – complex systems of classification.
Looking more specifically at the classification of plant or animal
species, Lévi-Strauss points out the intrinsic difficulties facing
the anthropologist who would understand any given system
based on polyvalent logics 'that draw simultaneously on several
formally different types of connection', working on several axes
simultaneously.[30] For the distinctions between animal species
and between plant species function not just as a formalization
of knowledge about these aspects of the environment; they
also function as 'concrete classifiers' that convey ideas and are
reciprocally convertible with abstract classifiers such as numbers,
directions and cardinal points, as well as other 'natural' categories such as seasons and elements (wind, earth, etc.):[31]

> We see, then, that in no case can an animal, the 'totem', or its
> species be understood as a biological entity; by its dual character
> as an organism – that is, a system – and the emanation of a species
> – which is a term in a system – the animal appears as a conceptual
> tool with multiple possibilities for detotalizing and retotalizing any
> domain, whether situated in synchrony or diachrony, the concrete or
> the abstract, nature or culture.[32]

29. Ibid., p. 77; see also *Wild Thought*, p. 128.
30. *Wild Thought*, pp. 70, 71.
31. Ibid., pp. 160–61.
32. Ibid., p. 168.

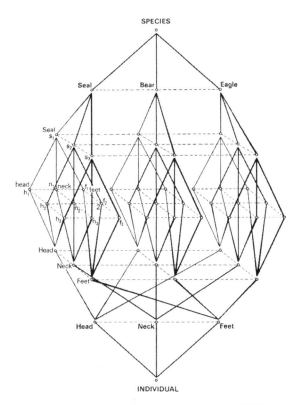

FIGURE 2 The totemic operator. The figure appears in *Wild Thought*, p. 172. It is attributed there to *Laboratoire de cartographie, École Practique des Hautes Études*.

The ideal dismemberment of the animal and the differences within any given species (what we would call varieties, but also stages of maturity, different colours, and so on) means that it is not the animal itself but 'a veritable system by means of an animal' that 'constitutes the object of thought [in the indigenous society] and furnishes the conceptual tool'.[33] The natural species – the animal or plant as 'totemic operator'[34] – is the privileged classifier both because it offers the most intuitive image of the

33. Ibid.
34. Ibid., p. 171.

discontinuity of the real and because, as a middle-level classifier, it offers so many opportunities to 'widen its network' upwards in the direction of abstract classifiers and downwards to the most concrete, to individuals and proper names.[35] The figure of the totemic operator in *Wild Thought* (FIGURE 2) represents, as Lévi-Strauss says, 'no more than a very small fraction of the ideal model', as it represents only a fraction of the number of natural species and shows only the skeleton of the conceptual tool, and neither the network generated by the conceptual tool nor the possible integration of domains by means of the 'logical power of the species-level operator'.[36] The animal or plant as a conceptual tool is not limited to its function as a totemic operator. Animals and plants are good to think with in more ways than this.

Freud: the logic of the dream

But, so what?

Lévi-Strauss's overarching project was to establish facts about the human mind, not about this or that society.[37] Sometimes this means that so-called 'wild thought' is also 'our thought', coexisting with 'forms of thought that take science as their authority'.[38] Here Lévi-Strauss should have said forms of thought that take *Western* science as their authority, because the distinction between wild thought and Western science is also cast in *Wild Thought* as the distinction between 'two distinct modes of scientific thought ... two strategic levels at which nature allows itself to be grasped by scientific knowledge – one approximately congruent with perception and imagination, and the other at a

35. Ibid., pp. 155, 169.
36. Ibid., p. 185.
37. Edmund Leach, *Claude Lévi-Strauss* (1970), University of Chicago Press, Chicago IL, 1974, p. 2.
38. Lévi-Strauss in Lévi-Strauss and Eribon, *Conversations with Claude Lévi-Strauss*, p. 110.

remove'.[39] The logic of sensation, on the one hand, and Kant's transcendental logic, on the other, perhaps, but not necessarily. Wild thought is not 'the thought of savages nor of a primitive or archaic humanity, but thought in the wild state, as opposed to thought that has been cultivated or domesticated with a view to yielding a return'.[40] Wild thought is 'always present and alive among us'.[41] But it is hard to see how this does not cast wild thought as the original form of thought, out of and alongside which the distinct path of Western scientific thought develops, which comes perilously close to the primitivist interpretation that Lévi-Strauss otherwise explicitly denies.[42] Elsewhere the universality of human thought is for Lévi-Strauss not wild thought itself but the universal structures of the mind, or an 'original logic, a direct expression of the structure of the mind (and behind the mind, probably, of the brain)', the 'logic of oppositions and correlations, exclusions and inclusions, compatibilities and incompatibilities, which explain the laws of association and not the reverse'.[43] Distilling this down to its purest essence, 'The logical principle is always *to be able to oppose* terms.'[44] This basic logical principle proliferates into systems in

39. Lévi-Strauss, *Wild Thought*, p. 18.
40. Ibid., p. 247.
41. See also Lévi-Strauss in Lévi-Strauss and Eribon, *Conversations with Claude Lévi-Strauss*, p. 110: 'I wanted to show that there is no gap between the way so-called primitive peoples think and the way we do. When strange customs or beliefs that offended common sense were remarked in our own societies, they would be explained as vestiges or survivals of archaic ways of thinking. On the contrary, it seemed to me that these ways of thinking are always present and alive among us. We often give them free rein. They coexist with forms of thought that take science as their authority, and by that right they are contemporaries.' Lévi-Strauss sees wild thought, 'always present and alive among us', in art among other phenomena.
42. Nevertheless, this is the position Boris Wiseman ('Structure and Sensation', in *The Cambridge Companion to Lévi-Strauss*, p. 302) attributes to Lévi-Strauss. Wiseman reads *Wild Thought* as based on a historical narrative according to which human thought remains entirely rooted in the logic of sensory properties, with an immediate relation to the perceptible world, until the neolithic. With the event of 'the Greeks', the birth of reason and of domesticated or abstract thought, we witness a bifurcation in human thinking 'whereby humanity discovered another way of accessing the necessary relations previously grasped at the level of sensory experience alone'. 'Oh, those Greeks!', as Nietzsche once said.
43. Lévi-Strauss, *Totemism*, p. 90.
44. Lévi-Strauss, *Wild Thought*, p. 85.

which operators function at a plurality of levels on a plurality of vertical and horizontal axes which, Lévi-Strauss implies, we can see more clearly in systems based on the logic of sensation than in our own systems, even though the same proliferating logical principle is at the basis of all thought, including the 'forms of thought that take [Western] science as their authority'. Indeed, we cannot see the universal structures from within any one system of thought alone, as Kant tried to do. Thought in the wild *is* this proliferating logical principle, and Lévi-Strauss's work shows it as it has developed into systems of knowledge and social classification in various indigenous cultures. The structures and logic of these systems can be understood as unconscious, transcendental *a posteriori* necessities, albeit ones vulnerable to the contingency of events, which can indeed be catastrophic for them. But where can we catch 'thought in the wild' in Western societies today?

Some, for example Boris Wiseman, would say you find it in popular culture. So let us be permitted a little joke about UK politics (FIGURE 3). Did we catch a glimpse of wild thought in the lettuce recently deployed as a conceptual tool in the demotic UK media, part of a system of differences in which the lettuce, which is not a cabbage, operates at the level of the ideal anatomy of the head and in relation to various sets of abstract classifiers (wet/dry, cold/hot, fresh/rotten, alive/dead, useful/useless, worthy/unworthy). Here the lettuce is a 'binary operator',[45] able to represent, simultaneously, both what is alive and what is dead. There is an affinity between the lettuce and the problem that it is evoked to signify – the enigma of a prime minister who is also not a prime minister.[46]

45. Claude Lévi-Strauss, *Myth and Meaning: Cracking the Code of Culture*, Schocken Books, New York, 1979 p. 22. This is the text of a series of talks broadcast on CBC Radio in December 1977.
46. Liz Truss became leader of the governing Conservative Party in September 2022, and thus prime minister of Great Britain and Northern Ireland. After a disastrous budget leading to immediate economic instability, and after intense pressure from politicians and

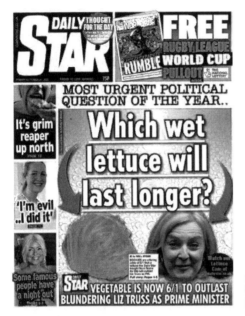

FIGURE 3 *Daily Star*, 14 October 2022. Lettuce vs Liz.

More seriously, perhaps, did Freud catch thought in the wild in Austria at the end of the nineteenth century in his own and his patients' dreams? Let us take as an example the famous analysis of the 'Dream of the Botanical Monograph'. Having one morning seen a monograph on the genus *Cyclamen* in the window of a book shop, Freud that night dreamed that he had written a monograph on a certain plant, that the book lay before him as he turned over a coloured plate. There were dried specimens of plants, as if from a herbarium, between the pages.[47] The analysis of this dream gives rise to a whole series of memories

---

public, she resigned after only fifty days in office, making her the shortest-serving prime minister in British history. When it was already obvious to everyone (except perhaps Truss) that she would have to resign, the *Daily Star* set up a live webcam with a 60p lettuce and a photograph of Liz Truss, to see which would last the longest. The lettuce won. (Thanks to the students in my Philosophy and Psychoanalysis class 2022–23 for the example of Liz and the lettuce.)

47. Sigmund Freud, *The Interpretation of Dreams* (1900), trans. James Strachey, Standard Edition, vols IV and V, Vintage, London, 2001, p. 169. This dream first appears in the discussion of 'Recent and Indifferent Material', in chapter 5, 'The Material and Sources of Dreams'.

and thoughts that he later calls the 'botanical group of ideas',[48] among them his wife's favourite flowers, not frequently enough remembering to bring her flowers, a patient whose husband forgets to bring her flowers on their anniversary, Freud's work on and use of the coca plant ('that business with the cocaine'), Professor Gärtner [Gardener] and his wife (whom Freud had met that day, commenting on their 'blooming looks'), a childhood task in a herbarium and his studies in botany, Freud's own favourite flower, the artichoke and a young woman named 'Flora' whom he had discussed with Professor Gärtner. These trains of thoughts and memories all lead Freud to the – at first apparently unconnected – memory of a significant conversation with a friend, Dr Königstein, which he had also had on the day of the dream.[49]

A major issue in the justification of the analysis of the dream concerns the contingency of the chains of thought that lead from his seeing the botanical monograph in the bookshop and talking to Dr Königstein. What if he had not also met Dr Gärtner and discussed a young woman named Flora? Freud accepts these contingencies: if the dream day had offered different material, then other 'chains of thought would no doubt have been selected'; if not enough intermediate links between the monograph and Dr Königstein could have been found then the dream would have been different. But '[s]ince it was the [botanical] monograph and not any other idea that was chosen to serve this function [that is, connect up the various elements], we must suppose that it was the best adapted for the connection.'[50] Revisiting the analysis of this dream in the later chapter on the dream-work, Freud notes that not only the compound 'botanical monograph' but also the elements 'botanical' and 'monograph' separately

---

48. Ibid., p. 176.
49. All of the 'trains of thoughts' (*Gedankengänge*) ultimately led, he says, 'to one or other of the many ramifications of my conversation with Dr Königstein'. Ibid., p. 173.
50. Ibid., p. 176.

'led by numerous connecting paths deeper and deeper into the tangle of dream-thoughts' – that is, into the latent content of the dream. They are each a 'nodal point' (*ein Knotenpunkt*), a junction, in the dream upon which numerous trains of thought (*Gedankengänge*) converged. As elements of the manifest dream content, they were, like all other elements in fact, 'overdetermined'.[51] Further, each of the dream thoughts is also represented by multiple elements in the manifest dream content. He concludes:

> Thus a dream is not constructed by each individual dream-thought, or group of dream-thoughts, finding (in an abbreviated form) separate representation in the content of the dream ... a dream is constructed, rather, by a whole mass of dream thoughts being submitted to a sort of manipulative process in which those elements which have most numerous and strongest supports acquire the right of entry into the dream content.[52]

Later, Freud says that the dream-thoughts emerge

> as a complex of thoughts and memories of the most intricate possible structure [*Aufbau*], with all the attributes of the trains of thought familiar to us in waking life. ... each train of thought is almost invariably accompanied by its contradictory counterpart, linked with it by antithetical association. The different portions of this complicated structure stand, of course, in the most manifold logical relations to one another.[53]

It is important that the idea of trains of thought, which suggests a movement from one place to another along tracks, not be allowed to dominate the way we think about this. What is suggested is altogether more multidimensional or multiplanar. Each element in the dream content – for example, the botanical

---

51. Ibid., p. 283.
52. Ibid., p. 284.
53. Ibid., pp. 311–12. In his first comment on this Freud maintains that the dream has no means of representing (*keine Mittel der Darstellung*) these logical relations between the dream thoughts (p. 312). Over the next few pages, however, he proposes various ways in which the dream-work does 'indicate' (*anzeudeuten*) them.

monograph – is not like the centre of a spider's web either. As a
sign, in its formal and plurilogical relations, it is more like the
totemic operator, or something functioning within the logic
of the totemic operator, to the extent that the figure of the
totemic operator as we see it in *Wild Thought* is a fraction of
the 'potential framework' of the system of differences of (here)
animal species, related off stage, as it were, to other systems of
differences, including those of groups of people and groups of
human-made objects.

It might be objected that whereas the totemic operator is a
sign in a shared system of differences, the botanical monograph
in the dream is a merely a sign that surfaces in the psyche of
an individual and that thus functions exceptionally idiomati-
cally, such that it cannot be compared to the totemic operator.
However, the botanical group of ideas (the genus *Cyclamen*,
bunches of flowers, artichokes, the names Gärtner and Flora,
the idea of blooming looks, and so on) is obviously intelligible
as a group to us as well as to Freud himself. We could say that
the dream makes use of something functioning with the logic
of the totemic operator, and the analysis of the dream lays this
out or makes this explicit. The dream is dreamed within the
constraints of the (quasi-transcendental?) *a posteriori* necessary
'unconscious structures' of the dreamer's society, not according
to what Lévi-Strauss in another context calls 'the apparent
arbitrariness of the mind, its supposedly spontaneous flow of
inspiration, and its seemingly uncontrolled inventiveness'.[54]
But the wild thought of the dream, we could say, makes use of
more of the systems of differences within which its elements are
located than do our usual waking constructions, or the dream
explores or manipulates these system of differences more than

---

54. Lévi-Strauss, *The Raw and The Cooked*, p. 10. It is on this basis that we can begin to
understand some of the otherwise contradictory and implausible discussion of symbols
in dreams in chapter V of *The Interpretation of Dreams*.

does the use of signs in other contexts. We could also say that
the dream and its analysis are a commentary on the systems of
differences that it mobilizes, testing its limits.

Metzger: futurethoughts

But, if so, what is 'wild' about wild thought? Are not these
systems of differences, because of their *a posteriori* necessity,
in danger of appearing somewhat static in Lévi-Strauss's and
Freud's analyses? Still too much like 'forms imposed on content',
as Lévi-Strauss says in 1949? Too much like transcendental *a
priori* forms (or structures) with or according to which thought
thinks, rather than wild thought or thinking in the wild itself?[55]

In 1930, while Lévi-Strauss was still a student, the French
philosopher and historian of science Hélène Metzger published
a critical essay on the work of Lucien Lévy-Bruhl that was
dedicated to the analysis of what he continued to call 'primitive'
thought. 'Primitive thought', according to Lévy-Bruhl, is 'the
mentality peculiar to undeveloped peoples', which is contrasted
with 'our own' '"Mediterranean" civilisation, in which a rationalistic philosophy and positive science have been developed'.[56]

55. When seen like this, these 'systems of differences' are structured like a language;
in the case of Freud's analysis of the 'Dream of the Botanical Monograph' we might
even say that what is analysed is reducible to linguistic groups. However, Freud's analysis
lays as much stress on the function of the psychical investment of ideas as on what
Saussure calls 'associative' linguistic relations; and, of course, the 'syntagmatic' relation
is either absent or severely disrupted by the dream-work. (See Ferdinand de Saussure,
Course in General Linguistics (1915), trans. Roy Harris, Bloomsbury Academic, London,
2013, ch. 5, 'Syntagmatic Relations and Associative Relations'.) The question is: what
'works' the dream-work? See Stella Sandford, 'The "Thought-Work"; Or, The Exuberance
of Thinking in Kant and Freud', in Panayiota Vassilopoulou and Daniel Whistler, eds,
Thought: A Philosophical History, Routledge, London, 2021, pp. 219–35. We might also
remember that 'wild' (*wilde*) was not a happy word for Freud. It was because of the
growing practice of 'wild' psychoanalysis that Freud felt he had 'no choice' but to found
the International Psycho-analytical Association in 1910, in order that its members might
'repudiate responsibility for what is done by those who do not belong to us'. Freud,
'"Wild" Psycho-analysis' [1910], trans. James Strachey, Standard Edition, vol. XI, Vintage,
London, 2001, pp. 226–7.
56. Lucien Lévy-Bruhl, *How Natives Think* (1922), trans. Lilian A. Clare, Martino
Publishing, Mansfield Centre CT, 2015, p. 29. This translation comprises both Lévy-Bruhl's
1922 *La mentalité primitive* and *Les fonctions mentales dans les sociétés inférieures* of 1910.

According to Lévy-Bruhl this primitive, animist, mystical, magical, prelogical thought is the thought of the childhood of humanity, more or less banished in the logical mentality of the European.[57] Three decades before Lévi-Strauss set about countering the presumptions of Lévy-Bruhl and this ilk of anthropology in general, Metzger criticized Lévy-Bruhl by denying that there existed a great gulf between what he called 'primitive' and 'civilized' thinking, arguing that Western logic is not the instrument of thought but of verification.[58] Metzger identified what she called 'spontaneous' thought as the basis of all thought, including the scientific – a spontaneous thought that was often 'choked' or 'repressed' by logical thought which takes as its task the disciplining of spontaneous thought.[59] Logical critique alone is 'insufficient to create philosophy and science'; spontaneous thought is also required because it furnishes the first inspiration for discovery and invention and reason derives its 'force' from spontaneous thought. Scientific thought is or needs to be 'grafted on' to spontaneous thought to become 'truly productive'. And while thought disciplined by logical critique can be studied formally, apart from its content, spontaneous thought cannot be cut in two; its form cannot be separated from its content. Spontaneous thought must be continually active and cannot stop to reflect back on itself without risking self-destruction.[60]

To some extent Metzger's conception of spontaneous thought suffers from the same problem with Lévi-Strauss's conception of wild thought. Metzger implies that Europeans in fact (or at least potentially) think both spontaneously and scientifically, but what about the others? The episodic nature of Metzger's work,

57. Ibid., pp. 97, 80.
58. Hélène Metzger, 'La philosophie de Lucien Lévy-Bruhl et l'histoire des sciences', in *La méthode philosophique en histoire des sciences: Textes 1914–1939*, Fayard, Paris, 1978, pp. 118, 119.
59. Ibid., p. 120.
60. Ibid., pp. 121, 122, 127. As such, the idea of 'spontaneous thought' may derive primarily not from Lévy-Bruhl's 'primitive thought', or even Lévi-Strauss's 'wild thought', but Kant's concept of spontaneity in *The Critique of Pure Reason*.

often in the form of book reviews, does not allow us to press the questions further with her. But Metzger's notion of 'spontaneous thought' is not a set of contents or a method. We can understand it to be the driving force of thought itself, the embodied vitality of thought. If Lévi-Strauss and Freud, in their different but overlapping ways, reveal the infinite possibilities contained within different multilevel systems of signifying differences, Metzger perhaps identifies what moves them, the force that mobilizes them in novel combinations and allows for innovation: perhaps that is 'wild thinking'? Neither form not content but process? Neither cause nor effect but driver?

When Lévi-Strauss says that wild thought is not 'the apparent arbitrariness of the mind, its supposedly spontaneous flow of inspiration, and its seemingly uncontrolled inventiveness', this might appear to be a rebuke to Metzger. But if he meant that it is not like the 'psychical anarchy' that some of Freud's predecessors saw at work in dreams, a kind of ultimately meaningless delirium,[61] then neither is Metzger's spontaneous thought like that. For Lévi-Strauss wild thought seems to be the name for the existing, open-ended complexity within the systems of differences with which we already think but which is from the standpoint of Western scientific rationality (the 'enclosure of the European mind', as Imbert put it[62]) more visible outside of it in other systems of thought; or, as we have suggested, more visible in dreams than in the usual run of waking thought. If so, then perhaps Metzger's idea of spontaneous thought is something like the vital motor of it all, what makes the logical possibility of new configurations within the systems of differences actual, which is also therefore what potentially actualizes the logical possibility of transformation in the history of philosophy.

61. See Freud, *The Interpretation of Dreams*, p. 55.
62. Imbert 'On Anthropological Knowledge', p. 126.

6

Climate catastrophe and the bomb

HOWARD CAYGILL

In their introduction to *Arts of Living on a Damaged Planet*, Anna Tsing and her colleagues on the Aarhus University Research on the Anthropocene Project wrote: '*Anthropos* has become an overwhelming force that can build and destroy, birth and kill all others on the planet.'[1] In a collection dedicated to ghosting, monstrosity, contingent entanglements and other ecological storytellings, this apodictic note sounds strangely out of place. For this answer to implied questions of 'what is *anthropos*?' and 'what is to become of it?' is not offered as a working hypothesis, or another story, or even as an argument, but as an axiom carrying complete conviction and assuming full assent from its readers. It brings with it demands that we can immediately recognize and perhaps even, unwisely, empathize with: demands, for example, to act as if there is 'no Planet B'. My question is not so much whether such claims about human destructive power are true or false but rather how we have become so certain about them: whence comes this conviction that the answer to 'know thyself' can be so unequivocally answered in terms of *anthropos*'s

---

1. Anna Tsing et al., *Arts of Living on a Damaged Planet*, Minnesota University Press, Minneapolis MN, 2017, G12.

'overwhelming force' and its alleged power over planetary life and death?

That sentence from *Arts of Living on a Damaged Planet* echoes in its rhythm and its sense the grotesque 'quotation' from the Bhagavad Gita by the director of the Manhattan Project, J. Robert Oppenheimer, after watching the Trinity explosion of the first atom bomb on 16 July 1945. He recollected later in a speech:

> I remembered the line from the Hindu scripture, the *Bhagavad Gita*: Vishnu is trying to persuade the Prince that he should do his duty and to impress him he takes on his multi-armed form and says 'Now I am become death, the destroyer of worlds.' I suppose we all thought that, one way or another.[2]

Oppenheimer's use of a part of chapter II, verse 32 of the *Gita* is usually cited with awe, as in Karen Barad's contribution to *Arts of Living on a Damaged Planet,* 'No Small Matter: Mushroom Clouds, Ecologies of Nothingness, and Strange Topologies of Spacetimemattering',[3] but both its widespread acceptance, bolstered by Christopher Nolan's 2023 film, and its obnoxious hubris is troubling.

It is troubling not only because the more accepted translation of Krishna's manifestation of this one of many of his universal forms to Arjuna is: 'I am time. I make worlds die, I have come to destroy worlds.'[4] Reading the verse with Krishna becoming time rather than death offers a far more nuanced sense of the affinity between time, death and the passing of worlds than could ever

2. In his definitive *The Making of the Atom Bomb*, Richard Rhodes cites a post-war lecture by Oppenheimer in which he remembers saying these words. Richard Rhodes, *The Making of the Atomic Bomb*, Simon & Schuster, New York, 1986, p. 676.

3. Tsing et al., *Arts of Living*, G106. The second atom bomb, dropped on Hiroshima, is also an important referent in Tsing's ethnography, *The Mushroom at the End of the World*: 'When Hiroshima was destroyed by an atomic bomb in 1945, it is said the first living thing to emerge from the blasted landscape was a matsutake mushroom.' Anna Tsing, *The Mushroom at the End of the World: On the Possibility of Life in Capitalist Ruins*, Princeton University Press, Princeton NJ, 2015, p. 3. That mushroom at the end of a world remains exemplary for all the others at the end of *the* world.

4. Amit Majmudar, *Godsong: A Verse Translation of the Bhagavad-Gita with Commentary*, Alfred A. Knopf, New York, 2018, p. 88.

be captured in an atomic detonation.[5] And not only because
Oppenheimer selectively cites the verse, deleting the humbling
second part that would have tempered his arrogance: 'All those
warriors, stationed in opposing ranks: / Even without you they
will cease to be.'[6] But surely most troubling is the hubris of the
blasphemous identification with Krishna: J. Robert Oppenheimer
and his accomplices did not become Krishna, they did not make
worlds die. They only augmented the power to destroy cities.
They did not come to destroy worlds but only provided the
means to murder Japanese people. So there is something very
wrong with this inaugural mythologizing of atomic weaponry
through an appeal to the *Bhagavad Gita*; a wrong path taken
from the very start. For with Trinity, then in the attacks on
Hiroshima and Nagasaki and in the 500 bomb tests that would
follow, in all this, *anthropos* did not become 'destroyers of worlds'
but at best (at worst) destroyers of themselves as part of a geopolitical and, in planetary terms, insignificant human civil war.

What if such mythologizing of human power through atomic
weaponry is related to, or even a condition of possibility for, the
mythologizing of human power to 'build and destroy, birth and
kill all others on the planet in the anthropocene'?[7] What if it
is a mythology that underwrites arguments for the collapse of
planetary geological time into human historical time, as formal-
ized philosophically by Dipesh Chakrabarty, and the prevailing
view of *anthropos* as an 'overwhelming' planetary force, proposed

5. My thanks to Varun Gopal Tiwari for the lesson on this verse of the Gita: 'The
phrase "I am Death" is an attempted translation of the phrase in Sanskrit – kaal asmi
(kaal – time , asmi – I am) ... The relation between kaal as time and kaal as death is
complex and does not lend itself to a simple synonymic translation where kaal = time =
death.' Personal correspondence.
6. Majmudar, *Godsong*, p. 88. Commenting on Nolan's film, Mani Rao sees in the
truncated citation of a 'moment' from the Gita as a simplification of its wider concerns;
kalo'smi is but one in a long list of self-revelations of Krishna, and in 'the broader context
of the Gita, we realise that war eventually proves catastrophic for everyone in the
Mahabharata'. Mani Rao, '"Now I am become Death, the Destroyer of Worlds": Truth and
Lies in Oppenheimer's Gita Moment', *Scroll.in*, 5 August 2023.
7. Tsing, *Arts of Living*, G12.

in Paul Crutzen's one-page 2002 article in *Nature*, 'The Anthropocene: Geology of Mankind'? What if the Anthropocene – one
of the first new concepts to be forged in the twenty-first century
– has its origins in the mythology of nuclear devastation? The
danger in uncritically accepting this mythology is that it abso-
lutizes and at the same time moralizes human power, the better
to conceal it and so surrender to melancholy resignation before
it. The fantasy of such planet-breaking power complicates and
renders almost inaccessible any possibility of sustaining a political logic of debate and real contestation of destructive power.
The delusion of imagining we have become like Krishna and can
destroy worlds forgets that the overwhelming force of anthropos
– that 0.01 per cent of planetary biomass – might be an all too
human illusion to which the planet is indifferent. And, perhaps
more controversially, might not the hubristic assumption that we
are such a destructive planetary force, along with the absolutist
salvational ethics and politics of environmental action to which
it gives rise to 'save the planet', be one of the main obstacles to
preserving the current set of planetary parameters favourable to
human life?

The historical narrative of the roots of environmentalist
discourse in the strategies of the cold war is by now uncontro-
versial. In *Arming Mother Nature: The Origins of Catastrophic
Environmentalism*, Jacob Hamblin made a strong case for the
significance of the International Geophysical Year of 1958 in
establishing the epistemological conditions for environmental
knowledge through systems of planetary surveillance and
measurement. This claim followed his 2010 work on the strategic
vision of environmental warfare in 'A Global Contamination
Zone: Early Cold War Planning for Environmental Warfare' in
J.R. McNeill's *Environmental Histories of the Cold War*, which describes the weaponizing of planetary forces against an adversary
entertained by both the USA and the USSR, along with the UN

conferences and treaties that attempted to limit it. Prominent among the conditions of possibility of imagining environmental catastrophe may be added the changing reflections, some of them philosophical, on the environmental impact of the atomic and hydrogen bombs.[8]

The immediate philosophical reflections on atomic warfare were limited and ambivalent; unwilling to surrender established philosophical positions in the face of a new and unprecedented destructive force. The focus on spectacular blast damage that immediately followed the attacks on Japan – which remain for some, including Mario Tronti, the *war crimes* committed on Hiroshima and Nagasaki – distracted even philosophical attention from the invisible threat posed by radiation. Regarding the bomb as a more powerful version of conventional ordinance enabled the extremes of Oppenheimer's 'we have become death' and a view that minimized the planetary impact of atomic blasts. Edward Teller and his associates planned to use nuclear explosions to reshape the Arctic and calculated that the risk of damage from nuclear blasts was outweighed by the economic benefits of opening a navigable passage through the Arctic Ocean.[9]

The obsession with the visible appearance of the destructive power of nuclear weaponry contributed to the frankly modest and limited achievements of philosophical discourses on nuclear war. The extraordinary documentation of John O'Brian's collection *Camera Atomica* chronicles this abiding fascination with the visible destructive effects of human power unleashed by nuclear weapons that was accompanied by relatively subdued attention to the effects of invisible radiation poisoning.[10] Efforts to think

8. Jacob Darwin Hamblin, *Arming Mother Nature: The Birth of Catastrophic Environmentalism*, Oxford University Press, Oxford, 2013; J.R. McNeill, *Environmental Histories of the Cold War*, Cambridge University Press, Cambridge, 2010.
9. Dan O'Neill, *The Firecracker Boys: H Bombs, Inupiat Eskimoes and the Roots of the Environmental Movement*, Basic Books, Philadelphia PA, 1994.
10. John O'Brian, *Camera Atomica*, Black Dog Publishing, London, 2015.

beyond the visible effects of nuclear explosions and to imagine a new transcendental aesthetic sensitive to the invisible workings of radiation, such as Joseph Masco's *The Nuclear Borderlands* and *The Future of Fallout, and Other Episodes in Radioactive World-Making* (2021) remain singular and largely unheeded calls to rethink the intricate complicities between visible and invisible destruction at a global scale.[11] The obsession with the visible power of nuclear blasts answered to a fascination with the spectacle of destruction that tended to overestimate human power at a planetary scale, and offered a fatal distraction from the more insidious and unspectacular threats posed by radioactivity and other invisible vectors of destruction such as greenhouse gases. It became easier to entertain the melancholy fantasy of total visible destruction than to work pragmatically with incremental, invisible threats.

The mythology of nuclear war promoted by Oppenheimer and his contemporaries intoxicated by the visible destructive force of nuclear weaponry was gradually challenged as the public became aware of the invisible and long-term dangers of radiation. By the late 1950s the object of nuclear threat slowly moved from the all-too-visible blasts and mushroom clouds of the H-bomb tests to the atmospheric radiation released by nuclear test explosions. This was in spite of official (US Atomic Energy Commission) re-assurance in 1955 that 'the radiation from the [Nevada] tests was "only slightly higher than normal radiation…"'.[12] Nevil Shute's 1957 novel *On the Beach* contributed to a growing awareness of the threats posed by radiation, which reached a climax with the 1959 strontium-90 cultural panic following what retrospectively should have been the wholly unsurprising discovery

11. Joseph Masco, *The Nuclear Borderlands: The Manhattan Project in Post-Cold War New Mexico*, Princeton University Press, Princeton NJ, 2006; Masco, *The Future of Fallout, and Other Episodes in Radioactive World-Making*, Duke University Press, Durham NC and London, 2021.
12. Fred Pearce, *Fallout*, Portobello Books, London, 2018, p. 25.

that strontium-90 radiation released by nuclear explosions
was detected in baby milk and other foods. Again, it was Jacob
Hamblin, in his *Poison in the Well: Radioactive Waste in the Oceans
at the Dawn of the Nuclear Age*, who showed how this cultural
panic emerged from new techniques for measuring radioactivity
from the mid-1950s.[13] With the invisible radioactivity manifesting
itself in scientific measurements and food chains, the rendering
visible of the invisible directly inspired protest movements,
including what would become CND.[14]

The immediate radiological effects of nuclear explosions were,
however, known and monitored from the outset. As early as 1949
David Bradley, a medical observer of the Bikini test explosions,
published a log of the tests with the unequivocal title *No Place
to Hide*. As a radiological monitor with the Radiological Safety
Section, or one of the 'Geiger men', Bradley described his mission
as 'to stand guard with Geiger counters for invisible danger from
radioactivity'.[15] Although written under the censorship of official
secrecy, Bradley was able to refer not only to the invisible 'poison'
of radioactivity but also indirectly to its geographical reach: the
'Geiger men's' 'assignment began at Bikini, but their mission
spread to include the neighbouring atolls, the hundreds of miles
to Eniwetok, Guam, the Philippines, Hawaii, and ultimately to

---

13. Jacob Darwin Hamblin, *Poison in the Well: Radioactive Waste in the Oceans at the
Dawn of the Nuclear Age*, Rutgers University Press, New Brunswick NJ, 2008.
14. For a sense of this change of cultural climate, listen to Peter LaFarge's 'Radioactive
Eskimo' (1965):
Bring on the Geiger counter
Bring on the old hard rain
Bring on the army engineers
The answer's just the same

I'm a radioactive Eskimo
With a radioactive mother
A radioactive sister
And a radioactive brother

My wife can't suckle our babies
The milk must come from cans
My wife's too radioactive
Say, we're real atom fans
15. David Bradley, *No Place to Hide*, Hodder & Stoughton, London, 1949, p. 14.

the seaports of the West Coast. Bradley was in no doubt about the global reach of the threat posed by radioactivity and its potentially devastating consequences for human and other forms of life.

No Place to Hide begins with the striking image of the return to San Francisco of the US Navy ship *Independence*, used as a target vessel in the Bikini tests. Bradley first described the visible blast damage – 'she looked less like a ship than a paper bag blown up and burst' – and then noted: 'what is most impressive, and likely to be overlooked, is that she remains an outcast ship. The disease of radioactivity lingers on her decks and sides and along her dingy corridors.' Bradley hoped his book would alert public opinion to the invisible 'overlooked' but no less 'lingering and insidious nature of the radioactive agent which makes it such an ideal weapon for use on civilian populations'.[16]

Yet while Bradley was already sounding the warning in 1949, it would be another ten years before the dangers of radioactivity would become a cultural fact and occasion for political mobilization.[17] However, the significance of strontium-90 remained ambivalent, as was evident in two influential books published in response to the strontium-90 panic: Hermann Kahn's 1960 *On Thermonuclear War* and Rachel Carson's 1962 *Silent Spring*.[18] Kahn argued for the survivability of nuclear war, even with casualties in the United States of over 50 million, and proposed some policy recommendations to address the problem of strontium-90 poisoning and the threat of civil disorder following a nuclear attack. In a characteristic passage, he wrote (and it will come as no surprise to learn that he was the model for Stanley Kubrick's Dr Strangelove):

---

16. Ibid., pp. 9, 11.
17. Fred Pearce describes the remarkable gap between official and public awareness of the dangers of radioactivity in *Fallout*, pp. 25–8.
18. Herman Kahn, *On Thermonuclear War*, Transaction Publishers, New Brunswick NJ, 1960; Rachel Carson, *Silent Spring*, Mariner Books, Boston MA and New York, 2002.

if you get a fatal dose of radiation the sequence of events is about like this: first you become nauseated, then sick; you seem to recover; then in two or three weeks you really get sick and die. Now just imagine yourself in the postwar situation. Everybody will have been subjected to extremes of anxiety, unfamiliar environment, strange food, minimum toilet facilities... Under these conditions some high percentage of the population is going to become nauseated, and nausea is very catching. If one man vomits, everybody vomits. Almost everyone is likely to think [they] have received too much radiation. Morale may be so affected that many survivors may refuse to participate in constructive activities, but would content themselves with sitting down and waiting to die – some may even become violent and destructive. However the situation would be quite different if radiation meters were distributed. Assume now a man gets sick from a cause other than radiation... You look at his meter and say 'You have received only 10 roentgens, why are you vomiting? Pull yourself together and get to work.'[19]

Speaking on behalf of the Rand Corporation – that is to say, the United States Airforce – Kahn recommended 'the immediate purchase of $100,000,000 worth of radiation meters'. Surviving nuclear war and radiation poisoning is viewed as above all a logistical problem solved through pre-emptive planning and careful self-measurement of radiation contamination.

On the other side of the strontium-90 panic we find Rachel Carson and her rightly esteemed environmentalist classic *Silent Spring*. This powerful title was chosen by Carson at her publisher's suggestion at the last minute; her own working titles were 'The War Against Nature' and 'At War with Nature'. All of the proposed titles pointed to Carson's conviction that nuclear radiation and DDT pesticides were part of the same arsenal, both developed for US military use. This conviction, already developing for Carson after the war with her work with the government Fish and Wildlife Service, was confirmed by the strontium-90 panic. Here is a passage from the first chapter, 'The Obligation to Endure':

19. Kahn, *On Thermonuclear War*, p. 86.

in this now universal contamination of the environment, chemicals
are the sinister and little recognized partners of radiation in
changing the very nature of the world – the very nature of its life.
Stronium-90, released through nuclear explosions into the air,
comes to earth in rain or drifts down as fallout, lodges in the soil,
enters into the grass or corn or wheat grown there, and in time takes
up its abode in the bones of a human being, there to remain until
their death. Similarly, chemicals sprayed on croplands or forests or
gardens lie long in the soil, entering into living organisms passing
from one to another in a chain of poisoning and death.[20]

Whether Carson poses – as I believe – a direct equivalence
between radioactive and chemical warfare, or whether this is a
rhetorical use of an analogy between them, it is clear that her
environmentalism is modulated by a maximalist view of the
radioactive effects of nuclear warfare. What is new is her emphasis on invisible destruction – tellingly manifested in the silence
of the birds.

In strategic and environmental discourses of the early 1960s
there is a persistent ambivalence about the effects of nuclear
explosions in both blast and radiation versions, along with a
growing conviction that the military and civilian assaults on
the planet are parallel and equivalent. The cultural anxiety
surrounding the visible and invisible destructive powers of the
Bomb crossed over into environmental thinking, with environmentalist discourse adopting many of the tropes used to think
about the Bomb. The crossover provides a historical condition of
possibility for the thought that humans are capable of destroying
the planet, a conviction that would return in the assumption
of planetarily significant human power in the anthropocene.
To imagine there is 'no planet B' is a claim whose origins and
confirmation lie in the mythology of nuclear war. And yet in
retrospect the response of philosophy to thinking the Bomb and
environmental destruction seems tardy and reactive.

20. Carson, *Silent Spring*, p. 6.

It is possible to track the emergence of a philosophical discourse of the atom bomb from the late 1940s. The attacks on Hiroshima and Nagasaki on 6 August 1945 did not provoke any immediate philosophical response. There was of course widespread shock and disgust, attested to by Gunther Anders among others, but also an inability to respond philosophically to the event. Heidegger in his 1949 Bremen Lectures provided one of the first reflections on the mediated experience of the Bomb via film and radio, regarding it as symptomatic of a wider breakdown of distance. His view of the Bomb's significance is at first sight unusual in emphasizing the ecocidal implications of atomic warfare:

> The human is transfixed by what could come about with the explosion of the atomic bomb. The human does not see what for a long time now has already arrived and even is occurring, and for which the atomic bomb and its explosion are merely the latest emission, not to speak of the hydrogen bomb, whose detonation, thought in its broadest possibility, could be enough to wipe out all life on earth.[21]

The play of seeing and not seeing, the visible and invisible, structures Heidegger's thought in the Bremen Lectures, but what he understands by the invisible is less radiation than the self-concealment of the *Gestell*. Not only is the Bomb cited as an example of a broader movement of technics, but the passage shows Heidegger's conviction that it is the *detonation* of the hydrogen bomb that is able to 'wipe out all life on earth'. His is the inaugural philosophical reflection that lingers in fascination before the consequence of the atomic *blast;* it would be followed by statements by Karl Jaspers, in 1956, and Günther Anders in 1957, which also remain entranced with the mushroom cloud and

21. Martin Heidegger, *Bremen and Freiburg Lectures: Insight into that which Is and Basic Principles of Thinking*, trans. Andrew J. Mitchell, Indiana University Press, Bloomington IN, 2012, p. 4.

its spectacle of devastating destruction. The latter, however, pull
back from Heidegger's ecocidal conclusions and are preoccupied
by the homicidal and suicidal consequences of nuclear blasts:
what Jaspers calls human *selbst-Vernichtung* or self-destruction.

In his *Commandments in the Atomic Age* Anders begins with
this advice: 'Your first thought upon wakening should be:
"Atom".' And the object of his meditation is the death of the
current generation of humans through nuclear *blasts*: 'For if the
mankind of today is killed, then that which has been dies with it;
and the mankind to come too.'[22] At this point, the significance of
Anders's slogan *Hiroshima ist überall* remains largely ballistic: we
are all targets, and the explosive force that destroyed Hiroshima
and Nagasaki could now be delivered anywhere on the planet.
Anders is unconcerned by the global reach of atmospheric
radioactivity or fallout, expressing a broader cultural ignorance
of the threat posed by radioactivity.

Similarly Karl Jaspers's *The Question of the Atom-bomb and
the Future of Humanity* remains largely concerned with the
self-destruction of humanity through visible atomic blasts, a
limitation that leaves open the possibility for political survival
expressed in the usually neglected subtitle, 'Political Consciousness in our Time'.[23] The limitation of destruction to visible
blast damage leaves open a space for politics and political
consciousness. This is not the political time granted by the delay
of radioactive decay or slow incremental destruction described
by Kahn but the time of surviving nuclear blasts. In her 1958
The Human Condition, Hannah Arendt would even subordinate
the epochal event of splitting the atom to the orbital flight of
the sputnik and the contemplation of the planet from without.
And even Anders's sombre 1959 *Theses for the Atomic Age*, which

22. Günther Anders, 'Commandments in the Atomic Age', in *Burning Conscience*,
Monthly Review Press, New York, 1957, p. 11.
23. Karl Jaspers, *Die Atombombe und dir Zukunft des Menschen*, Piper Verlag, Munich
and Zurich, 1982.

defines our mode of being in the atomic age as 'not yet being non-existing', still restricts himself to imagining the end of mankind through a nuclear *blast* – visible 'radioactive clouds' are mentioned in Thesis 6 but they are not the focus of the meditation. There is plenty of melancholy ambivalence in Anders at this point, as there will be in Jeff Nuttall's 1968 *Bomb Culture*. But his philosophical reflections remain largely innocent of radiation, as were those of Heidegger and Jaspers. The reflections of the 1950s seem to issue from a different epoch, but their lesson of human self-destruction rather than planetary destruction remains to be heeded.

An explicit philosophical confrontation with the destructive effects of radiation occurs in Anders's *Ten Theses on Chernobyl* from 1986. Here he reworks his *Hiroshima ist überall* thesis to mean not only that we are all potential targets of atomic and hydrogen bombs, but also – following Kahn and Carson – that we are potential victims of even the peaceful use of radiation: not only Hiroshima but also Chernobyl is now for Anders *überall*. This new sensitivity to the threat of radiation and its environmental consequences brings Anders to add to the crime of genocide the crime of '"globicide": the destruction of the terrestrial globe'. Not through 'an immense Hiroshima', a spectacular blast, but through 'something worse, the invisible destruction of radiation poisoning'. (Perhaps perversely, in Thesis 4 Anders considers the hypocritical constructors of 'peaceful' nuclear power plants 'no better' than Truman.) Anders now considers that 'the real danger consists in the invisibility of the danger'.[24]

The space for politics kept open by Jaspers in the mid-1950s has now collapsed: citing Clausewitz's 'war is politics by other means', Anders calls for a war of terror against nuclear terror and its nihilistic advocates:

---

24. Günther Anders, 'Ten Theses on Chernobyl', *Tageszeitung*, 10 June 1986, Thesis 1.

In the interests of the people who currently exist and those of tomorrow, we cannot allow an order to be issued like the one that caused the destruction of Hiroshima and Nagasaki some forty years ago. Such orders and such order-givers must not exist. Anyone who disputes the need to obstruct in this way those who give such orders becomes their accomplice.[25]

The melancholy of imagined total destruction – globicide – brings with it the transformation of politics into war, a war of terror against terror, a war that is so desperately asymmetrical that it no longer makes a lot of sense to be described as 'war'.

The invention of the concept of globicide was consistent with a largely moral consensus over its effects emerging in the work of Hans Jonas and even Karl-Otto Apel.[26] But now the case for an atomic geocide or ecocide is supplemented by the addition of another layer of argument addressing the destructive effects of invisible radiation. At the same time, the fascination with the visible blast damage of nuclear detonations was extended in the influential argument of a scientific report published in 1982 by a leading authority on the atmospheric effects of nuclear war in an article entitled 'The Atmosphere after a Nuclear War: Twilight at Noon'. This authority was none other than Paul J. Crutzen. Crutzen was a specialist in (invisible) ozone and nitrogen imbalances in the atmosphere, and his first line of inquiry into the environmental effects of visible nuclear war addressed the impact of the nitrogen released by nuclear blasts on the ozone layer, 'which would allow increased levels of harmful ultra violet radiation to penetrate to the surface of the earth'. Given the most likely scenario for nuclear war in the early 1980s and still today – 'the detonation of large number of smaller yield weapons' – this would probably be insufficient to provoke a

25. Ibid., Thesis 10.
26. Hans Jonas, *Das Prinzip Verantwortung. Versuch einer Ethik für die technologische Zivilization*, Insel Verlag, Frankfurt am Main, 1979; Karl-Otto Apel, *Diskurs und Verantwortung. Das Problem des ubergangs zur postkonventionellen Moral*, Suhrkamp Verlag, Frankfurt am Main, 1988.

collapse of the ozone layer (and potential end of life on earth). But that was not the only effect of nuclear detonation addressed by Crutzen; there is also the effect of 'the many fires that would be ignited by the thousands of nuclear explosions in cities, forests, agricultural fields, and oil and gas fields', which would produce 'photochemical smog'.[27]

> [S]uch fires would strongly restrict the penetration of sunlight to the earth's surface and change the physical properties of the earth's atmosphere. The marine ecosystems are probably particularly sensitive to prolonged periods of darkness. Under such conditions it is likely that agricultural production in the Northern Hemisphere would be almost totally eliminated, so that no food would be available for the survivors of the initial effects of the war. It is also quite possible that severe worldwide photochemical smog conditions would develop with high levels of tropospheric ozone that would likewise interfere severely with plant productivity. Survival also becomes more difficult if stratospheric ozone depletions also take place.[28]

Interestingly the play of the visible and the invisible is here engaged at the level of the interaction between blast and ozone depletion rather than between blast and the radioaction released directly by the use of nuclear weapons.

Of course Crutzen is morally opposed to nuclear war, but this article sets his *Anthropocene: The Geology of Mankind* manifesto in a new setting. First is the claim that nuclear war offers a proof of concept for the claim that *anthropos* is capable of destroying life on the planet. We can see in Crutzen's important work on the depletion of the ozone level through chlorofluorocarbons, and the successful ban on their use, that he works across connections between military and civil threats to the atmosphere. It is also interesting that his work focuses on nitrogen as a

---

27. Paul J. Crutzen, *Paul J. Crutzen: A Pioneer on Atmospheric Chemistry and Climate Change in the Anthropocene*, Springer International Publishing, Cham, 2016, pp. 125–6.
28. Ibid., pp. 145–6.

greenhouse gas, making him a crypto-proponent of the nitrogen rather than carbon anthropocene.

Perhaps all this adds up to no more than a scruple about the concept of the anthropocene unleashed by Crutzen's 2002 manifesto. A concept that emerged from a matrix of nuclear war in which humans were mythologized as possessors of a planetary destructive power is far from neutral and should not be uncritically adopted. Such a view of destructive human power emerged from the spectacle of a nuclear explosion and its destructive blast that with time mutated into the insidious and incremental destruction of life by radiation poisoning. The phantasm of the destruction of the planet through a nuclear blast provided a condition of possibility for imagining that human beings have the power to destroy the planet. Military apocalyse is translated into environmental apocalypse, and all with very little critical reflection. The human possession of such destructive power may or may not be the case, but it should be treated as a hypothesis to be critically assessed rather than an unquestionable axiom of environmentalist thinking. At the very least we should keep a question mark after statements such as: 'Anthropos has become an overwhelming force that can build and destroy, birth and kill all others on the planet'?

OUTTAKES

7

'The modern partisan of many histories': Jacob Taubes and the critique of Reinhart Koselleck's new *Historik*

DANIEL GOTTLIEB

Reinhart Koselleck's pursuit of a theory that would allow 'historical experience ... to be transformed into historical science' was never intended to be a critical history of philosophy.[1] His programme for a new *Historik* did, however, constantly deploy the findings of the changing temporal structures of historical experience to criticize modern philosophies of history.

Koselleck's warnings against the prophetic pretensions and predictions of modern philosophies of history are a recurring feature of his authorship. According to Koselleck, the inflated ambitions of such philosophies reside in the claim to have discovered certain processes within history that would 'clarify history from out of itself'.[2] Unlike the measured prognostications and instruction of the old *Historie*, geared towards recognizing the repetition of forms that could inform concrete political action, philosophies of history leap over the cognition of historical situations and lay claim to the knowledge of history

1. Reinhart Koselleck, '"Space of Experience" and "Horizon of Expectation": Two Historical Categories', in *Futures Past: On the Semantics of Historical Time*, Columbia University Press, New York, 2004, p. 275.
2. Reinhart Koselleck, 'Geschichte, Geschichten und formale Zeitstrukturen', in Reinhart Koselleck and Wolf-Dieter Stempel, eds, *Geschichte – Ereignis und Erzählung. Poetik und Hermeneutik V*, Wilhelm Fink Verlag, Munich, 1973, p. 221. This essay appears in English as 'History, Histories, and Formal Time Structures', in *Futures Past*, ch. 6.

as such. Koselleck dedicates numerous essays to tracing how this overarching claim to knowing history as a whole (which, for him, amounts to claiming 'to know history [*Geschichte*] as process'[3]) consequently led to a transformation in the concepts that constitute the historical semantics of how we understand and speak of historical change itself. Progress, development, planning, crisis, reaction and revolution (to name just a few of the categories to which Koselleck returns) begin to take on different political and semantic valence once history's processual nature outstrips concrete situational emplotment. The changing political texture of these concepts, which Koselleck studies in his *Begriffsgeschichten*, are taken to circle around the same impermissible premiss: that 'history in and for itself' could be conceptualized – and thereby altered – as such. When history is philosophically rendered as 'design', its attendant concepts are subject to a political instrumentalization and historical efficacy which, according to Koselleck, disavows the fundamental alterity and unknowability of a future that cannot be collapsed into the historical expectations the philosophers of history may impose upon it.

The exaltation of the singular

Koselleck's concern with the extension of historical prognosis beyond the limit of what history permits us to cognize – to displace, that is, the question of what constitutes a historical event and its experience onto the management of history as process with a determined pattern – is a threefold discontent. The first gripe is that philosophers who speculate on history as a whole (*Ganzheit*) fail to grasp the proper result of modernity (*Neuzeit*), upon which they nevertheless rely for their prognostication.

---

3. Koselleck, 'Geschichte, Geschichten und formale Zeitstrukturen', p. 221.

Once the past is transcended by virtue of the criterion of the present being qualitatively and in principle constantly 'new', the object of enquiry for the historian becomes historical time itself. This result lends to the historian the proper criterion by which history can be disciplinarily unified as the shifting experiences of time. The burgeoning awareness, from the Enlightenment onwards, that history can be spoken of in the singular (that *Geschichten* become *Geschichte*) permits the modern historian and historiographer to speak of properly historical *time*. Once time is revealed as constitutive of historical passage *and* the assured methodological object of historical study, historical science has in principle reached its solid ground. Time then exists as transcendental condition for all possible histories and as the basis to inquire into shifting synchronizations at the level of empirical content. *Historik* was Koselleck's attempt to build a historical science on the basis of this philosophical and historical achievement.

Opposed to this coherence of transcendental condition and empirical content it is, ironically enough, the philosopher of history who sustains the alienation of history from philosophy. For Koselleck, the philosopher of history attempts to reveal the laws of development of history itself. What is missed in this transition to a singular tenor of history is its temporalization: each historical experience will 'embody past and future' in a manner that is indeterminate and infinitely varied.[4] Philosophers of history, in their speculative 'self-exaltation', occlude this study of the temporalization *of* history and instead claim to speak *for* history itself. This first discontent resonates with what Koselleck had already diagnosed in the Introduction to *Critique and Crisis* as the 'crisis caused by morality's proceeding against history'.

---

4. Reinhart Koselleck, 'Transformations of Experience and Methodological Change: A Historical-Anthropological Essay', in *The Practice of Conceptual History: Timing History, Spacing Concepts*, Stanford University Press, Stanford CA, 2002, p. 258.

With a certain subdued prophetic undertone, Koselleck declares that this 'will be a permanent crisis as long as history is alienated in terms of its philosophy'.[5]

Koselleck's attempt to methodologically rein in philosophy to bring it back into the enclosure of actual history immediately leads to his second major grievance. The philosopher's enthusiastic supplement to the epochal significance of modernity forecloses the open temporality that must be acknowledged. Human finitude that lies at the base of any act of temporalization is undermined by the projection of a future rendered achievable. The following passage, at the conclusion of his rightly celebrated essay 'Modernity and the Planes of Historicity', first published in a 1968 *Festgabe* to Carl Schmitt, brings both these elements into relief:

> This alternation of Revolution and Reaction, which supposedly heralds the attainment of an ultimate paradise, has to be understood as a futureless future, because the reproduction and necessarily inevitable supersession of the contradiction brings about an evil endlessness. In the pursuit of this evil endlessness, as Hegel said, the consciousness of the agent is trapped in a finite 'not yet' possessing the structure of a perennial imperative (*Sollen*). It has been possible since Hegel's time to convey into historical reality fictions such as the Thousand-year Reich or the classless society. This fixation on an end-state by historical actors turns out to be the subterfuge of a historical process that robs them of judgment. Needed, therefore, is historical prognostication that goes beyond the rational prognoses of the politicians and, as the legitimate offspring of historical philosophy, can moderate the historical-philosophical design.[6]

This passage shows how intimately linked the methodological and temporal problematics are. Once history as such becomes the projected surface for the 'fictions' of a future paradise, the

---

5. Reinhart Koselleck, *Critique and Crisis: Enlightenment and the Pathogenesis of Modern Society*, MIT Press, Cambridge MA and London, 2015, p. 11.
6. Reinhart Koselleck, 'Modernity and the Planes of Historicity', in *Futures Past*, ch. 1, p. 23.

future is stripped of its indefinite and modulated temporality that interests the historian. It becomes 'futureless' and the present a prison of planned deferral. For Koselleck, the notion of concrete 'judgment' too begins to lose its centrality. The philosopher's wide-screen historical vision might be historically efficacious in proposing a reservoir for instruction towards the perfection of a future state, but this is history read through the prism of hope. The *historia magistra vitae* which once was the 'teacher of the art of making political prescriptions' and thus informing political action is trammelled by 'historical-philosophical design'.[7] Once historical design announces a future abbreviated from its past, the gulf between past and future widens. The more historical time internalizes temporalization of the present within modernity – an occurrence the historian can compare and retrace versus earlier times – the less an authentic politics of history is discernible. For Koselleck's politics is based fundamentally on the possibility of delimiting expectations and experience and thus the recognition of 'the aporias of human finitude in its temporality'. Telic ends of history, such is the claim, makes the authentic experience of historical time a receding and dwindling resource in inverse proportion to its possible incitement of political enthusiasm and moralism.[8]

It is at this point that Koselleck's political discontent becomes clear. Beyond the metahistorical concerns regarding method, Koselleck's *Historik*, which seeks 'the thematization of possible histories (Geschichten)',[9] is as much a political intervention. For in his presentation of the transformations in the institutional and conceptual separations (and intersections) of philosophical critique and politics, it is clear that Koselleck's major concern

7. Reinhart Koselleck, 'Historia Magistra Vitae: The Dissolution of the Topos into the Perspective of a Modernized Historical Process', in *Futures Past*, pp. 41–2.
8. Reinhart Koselleck, '*Historik* and Hermeneutics', in *Sediments of Time: On Possible Histories*, Stanford University Press, Stanford CA, 2018, p. 42.
9. Ibid.; emphasis added.

is the collision between two utterly divergent forms of political judgment in and of history. While Koselleck broadly speaks of *geschichtsphilosophisch* reasoning, the reference to the 'classless society' above (a reference which quickly folds it into the same formal fictionality of the 'Thousand-year Reich') betrays his real political foe. Marxist history is anathema for Koselleck, for it appears as the zenith of all philosophies of history condensed into the singular. Marxism bears within it those ambivalences which are equally the core of its combustible political effectivity: it supersedes the present historical experience of time to lay judgment on the future, and thus lend meaning, as judgment, over the course of history as such (from its many histories), just as the permanence of its revolutionary prognosis outdoes political judgment to nevertheless exacerbate the political situation.[10] Both the neutralization of politics and its exacerbation, the philosophical valorization of the future and its suspension, Marxism qua philosophy of history rubs up against the method of a *Historik* that studies the shifting possibilities of historical experience.

It is this implicit move that provoked Jacob Taubes to name Koselleck 'a modern partisan of many histories in the plural'.[11] The seething response to Koselleck's essay 'History, Histories, and Formal Time Structures' by the philosopher and scholar of

---

10. This is one of the central themes of *Critique and Crisis*, although in that book Koselleck traces the tension back to its origins in the Enlightenment when 'eschatology recoils into Utopianism'. Studying the history of what Koselleck calls criticism's moralism (a criticism that *had* to become moral as a reflex to its actual political ineffectiveness), Koselleck tells us that the great error of the moralists was believing that 'planning history' was consistent with the political. Planning, however, is 'unable to integrate politics' and thus 'moral man stands in a void and must make a virtue of necessity'. At once historically utopian, morally virtuous and politically anodyne, the burgeoning realm of the philosophy of history for the enlighteners centrally forgot 'That politics is fate, that it is fate not in the sense of blind fatality.' Politics, that is, is entirely non-contiguous with fate seen as 'progress'.

11. Jacob Taubes. 'Geschichtsphilosophie und Historik: Bemerkungen zu Kosellecks Programm einer neuen Historik', in Koselleck and Stempel, eds, *Geschichte – Ereignis und Erzählung*, p. 493; reprinted in Jacob Taubes, *Apokalypse und Politik: Aufsätze, Kritiken und kleinere Schriften*, Wilhelm Fink Verlag, Paderborn, 2017, p. 238. All subsequent citations refer to the latter edition.

religion brings the politics of *Historik* to the fore. Taubes, the
apocalyptic Marxist, recalls in his written response a key passage
from Koselleck's earlier essay on revolution: '*Begriffsgeschichte*
reminds us – even when it becomes involved with ideologies
– that words and their usage are more important for politics
than any other weapon.'[12] According to Taubes, Koselleck's
presentation of the various temporal indices condensed into
history's fundamental concepts (*Grundbegriffe*) are themselves
exemplary salutations to the politics these studies attempt to
demonstrate. For if 'words and their usage' are politics' greatest
weapon, Koselleck's tactic is to reduce the political resources
and possibilities opened up by philosophies of history to a mere
semantics. Marxist philosophy is thus treated as a lexical reflex
to modernity (albeit with particular political virulence) that
attempts to dissimulate the widening cleft between experience
and expectation in the *Neuzeit*. Taubes will respond by intensify-
ing this encounter between two forms of historical partisanship.
He mines the resources of an 'apocalyptic expectation' that
emphasizes the temporal category of the *end*, irreducible to the
limited horizons of an expectation of the *future*. Marxism in
its apocalyptic mode thus combats Koselleck's politics with an
experience of time and a semantics that, so is the claim, cannot
be neutralized by the iterative motion of Koselleck's expected
futures.

Formal time structures and Koselleck's prehistorical anthropology

Koselleck first presented 'History, Histories, and Formal Time
Structures' in 1970 at the fifth colloquium of the Poetik und Hermeneutik research group. The working theme of the colloquium

12. 'Der Neuzeitliche Revolutionsbegriff als geschichtliche Kategorie', translated as
'Historical Criteria of the Modern Concept of Revolution', in *Futures Past*, ch. 3 (p. 57).

was 'Geschichten und Geschichte', which became *Geschichte
– Ereignis und Erzählung* (History – Event and Narration) by the
time the volume was printed in 1973, with Koselleck as one of
the co-editors. Alongside presentations by prominent German
academics such as Hans Robert Jauss, Peter Szondi, Christian
Meier, Odo Marquard and Hermann Lübbe, the editors decided
to publish written responses based on the subsequent discussion
to the presentations. Jacob Taubes, Jürgen Habermas and Dieter
Henrich all wrote responses, taking issue with various aspects
of the subject matter discussed at the colloquium, including
criticism of Koselleck's work in particular. How could this essay,
apparently more concerned with historical method than its
politics, so rile its respondents?

At the outset, Koselleck presents in broad strokes his account
of the modern notion of historical time we have outlined above.
In doing so, he is faced with the following problem: how to
derive a unity to historical science when the defining experience
of modern historical time is a ruptural relation to the past, and
thus appears to be discontinuous with previous accounts of
historical temporality? Koselleck's response is to project coherence on the stability of man: all time, no matter how various its
synchronizations or combinations, must be refracted through
an 'anthropologically pregiven circle'. Koselleck cites Plato,
Augustine and Bossuet as examples of thinkers whose 'structural
long-term statements' employ 'substantial determinations [that]
are always related to the finitude of historical constellations and
hence to their temporality'.[13] Whether it is 'natural' time and its
cycles in the context of the Greeks, or the salvational doctrine
in Augustine that enabled the *ordo temporum* to be decoupled

---

13. Koselleck, 'Geschichte, Geschichten und formale Zeitstrukturen', p. 219. And
further: 'The naturalistic attachment of historical process in the world of Greek
cosmology or in the theological *ordo temporum* of the Judeo-Christian salvational
doctrine involved historical knowledge which could be attained only by turning away
from history as totality.'

from 'history as totality', the difference between time and history actually enables the practical character of historical statements. It is the acceptance of other modes of temporality which ensures that both mankind and its history are kept within certain limits, and lent those philosophers their claims to historical knowledge. Since the eighteenth century, however, there has been a 'convergence' of historical knowledge and experience, such that history is 'known from itself' as a process *sui generis*. This historical occurrence appears to have disrupted the anthropological circle: 'transcendental meaning' as a 'space of consciousness' has now been 'contaminated' with history as a 'space of action'.[14]

One might be surprised that Koselleck does not consider a 'space of action' to be part of any anthropologically pregiven circle. Droysen's attempt to establish a scientific *Historik*, for example, had made the 'space of action' central to the task of systematizing the special nature of historical material that has been 'formed, stamped and moved by the human mind *and* human hand'. But Koselleck is reluctant to follow Droysen in positing a 'general', continuously self-developing 'ego' as constitutive of this pregiven anthropological unit. Droysen took this ego to be the 'subject of history', the continuity of which the historian can deduce in 'feel[ing] ourselves to be essentially similar and in relations of reciprocity' to those products.[15] To concede the unity of history as the product of the 'human hand' or a 'space of action' risks implying that laws could be found that would make history structurally, and not just temporally or semantically, unified. The temporalization of modern history could thus be based on changing forms of historical and social relations that inform this activity. Were Koselleck to accept this premiss to historical science, however, he would have to concede

14. Ibid., p. 211.
15. Johann Gustav Droysen, *Historik*, cited in Alfred Schmidt, *History and Structure: An Essay on Hegelian-Marxist and Structuralist Theories of History*, MIT Press, Cambridge MA 1981, p. 8; emphasis added.

that historical knowledge is indeed derived from the knowledge of 'history itself'.

Koselleck seems to be aware of this problem. He warns the reader almost immediately that 'the semantically demonstrable process involving the emergence of modern historical philosophies should not itself be exaggerated in a historico-philosophical manner.'[16] That is to say: the concepts of modern historical philosophies should not be taken to be derived truthfully from a 'space of action' that would establish the immanent necessity of those concepts for a process of history itself. Rather than widen his anthropological circle to include a 'space of action' – a deepening which, across time, might put into question the very stability of that anthropological unit and its institutions that could subtend history – he calls for the reduction of the 'premises of our own historical research by this once-formulated experience of history'.

Koselleck 'steps back' from historical time and the objective processes that might explain it to enquire into the purely temporal coordinates that all historical times share. What is 'common' to all histories for Koselleck, no matter their foreignness, are certain underlying 'temporal structures' that remain 'characteristic of history in the singular and histories in the plural'.[17] The temporal experiences of 'irreversibility', 'repeatability of events' and the 'contemporaneity of the non-contemporaneous' can be used as formal coordinates by the historian to gather history 'in the plural' on behalf of studying history 'in general'. From that step back, temporal experiences become the minimal condition of all history. Because that basic temporal schema can only be experienced in consciousness, the space of action is relegated to a secondary position – action becomes a reaction to certain frictions and combinations of those basic structures. In doing

16. Koselleck, 'Geschichte, Geschichten und formale Zeitstrukturen', p. 212.
17. Ibid.

so Koselleck preserves the 'transcendental meaning of history
as the space of consciousness'. The rhetorical force of the word
'contamination' signposts Koselleck's vehemence on this point.
Action is annexed from the production of new forms of temporalization; it is at best a political response articulated at the level
of historical concepts. To suggest otherwise is to undermine the
stability of the anthropological circle which ensures the unity of
Koselleck's historical science.

In his interest to sustain the continuity of historical science,
Koselleck promotes the trifold schema of 'pre-historical'
(*vorgeschichtlich*) temporal experiences to which the 'space of
consciousness' is beholden and produces various matrixes of
historical knowledge. Differences in historical knowledge can
he noted, and thus drawn into the continuity of history as a
'genuine' field of research, because all experience is projected
against, and thereby refracts, the transcendental plane of shifting intersections of these temporal structures. These structures
are 'registered' in experience, and transformed into knowledge,
contained within this anthropologically given circle. Once the
anthropological general circle of meaning is defined in terms of
the 'transcendental meaning of the space of consciousness', the
phenomenological categories of expectation and experience are
understood with such breadth by Koselleck to be both anthropologically vague and to carry with them the historical legacy
of European modernity, as a temporal and territorial selection.
It is therefore telling that the 'many histories in the plural'
Koselleck wishes to recover remain *past* histories that, despite
their infinite variation, all come from European historiography.
The dispersal of infinite histories is nevertheless gathered up
into the prevailing notion of history stamped by transcendental
phenomenological anthropology.[18] This fusion of transcendental

18. One is tempted to formulate this along Kantian lines: *Historik* demands a
purposiveness at the level of historical science (i.e. temporal experience) to systematize

and anthropological breadth permits Koselleck to enquire into 'past and alien' histories 'we no longer know how to recount'. But it also stops him from having to enquire further into the notion of distance, namely how the historical experience of distance could relate to this anthropological pregivenness, and thus how histories appear in its foreignness, or the fading form of their recuperability. Rather than the 'space of consciousness' itself having a historical valence which would deepen the changes to consciousness in historical forms such as personhood, subjectivity, citizenship or the 'self', consciousness is left vastly underdetermined, ensconced within a restrictive understanding of preconscious and prehistorical anthropological givens. Or, rather, experience is temporalized, but the consciousness that experiences is thereby withdrawn from modification.[19] For the historian equipped with the historical science of *Historik*, that distance is sutured by embedding their own knowledge into the broad but indeterminate realm of the human.

Koselleck wants to maintain an aperture in the anthropological pregiven circle that would leave mankind open to many possible histories. But because this infinity is presented as a manifold of different structures of time, time 'happens' to 'man' more than it is something that comes within the circumference of action. In any case, the possibility of histories is held in anthropological perpetuum. The implicit argument is that the 'convergence' or 'contamination' of modern philosophies of

the possibly infinite multiplicity of histories, but does not want to concede any purpose to history as such.

19. Dieter Henrich's objection to Koselleck in the volume touches on this point. Henrich takes issue with the way in which 'self-preservation' is perceived as a pre-historical constant (which could lead to a particular kind of naturalization of institutions that apparently sustain 'man'). This, however, fails to register the modern transformation of *Selbstsein* and *Subjektivität*, which, due to their historicity, change the terms of self-preservation from, for example, the Stoic theory of the *conservation sui*. It is the historicity of consciousness as a modern achievement that allows us to historically refer to its history and its difference according to the expanding possibilities retained in it, but not to anthropological continuities as such. See Dieter Henrich, 'Selbsterhaltung und Geschichtlichkeit', in Koselleck and Stempel, eds, *Geschichte – Ereignis und Erzählung*, pp. 456–63.

history have actually delimited possibilities for new histories in the present, all the while providing *Historik* the chance to acknowledge their existence in the past. Koselleck holds fast to a possibility for many histories as a transcendental condition while (perhaps, mournfully) noting their empirical homogenization over time.

Given this account, Koselleck is left to explain how the natural 'outside', which prevented the 'structural long-term statements' laying claim to history 'as totality', came to be reduced to a single plane of action. But accounting for this as a process is impossible if Koselleck is determined not to explain history out of itself, which would 'contaminate' the transcendental temporal structures with the intersecting, but independent, realm of historical time itself. Koselleck avoids this position by claiming that the 'political and social space of action has become denaturalized by the systematic compulsion (*Systemzwang*) of technology'.[20] *The 'force' of technology is made to fill the explanatory gap left in the refusal to consider history as a 'process'.* A quasi-natural account of technology's 'denaturalization' of time serves as that additional factor that begins to shift the dynamics of modernity. This is more posited than explained. Koselleck's fails to explain the particular mode of this technical-administrative world's compulsion or, for example, how the multiple temporalities proper to technology's genesis intersect with the expansion of global markets (despite noting its global efficacy), nor the particular form it has taken in the production process.[21] This also leaves unexplained the degree to which technology has its bearing on

20. Koselleck, 'Geschichte, Geschichten und formale Zeitstrukturen', p. 214.
21. In contrast, Habermas explains the same general dialectic more concretely. For example: 'In light of the growing need for control, planning competencies have been consolidated in a state apparatus that is subject to the imperatives of the economic system and must translate all conflictual content into a form that can be processed administratively. This results in the contradiction between the growing scope for manipulation of the planning authorities on the one hand and what they produce as a *secondary natural growth*: not only the uncontrolled side effects that have become *plannable in principle*, but on the other hand, the *risks* of life of *those that have not yet been brought under control*.' 'Über das Subjekt der Geschichte: Kurze Bemerkung zu

the human itself, and thus put into question the stability of that anthropological circle that remains beyond history.

Koselleck claims that modernity's 'break' is determined by the asymptotic shrinking of the structural difference between natural time and historical time through technology, without them ever wholly becoming identical. Once natural or salvational time indexes no longer provide a limit to the forces of technologized historical time, there is no structural limit to the extension of that history other than technology itself. 'Coefficients of motion and acceleration ... are no longer derived from expectations of the Last Judgement (as was earlier the case), but instead remain adequate to the empirical factors of a world increasingly technical in nature.'[22] This produces the distinctive dialectic of the modern experience of historical time for Koselleck in the 'Zeitstrukturen' essay: a dialectic of the possible infinite and finite totality of history:

> A previously divine teleology thus encounters the ambiguity of human planning, as can be seen in the ambivalence of the concept of progress, which must all at once prove itself both finite and infinite if it is not to relapse into the naturalistic and spatial sense it earlier embodied.

Concepts such as progress attempt to neutralize this pulsing between an infinite and finite understanding of history, opened up by the coefficients of acceleration and crisis. But progress unknowingly reproduces the dialectic by which it is conditioned, for progress is both theoretically infinitely applicable and finite in that it must respond to the empirical novelties it is to incorporate into its philosophical projection. 'This involves a process of temporalization whose subject or subjects are only to be investigated through reflection on this process, without this, however,

---

falsch gestellten Alternativen', in Koselleck and Stempel, eds, *Geschichte – Ereignis und Erzählung*, p. 471; emphasis in original.
22. Koselleck, 'Geschichte, Geschichten und formale Zeitstrukturen', p. 203.

making the process determinable.'[23] It is the very undecidability
of the dialectic between infinite and finite that leaves it vulnerable to a type of political calculation of the future that closes
off its irreducible openness. Previous histories made substantial
historical claims on the condition that the infinite and finite
were kept apart from one another despite their possible moments
of intersection. The modern dialectic under the compulsion of
technology has folded those two realms into mutual conditions
of one another, inviting the 'space of action' to neutralize that
broken mechanism. The infinite collapses into finite history but
dissimulates that historical realm as possibly infinitely graspable.
Although he does not mention it, the implication is clear: against
this virulent oscillation between the infinite and finite constitutive of all Utopia, a countervailing politics to history must be
found that would institutionally stabilize, through their separation, these two temporal realms. Jacob Taubes senses precisely
this implicit argument. In his response to the 'Zeitstrukturen'
essay, 'apocalyptic expectation' is used to retain the irruption of
the infinite into history against Koselleck's neutralization of that
sphere.

Apocalyptic expectation: Taubes's response

The first section of Taubes's 'Philosophy of History and *Historik*:
Remarks on Koselleck's Program for a new Historik' sets up a
virtual confrontation between Koselleck and Marx and their
varying accounts of the emergence of history as a whole. Taubes's
critique begins with a discontent regarding Koselleck's vague use
of 'technology' as a principle of historiographic change. Taubes
writes: '"Technical progress", abstractly understood, provides
Koselleck with "the empirical substrate" of that constitution of

---

23. Ibid., p. 214.

a '"history as such".'[24] Technology's denaturalization of natural
time – the reduction of a structurally different temporality to
a time 'internal' to history's own account of itself as process –
provides the historian with the principle subtending changes such
that he or she can determine different historical experiences and
histories. For all his ambivalence towards modernity's unique
conception of history conceived as process, Koselleck's *Historik*
is thus still parasitic on that reduction of structurally different
times to the historical plane. As we have noted, Koselleck can
identify many different histories in the plural in the past, because
'history as such' has provided the conditions in which all those
histories are levelled to one disciplinary field and yet, in terms of
historical experience, have simultaneously been eclipsed.

Technology is conceived by Koselleck as a principle of temporal synchronization that is registered in its historical efficacy
at the level of semantics. According to Taubes, the deficit in this
account can best be seen in how Koselleck explains the distinc-
tiveness of the modern concept of 'world history'. For Koselleck,
world history 'as a system' was first registered as 'history's need
for theory and relating it to the entire globe as its place of action'.
Because the European 'world' now spans the globe, the sedimen-
tation of previous historical experience no longer corresponds
to the horizon of expectation. Theory comes to articulate the
'interdependence of events and the intersubjectivity of actions'.[25] In defining 'world history' as a need, it merely becomes
the fulfillment of a modern semantic 'lack' once no outside is
posited to history. World history as itself a historical – and not
theoretical-semantic – reflex is occluded in the process.

Taubes opposes this to the account that Marx gives of a
world history grounded within history itself, summarized in the

---

24. Taubes, 'Geschichtsphilosophie und Historik: Bemerkungen zu Kosellecks
Programm einer neuen Historik', in Koselleck and Stempel, eds, *Geschichte – Ereignis und
Erzählung*, p. 495.
25. Koselleck, 'Geschichte, Geschichten und formale Zeitstrukturen', p. 221.

famous line in the Introduction to the *Grundrisse*: 'World history did not always exist; history as world history is a result.' If this is accepted, the stakes of modernity's specific synchronization of time also shifts. For it questions whether Koselleck's definition of modernity as a *plurale tantum* – that is, a semantic-conceptual unity that is determined by pluralities that are actually irreducible to the concept – can really be properly grounded without addressing the determining unity of activity occurring at the level of the objective self-development of capital. This latter investigation displaces the Koselleckian process of how *Geschichten* precede and are subsequently overcome by *Geschichte*. Rather, it takes as its frame of reference how global markets driven by the expansion of capital produced not just social homogenization but also the differentiation of historically specific localities that in turn produce their new temporalizations and possible synchronizations. That is, world history produces *Geschichten*. Only from the position of world history (in the singular) do the multiple histories incorporated into that process become discernible and comprehensible. And not just for the retrospective gaze of the historian, but also for the theorist equipped with the principle of immanent critique that this emergence has permitted. The 'civilizing influence of capital' is its capacity to integrate different local histories and spatial relations, which can be aligned both according to a stagism of subsumption to capital and ideologically naturalized to a single, historical plane of 'humanity's development':

> Thus capital creates bourgeois society, and the universal appropriation of nature as well as of the social bond itself by the members of society. Hence the great civilizing influence of capital; its production of a stage of society in comparison to which all earlier ones appear as mere *local developments* of humanity and as *nature-idolatry*.[26]

26. Marx, *Grundrisse*, quoted in Taubes, 'Geschichtsphilosophie und Historik', p. 495.

The temporal and spatial pluralities that Koselleck ostensibly celebrates have their generative impulse in an objective development of capital that exceeds semantic form. The historical scientist à la Koselleck may be able to flatten and unify their plural temporal indices within a virtual common time of the 'historian', but *Historik* fails to see in these multiple temporalizations a product of a present moment. While Koselleck attempts to outflank Marx by presenting world history as a semantic result, Taubes reintegrates Koselleck's semantic findings into the process of Marxist history itself:

> Marx (and, as a consequence, Marxist historiography) attempts to make transparent why and how the turn from archaic 'local developments of humanity' (from *Geschichten* in Koselleck's sense) that still remain naturally bound ('appear as natural idolatry' in Marx's sense) is consummated in world history (to the collective-singular *Geschichte* in Koselleck's sense) that 'tears down all borders'. Koselleck, however, merely wants to develop a 'grid' – theoretical premises in a formal sense – in order to 'preserve the unity of history as a science' capable of containing both the experiences of time and history of completely other pasts as well as that of the characteristically modern.[27]

Taubes senses in Koselleck's attempts to valorize those pasts 'we no longer know how to recount' a celebration of pasts within a continuum of what we might call an abstract 'historiographic time' which fastidiously notes their structural differences in terms of certain combinations of time. Despite possessing their own forms of temporalization, those pasts remain ultimately past to this new *Historik*, without thereby having accounted for the activity that constitutes them as past in relation to modern historical experience. In doing so, Taubes accuses Koselleck of having shifted, but ultimatedly retained, certain premises of nineteenth-century historicism: if, for Ranke, all epochs were

---

27. Taubes, 'Geschichtsphilosophie und Historik', pp. 495–6.

immediate to God, then for Koselleck the expanding grid of
formal time structures are made immediate to the practitioner of
Historik. This immediacy to time is achieved by neutralizing the
genealogical approach to history, in which the present is a site
of action whose critical narrativization of the past is informed
by the constitutive rupturing of the present. In reading the
past genealogically, the possibilities (and a politics) of form are
glimpsed in paying attention to the institutional forms in which
they have been effaced. If Koselleck wants to retain only formal
time structures from the moment of rupture, it is to salvage
the role of the historian who can then silently judge, on the
basis of past examples, the intent of that genealogical approach.
However, for Taubes, the point would be to formulate a concept
of history that takes rupture as its locus, and expound a different
notion of experience according to it.

This last claim is what pushes Taubes's initial Marxist critique
towards the apocalyptic. The apocalyptic strain of the response
is directed towards undermining what Koselleck ultimately
wants to 'save': the achievements of the historical school and
historicism, albeit under modified conditions. The basis of
this claim centres on Koselleck's indebtedness to Heidegger's
'existential-ontological exposition of the problem of history' and
Gadamer's hermeneutical phenomenology. Heidegger's intention
to ground history in the 'existential-temporal condition' of
Dasein's being '*between* birth and death' provides the schema by
which 'one's factical being-there' is also 'a potentiality-for-being'
that 'is in each case projected in the horizon of the future'.[28]
The temporal categories of anticipation and expectation are
authentic or inauthentic modes respectively of being oriented
towards a finite horizon within which entities are disclosed as
possibly actualizable or as 'pure possibility'. For Taubes, then,

---

28. Martin Heidegger, *Being and Time*, trans. John Macquarie and Edward Robinson, Blackwell, Oxford, 1962 (1927), p. 416.

'"being-towards-death" functions in Heidegger as the Eschaton',
reduced to the horizon of Dasein's facticity and finitude.[29] But
this indicates for Taubes that Heidegger's break with theological presuppositions of prophecy coincides with a relapse to
mythology. (The 'anticipation towards death' is what delivers to
human 'Dasein its destiny [Schicksals]', Heidegger writes.) Dasein
'temporalizes itself originally from the future', but this future is
reduced to the natural limits of being towards death. Heidegger's
post-Kehre concept of history is then developed, as a kind of
phenomenologically ephemeral but nonetheless organizing
structure of destiny: 'History [Geschichte] is "das Geschicht",' as
the mountain range is for the mountains, the originally unifying
and determining feature of fate [Schicksals].'[30] According to this
manner of proceeding, world history can only be glimpsed in
the Verlorenheit in das Man – that non-authentic leaping over
the destinal sending that can only ever disclose a series of finite
possibilities ultimately grounded in death.

In Taubes's estimation, Heidegger enacts a threefold move:
of ontologically grounding 'end' in 'death', by which Dasein's
temporal extension towards death is repurposed as 'destiny', and
history is thereby remythologized as the arrangement of those
destinies into some phenomenal coherence. While Koselleck's
Historik avoids the fundamental ontological interpretation of
history on those terms, his transposition of the horizonal quality
of Heidegger's thought onto historical experience cuts history
short from exceeding a certain temporally determined constellation of experience and expectation. These two anthropological
givens are formally elastic to make all history legible, but they
are never disjunctive enough to permit history to exceed the
phenomenological circle that would problematize the continuity
between expectation and experience. As Koselleck writes:

---

29. Taubes, 'Geschichtsphilosophie und Historik', p. 241.
30. Heidegger, Erläuterungen zu Hölderlins Dichtung, quoted in ibid., p. 242.

> Only the unexpected has the power to surprise, and this surprise involves a new experience. The penetration of the horizon of expectation, therefore, is creative of new experience. The gain in experience exceeds the limitation of the possible future presupposed by previous experience. The way in which expectations are temporally exceeded thus reorders our two dimensions with respect to one another.[31]

'Reordered' with respect to one another, but never in a way that something outside the circle would be permitted as constitutive of history. For, as we have seen, Koselleck's transposition of horizonal phenomenology onto history means that any derivation of the future based on history 'as such' – the methodologically impermissible lapse when expectations exceed what previous experience tells us is actually possible within the circumference of finite horizons – is dismissed as abstract prophesy. Koselleck is focused on the subjective constitution of meaning of historical experience, and it takes precedence over any objective historical factors that would determine meaning from 'something' that would negate previous experience. Contradictions are thus reduced to waxing and waning engagements with historical space, without having to deal with objectivities that indeed inform experience and expectation and simultaneously cause them to fissure;[32] all the while neutralizing any basis of critique established on that fissuring on the basis of history itself (be it 'equality' under the conditions of society of equal exchange, 'justice' under conditions of domination, and so on). The

---

31. Koselleck, '"Space of Experience" and "Horizon of Expectation"', in *Futures Past*, ch. 14, p. 262.

32. This could be contrasted to Adorno's reflection on the vanquishing of accumulated memory and recollection – and thus a consciousness aware of historical continuity – which is grounded in an 'objective developmental law' that need not be 'experienced' for it to nevertheless shatter experience. This law and its 'irrational residue' lie on a different plane than a possible contradiction in man's anthropological facility to sustain a situated connectedness between possible experiences and expectations. See Theodor W. Adorno, 'The Meaning of Working Through the Past', in *Critical Models: Interventions and Catchwords*, trans. Henry W. Pickford, Columbia University Press, New York, 2005, pp. 344–5.

contradiction is instead said to lie within those anthropological constants as they appear in modernity.

For Koselleck, according to Taubes, 'the contradiction derives its brilliance from the fact that beyond histories and history it always the signature of human Dasein'.[33] 'Man' can fall into contradiction in its mode of deriving subjective meaning from history, but history itself is tamed of all contradiction. Because of this, there is a sense that this iterative horizon of expectation is sustained in continuity by phenomenologically foreclosing interruption of expectation as such. The phenomenological horizon gestures towards its preservation. But it is only within that interruption of anthropological and institutional residues, which had contained experience and expectation, that for Taubes one could glimpse the possibility of new forms of human existence – both as vanquished in the past, and possibly redeemable in the future.

This is where Taubes's own idea of history begins to become explicit. He cites Benjamin's description of the chronicler to mark his divergence from Koselleck:

> The chronicler who narrates events without distinguishing between major and minor ones acts in accord with the following truth: nothing that has ever happened should be regarded as lost to history. Of course only a redeemed mankind is granted the fullness of its past – which is to say, only for a redeemed mankind has its past become citable in all its moments. Each moment it has lived becomes a *citation à l'ordre du jour*. And that day is Judgment Day.[34]

Benjamin's chronicler would also find his or her place among those 'many histories in the plural' which we no longer know how to recount. Koselleck, the historian, would presumably see in this form of presentation a delimited experience of historical

---

33. Taubes, 'Geschichtsphilosophie und Historik', p. 239.
34. Benjamin, *On the Concept of History*, quoted in Taubes, ibid., p. 244. Here in Howard Eiland's translation: Walter Benjamin, *Selected Writings*, Volume 4: *1938–1940*, Harvard University Press, Cambridge MA, 2006, p. 390.

time incompatible with the torsion of modern experience.
Benjamin (and by extension Taubes) finds instead an instance
of the element of redemption that all histories bear. The Day of
Judgement which would be the seal on that redeemed humanity
is not inscribable as historical expectation because it provides the
limits to history as such. It is an emphatic notion of 'end' that is
never wholly reducible to the notion of 'future' which is subject
to taming by the phenomenological limits of historical expectation. It can never be expected within the horizon of expectation
and is therefore neither a prognosis nor a prophecy. Taubes calls
this 'apocalyptic expectation'. As radically discontinuous with
what history presents as historical sequence, it is the irruption
of historical sequence as the experience of historical time itself.
Apocalypse prevents all historical events being buried under the
course of how things 'really were' – the phantasm and fatalism
of historicism. Rather, from apocalyptic expectation, history
is compelled to provide an account of mankind that strives to
make its past referenceable to a meaningful future that cannot
be simply circumscribed within the accumulation of past
experiences in their given sequence. Were we to search for an
anthropological qualification of this apocalyptic experience that
departs from Koselleck's anthropological circle, it could come
from the anthropologist Ernesto de Martino's description of an
'ethos of transcendence' proper to Apocalypse:

> The image of a single human face that bears the signs of violence
> and offence at the hand of another should be enough to put into
> motion the dramatic tension of a world that 'can' and 'must not' end
> in the person looking at that face.[35]

The pressure of a world that 'can' and 'must not' end intro-
duces a different modal and speculative injunction into the

---

35. Ernesto De Martino, *The End of the World: Cultural Apocalypse and Transcendence*,
University of Chicago Press, Chicago IL, 2024, p. 3.

expectations of historical experience. This 'must' is not the must of historical of systematic compulsion. It is the fissure within phenomena that rescues them from their blank transmission. Accordingly, it allies itself with the principle of citability mentioned in the Benjamin quotation above, and with the way Benjamin describes it in Convolute N of the Arcades Project: 'It belongs to the concept of citation ... that the historical object in each case is torn from its context.'[36] According to Taubes, something can be torn from its historical context only in so far as the discontinuity that apocalypse assures as image has become immanent to the temporalization of the present itself. 'In order for a part of the past to be touched by the present instant (*Aktualität*), there must be no continuity between them.'[37]

For Taubes, 'apocalyptic experience' is summarized in the question of a *Wozu* – a 'where-to' or 'towards-which' within history. 'A part of this *Wozu* of "history as such" is hidden in all *Geschichten* (in the plural)' and this '*Wozu* ... is the theme of all history and therefore of all history-writing [*Geschichtsschreibung*].'[38] On this basis, Taubes calls for an explicit inversion of Koselleck's thesis. One does not proceed from 'history' in order to glimpse the existence of other 'histories' that are somehow more measured or hermeneutically coherent with the consolidated space of accumulated experience. On the contrary, 'in the passage through histories – those earlier and those from today – "history" (in the collective-singular), the historico-philosophical index of all histories, is rediscovered.'[39] This second passage – not from history to the past histories, but from histories to rediscovering the *Wozu* common to them all – has more to do with the process by which remembrance modifies

36. Walter Benjamin, *The Arcades Project*, trans. Howard Eiland and Kevin McLaughlin, Harvard University Press, Cambridge MA, 2002, [Convolute N11,3], p. 476.
37. Ibid., [Convolute N7,7], p. 470.
38. Taubes, 'Geschichtsphilosophie und Historik', p. 250.
39. Ibid., p. 244.

those previous histories by introducing that completely 'other' apocalyptic experience as an interruption or destruction that would compel construction on the basis of an end.

What is distinctive about 'history as such' for Taubes, then, is not the radical disjuncture between its experience and expectation as it runs against the limits of a vanishing difference to other 'external' time structures, whether that be due to technology, secularization or any other vaguely determined thesis. It is rather that apocalypse has become a topos for history, as historically (and not theologically) actual. Modernity can glimpse a *towards-which* which is derived out of the precise experience of its own historical time, as a time of irruption. History as such holds within it the possibility of experiencing the future derived from, and thus dialectically intensified by, the notion of an end (the strain of apocalyptic Marxism to which Taubes adheres) *or* experience historical calamities and crises as expected futures stripped of ends, and thus without end. The latter is Koselleck's position, against which the former stance responds. In Koselleck's *Historik,* 'the last remnants of [this] apocalyptic experience are driven out from our historical consciousness'. Koselleck wants to contain discontinuity on the basis of continuity. Koselleck's position is allied with what, in de Martino's critical words, could be described as 'apocalypse without eschaton' – the tamed and bounded subjection to a fateful future that Western colonialism has writ large on the globe.

For Taubes, the paradoxical introjection of apocalyptic expectation back into the field of the horizon of expectation disrupts the 'transcendental meaning of history as the space of consciousness'. The 'must' beyond any circumscribable horizon, as well as the discontinuous and unexpected that apocalypse discloses as idea, is instead an 'an intense stimulus to action'.[40]

---

40. Jacob Taubes, *From Cult to Culture: Fragments toward a Critique of Historical Reason*, Stanford University Press, Stanford CA, 2009, p. 20.

The plane of history as one of action persists beyond any
foreclosure of history by laws or institutions that try and return
the irruptive nature of historical time to continuity. In this, that
eternal disruption which Koselleck laments when it is bound to
a dialectic of finitude could instead be inverted. This apocalyptic
expectation, which brings the eternal in relation to the finite so
that finite humans are never reduced to history as it has been,
could instead aim in the opposing direction. It could, in Taubes's
words, 'connect up with those last remnants of apocalyptic
experience – without recourse to a schema of salvational history
[*heilgeschichtliche*] – in order to serve a profane analysis of now-
time [*Jetztzeit*]'.[41]

---

41. Taubes, 'Geschichtsphilosophie und Historik', p. 245.

8

Between tradition and new beginnings: the genesis of Hannah Arendt's category of natality

ANNA ARGIRÒ

In the Western tradition, mortality has been conceived as a constitutive part of human existence since at least the thought of the Ancient Greeks. In the twentieth century, Heidegger, Levinas and Derrida foregrounded it once again.[1] In this context, Hannah Arendt's introduction of the concept of 'natality' questions the centrality of death in framing human existence. As Adriana Cavarero points out, the Arendtian category of natality cannot simply be added to Western philosophical thought as a new concept that enriches and completes it, but is a category that radically changes this thought, by transforming it at its roots.[2] The concept of natality emerges in Arendt's thought in dialogue with Aristotle, Plato, Augustine, Kant, Benjamin, Jaspers and Heidegger, but Arendt draws very different conclusions.

The secondary literature on Arendt's concept of natality is now quite extensive. A systematic reconstruction can be found

---

1. This essay is based on the PhD project on Hannah Arendt and natality I am carrying out at the Centre for Research in Modern European Philosophy, Kingston University. I also address the topic in Anna Argirò, 'Arendt and Natality: Including Maternity in the Discourse around Birth', in *HA: The Journal of the Hannah Arendt Center for Politics and Humanities at Bard College* 11, 2023, pp. 95–110. I am grateful to Stella Sandford for her supervision and support.
2. Adriana Cavarero,'Dire la nascita', in *Diotima. Mettere al mondo il mondo. Oggetto e oggettività alla luce della differenza Sessuale*, La Tartaruga, Milan, 1990, pp. 93–121; p. 110.

in Silvano Zucal[3] and, most notably, in Patricia Bowen-Moore. In *Hannah Arendt's Philosophy of Natality*, Bowen-Moore detects a tripartite concept of natality in Arendt: 'primary natality', referring to factual birth into the world; 'secondary' or 'political natality' – birth into the realm of action; and 'tertiary/theoretical natality' – birth into the timelessness of thought.[4] (It is worth noting that Bowen-Moore wrote this book before the publication of Arendt's *Denktagebuch* in 2002, and before the essays included in the collections *Jewish Writings* and *Essays in Understanding 1930–1954*.[5]) Anne O'Byrne offers an existential account of natality in her book *Natality and Finitude*, while Dana Villa investigates the Heideggerian roots of Arendt's political thought.[6] Arendt's notion of natality has been explored in connection with biopolitics by Agamben, Diprose and Ziarek, and Bottici.[7] Vatter offers a valuable account of the genesis of the concept, but limits this to retracing when Arendt first began to employ this term in her published works and in her *Denktagebuch*.[8] Feminist interpretations and critiques of this concept can be found in texts by Durst, Söderbäck, Fulfer, Cavarero, Rigotti, Dietz and Kristeva.[9] In her 2006 book *Hannah Arendt and Human Rights*,

---

3. Silvano Zucal, *Filosofia della nascita*, Morcelliana, Brescia, 2017.
4. Patricia Bowen-Moore, *Hannah Arendt's Philosophy of Natality*, Macmillan, London, 1989, p. 1.
5. Hannah Arendt, *Denktagebuch*, Volume 1: *1950–1973*, Volume 2: *1973–1975*, ed. Ursula Ludz and Ingrid Nordmann, Piper Verlag, Munich, 2002; Arendt, *The Jewish Writings*, ed. Jerome Kohn and Ron H. Feldman, Schocken Books, New York, 2007; Arendt, *Essays in Understanding: 1930–1954*, ed. with an introduction by Jerome Kohn, Harcourt, Brace, New York, 1994.
6. Anne O'Byrne, *Natality and Finitude*, Indiana University Press, Bloomington IN, 2010; Dana Villa, *Arendt and Heidegger: The Fate of the Political*, Princeton University Press, Princeton NJ, 1996.
7. Giorgio Agamben, *Homo Sacer: Sovereign Power and Bare Life*, Stanford University Press, Stanford CA, 1998 (1942); Rosalyn Diprose and Ewa Plonowska Ziarek, *Arendt, Natality and Biopolitics: Toward Democratic Plurality and Reproductive Justice*, Edinburgh University Press, Edinburgh, 2018; Chiara Bottici, 'Rethinking the Biopolitical Turn: From the Thanatopolitical to the Geneapolitical Paradigm', *Graduate Faculty Philosophy Journal*, vol. 36, no. 1, 2015, pp. 175–97.
8. Miguel Vatter, 'Natality and Biopolitics in Hannah Arendt', *Revista de cienciapolítica*, vol. 26, no. 2, 2005, pp. 137–59.
9. Margaret Durst, 'Birth and Natality in Hannah Arendt', in *Analecta Husserliana* 79, 2003, pp. 777–97; Fanny Söderbäck, 'Natality or Birth? Arendt and Cavarero on the Human Condition of Being Born', *Hypatia*, vol. 33, no. 2, 2018, pp. 273–88; Katy Fulfer, 'Hannah Arendt and Pregnancy in the Public Sphere', in H. Fielding and D. Olkowski,

Peg Birmingham investigates the concept of natality in relation
to the question of human rights.[10]

'Natality' is like a red thread crossing most of Arendt's work;
yet, as many interpreters have pointed out, Arendt does not
develop a systematic account of this notion.[11] The first task is
thus to reconstruct the genesis of the concept in Arendt's work,
drawing the fragmentary references to it together and trying
to puzzle out their connection. In this essay I reconstruct how
the concept of natality spans Arendt's work, from her doctoral
thesis on *Love and Saint Augustine* (which Arendt revised for
publication from the late 1950s to the early 1960s) to her last,
unfinished work *The Life of the Mind*. I aim to show how it may
be considered a key to understanding and reinterpreting some
other Arendtian concepts. In contrast to Bowen-Moore and other
interpreters, I try to show the interconnectedness of the various
meanings of 'natality' that can be detected throughout Arendt's
oeuvre, rather than following a tripartite schema of separate
biological, political and theoretical meanings.

In particular, I make explicit how the concept is informed by
the dialogue between Arendt and twentieth-century German
Existenzphilosophie, Heidegger and Jaspers in particular, and
via them St Augustine. I argue that this background persists in
Arendt's mature reflections on the political significance of the
concept of natality and can help rethink the distinctions she
makes in *The Human Condition* and *The Life of the Mind*. This also

eds, *Feminist Phenomenology Futures*, Indiana University Press, Bloomington IN, 2017,
pp. 257–74; Adriana Cavarero, *Inclinations: A Critique of Rectitude*, trans. Adam Sitze
and Amanda Minervini, Stanford University Press, Stanford CA, 2016 (2014); Francesca
Rigotti, *Partorire con il corpo e con la mente. Creatività, filosofia, maternità*, Bollati
Boringhieri, Turin, 2010; Mary Dietz, *Turning Operations: Feminism, Arendt, and Politics*,
Routledge, New York and London, 2002; Julia Kristeva, *Hannah Arendt*, Columbia
University Press, New York, 2001.

10. Peg Birmingham, *Hannah Arendt and Human Rights: The Predicament of Common
Responsibility*, Indiana University Press, Bloomington IN, 2006.

11. See, among others, Durst, 'Birth and Natality in Hannah Arendt'; Vatter, 'Natality
and Biopolitics in Hannah Arendt'; Birmingham, *Hannah Arendt and Human Rights*.

allows for the outline of a concept of time that remains largely implicit in her work.

A red thread

One of Arendt's earliest works is a biography, *Rahel Varnhagen: The Life of a Jewish Woman*, dedicated to the figure of Rahel Levin-Varnhagen, a German-Jewish writer who, between the eighteenth and nineteenth centuries, hosted one of the most famous salons in Europe, gathering together artists and intellectuals such as Schelling, Schleiermacher, Alexander and Wilhelm von Humboldt, and Heinrich Heine. Begun by Arendt when she was barely 19, interrupted eight years later, in 1933, when she was forced to leave Germany due to the Nazi regime's persecution,[12] this project took shape over many years, finally being published in English in 1957.[13] Through Rahel's biography, Arendt reflects on the existential significance of being a Jew in the hostile climate of Nazi Germany, a reflection that anticipates her mature considerations on the questions of assimilation, on the figures of the pariah and the parvenu, and on statelessness.[14] In a letter to Jaspers in 1930, Arendt writes:

> It seems as if certain people are so exposed in their own lives (and only in their lives, not as persons!) that they become, as it were, junction points and concrete objectifications of 'life'. Underlying my objectification of Rahel is a self-objectification that is not a reflective

12. In 1933, after spending eight days in a Gestapo prison, Arendt fled from Berlin to Paris. At the age of 27 she became a stateless person.
13. Hannah Arendt, *Rahel Varnhagen: The Life of a Jewish Woman*, rev. edn, trans. Richard and Clara Winston, Harcourt Brace Jovanovich, New York, 1974. (A critical edition, ed. Liliane Weissberg, Johns Hopkins University Press, Baltimore MD, appeared in 1997.)
14. See, for example, Hannah Arendt, 'We Refugees', *Menorah Journal*, vol. 31, no. 1, January 1943, pp. 69–77.
Arendt started working on the book on Rahel after leaving Marburg in 1925 and moving to Heidelberg, where she wrote her doctoral thesis under the supervision of Karl Jaspers. In her biography Arendt often refers to Rahel Varnhagen as 'Rahel'. This is because Rahel Varnhagen often changed her name during her life, but kept 'Rahel' as her preferred signature. See Maria Tamboukou, *Epistolary Narratives of Love, Gender and Agonistic Politics: An Arendtian Approach*, Routledge, London, 2023, p. 34.

or retrospective one but, rather, from the very outset a mode of 'experiencing', of learning, appropriate to her. What this all really adds up to – fate, being exposed, what life means – I can't really say in the abstract (and I realize that in trying to write about it here). Perhaps all I can try to do is illustrate it with examples. And that is precisely why I want to write a biography. In this case, interpretation has to take the path of repetition.[15]

As Elizabeth Young-Bruehl suggests in her biography of Arendt, the book on Rahel Varnhagen can be considered an example of 'biography as autobiography'.[16] For Arendt, it was not only a way to re-elaborate her own personal story, placing it at distance, but also a laboratory, as it were, where her mature reflections on love, alienation from the world and the solitude of the activity of thinking were coming to life.

In Rahel's biography, the topic of birth takes on a central importance. Arendt begins the reconstruction of Rahel's life stages and of her interior path with her last words. On her deathbed, Rahel exclaims:

> WHAT a history! – A fugitive from Egypt and Palestine, here I am and find help, love, fostering in you people. With real rapture I think of these origins of mine and this whole nexus of destiny, through which the oldest memories of the human race stand by side with the latest developments. The greatest distances in time and space are bridged. The thing which all my life seemed to me the greatest shame, which was the misery and misfortune of my life – having been born a Jewess this I should on no account now wish to have missed.[17]

15. *Hannah Arendt/Karl Jaspers, Correspondence 1926–1969*, ed. Lotte Köhler and Hans Saner, trans. Robert and Rita Kimber, Harcourt, New York, 1993, pp. 11–12.

16. Elizabeth Young-Bruehl, *Hannah Arendt: For Love of the World*, Yale University Press, New Haven CT and London, 2004 (1982). Young-Bruehl was a former student of Arendt at the New School for Social Research in New York.

17. Arendt, *Rahel Varnhagen*, p. 3. This passage echoes Arendt's own words reported in her correspondence with Scholem: 'I have always regarded my Jewishness as one of the indisputable factual data of my life, and I have never had the wish to change or disclaim facts of this kind. There is such a thing as basic gratitude for everything that is as it is.' However, as Arendt herself remarks in her interview with Günter Gaus, the recognition of her origin was not an easy task: 'the word "Jew" never came up when I was a small child. I first met up with it through anti-Semitic remarks ... from children on the street. After that, I was so to speak "enlightened".' Hannah Arendt, 'An Exchange of Letters between Gershom Scholem and Hannah Arendt', in *The Jew As Pariah*, ed. Ron

Throughout Arendt's text, Rahel Varnhagen often refers to her 'infamous birth'.[18] Rahel's is a story of guilt, of shame, of self-denial and of continuous attempts to cover up this birth, through love, marriage or assimilation. Only *in extremis* does she recognize herself in her origin, intended as the starting point of everyone's life. As Cavarero suggests in 'Dire la nascita', Arendt combines two *atopies* in this biography: birth and Jewishness. In Cavarero's account, birth and Jewishness are *'a-topos'*, literally 'out of place' or 'extraordinary' to the extent that they exceed the established – symbolic, philosophical and political – order that overlooks the beginning of human life (especially if connected to a Jewish origin), by focusing rather on its end. In this sense, for Cavarero, birth and Jewishness are not simply placed outside of the established order or the mainstream Western philosophical tradition, but they retain a peculiar relationship with respect to them, by virtue of which they are capable of decentring and questioning their assumptions.

The category of natality will become central in Arendt's mature thought, and it is not irrelevant that it was initially connected to a Jewish origin. Indeed, Cavarero remarks that in her later works Arendt employs the category of natality purified from biographical and autobiographical references. In spite of this abstraction, the importance of the (auto)biographical and existential perspectives on political and philosophical reflection remain central in Arendt's thought. For Arendt, general concepts can be exemplified through and take on (different) meaning(s) when they are tied to a concrete life.

As the correspondence with Jaspers shows, the work on Rahel Varnhagen goes hand in hand with Arendt's elaboration in her

---

H. Feldman, Grove Press, New York, 1978, p. 246; Hannah Arendt, '"What Remains? The Language Remains": A Conversation with Günter Gaus', in *Essays in Understanding*, ed. Jerome Kohn, Harcourt, Brace, New York, 1994, p. 6.
18. Arendt, *Rahel Varnhagen*, pp. 8, 71.

doctoral thesis of the concept of love in St Augustine.[19] As Judith Chelius Stark points out in her preface to the 1996 English edition of Arendt's thesis, it should not be surprising that Arendt decided to focus her doctoral thesis on a Christian thinker like St Augustine. Stark reports that Hans Jonas, when asked why this was so, replied that 'such a topic would not have been all that unusual in the German universities of the time.' In the German universities particular attention was devoted to Augustine's *Confessions*, which, as Jonas recalls, prompted students to 'self-exploration and the descent into the abyss of conscience.'[20]

In her doctoral thesis, Arendt investigates three concepts of love in Augustine: love in the sense of *cupiditas*, the love between Creator and creature (*caritas*), and neighbourly love. All three types of love are characterized by craving (*appetitus*), desire for some good that can guarantee the actualization of a happy life (*vita beata*) or happiness (*beatitudo*). The idea of neighbourly love drives Arendt's reflections, as she seeks to render clear the meaning of the evangelical command 'love they neighbour as thyself'.

As Arendt remarks, in Augustine's view, love in the sense of *cupiditas* is constantly threatened by the possibility of losing the object of desire, as it is directed towards worldly and temporal goods ('love of the world'). This type of love prompts human beings to seek an object or good which is outside of the world and its mutability (transmundane). At this stage, the relation to God is found in the anticipation of an absolute future (oriented by human beings' mortality) which anticipates the 'timeless present' of eternity.

---

19. See the early letters published in *Hannah Arendt/Karl Jaspers, Correspondence 1926–1969*.
20. Hannah Arendt, *Der Liebesbegriff bei Augustin*, Julius Springer Verlag, Berlin, 1929. Translated as *Love and Saint Augustine*, with an interpretive essay by Joanna V. Scott and Judith C. Stark, University of Chicago Press, Chicago IL, 1996, p. xv.

By contrast, in the love of the creature for the Creator happiness is found not in the anticipation of an absolute future, but in the remembrance of a past which has never been present in our worldly existence. This is the perfect reunion with God intended as the *matrix* or origin of human beings' lives. From this perspective, human beings' lives are oriented not by the anticipation of an absolute future, but by the remembrance and repetition in a quasi-Freudian sense (in the literal sense of *re-petere*, re-seeking) an absolute past.

Both in the anticipation of an absolute future and in the remembrance of an absolute past, the present of worldly human existence is annihilated, and, with it the relation to anything mundane. Arendt seeks to reconcile neighbourly love with the isolation prescribed by the exclusive relation to oneself and to God by pointing to a twofold origin of human life: Christ's redemptive death and Adam's original sin.[21] In Augustine's view, through faith in Christ's redeeming grace, human beings are able to love their neighbours as they love themselves. What each one loves in the other is the recognition of a common createdness and desire to return to their origin.[22]

It is in the context of the discussion of the love of the creature for the Creator, and of the possibility of reconciling this love with neighbourly love, that Arendt's critique of the primacy of death for the understanding of human life appears, as well as early references to the concepts of birth, natality and plurality. In a passage from part II we read:

---

21. It is worth noting that, in her doctoral thesis, Arendt follows Augustine's overlooking of the figure of Eve in the narration of the Creation story, focusing on Adam. As Augustine remarks in the *De Civitate Dei*, differently from other species that were ordered 'to come into being several at once', Adam was created *unum ac singulum*. This will change in the first pages of *The Human Condition*, where Arendt points to 'two biblical versions of the creation story': I Cor. 11:8–12 and Genesis 1:27 'male and female created He them'. Hannah Arendt, *The Human Condition*, University of Chicago Press, Chicago IL, 1958, p. 8.
22. Bowen-Moore, *Hannah Arendt's Philosophy of Natality*, p. 11.

man's dependence rests not on anticipation and does not aim at something, but relies exclusively on remembrance and refers back to the past. To put it differently, the decisive fact determining man as a conscious, remembering being is birth or 'natality', that is, the fact that we have entered the world through birth. The decisive fact determining man as a desiring being was death or mortality, the fact that we shall leave the world in death. Fear of death and inadequacy of life are the springs of desire. In contrast, gratitude for life having been given at all is the spring of remembrance, for a life is cherished even in misery.[23]

As Vatter emphasizes, Arendt adds the passages explicitly mentioning the concepts of birth and natality in the period from 1958 through 1964, when she revises her thesis with the aim of publishing it in English; as well as adding, later in the text, the famous citation *Initium ut esset homo creatus est ante quem nullus fuit* from Augustine's *De Civitate Dei* and explicit references to Heidegger's *Being and Time*.[24]

In these pages from her doctoral thesis, Arendt begins to ask about an origin which stands outside the human condition and yet is the source of human beings' capacity to begin something new in the common world. Arendt proposes a concept of human life and of temporality primarily oriented not by expectation or anticipation, but by remembrance of a past that is never wiped out. For Arendt, human beings retain a special relation to this absolute past by virtue of being-born or 'having-been-created'. This origin, though not properly experienced, remains stored up in the human mind and prompts a response to and recollection of it by originating/initiating something new. In Arendt's view, human beings' capacity to act is indeed an actualization of 'the human condition of natality' to the extent that it depends on and responds to 'the beginning that came into the world when

---

23. Arendt, *Love and Saint* Augustine, pp. 51–2.
24. 'That there be a beginning, man was created, before whom there was nobody.' Augustine, *De Civitate Dei*, XII, 20.
See Vatter, 'Natality and Biopolitics in Hannah Arendt', p. 140; Arendt, *Love and Saint Augustine*, pp. 55–6, 132.

we were born'. For Arendt, this capacity is not metaphorically or symbolically connected to birth, but it is *ontologically* rooted in the fact of being born.[25]

An explicit critique of Heidegger's analytic of *Dasein* oriented by death can be found in Arendt's 1946 essay 'What Is Existenz Philosophy?' In the section 'The Self as Being and Nothingness: Heidegger', Arendt insists on the solipsism of *Dasein*, which relates to its own death to reach its authentic 'Self'.[26]

In notes from the 1950s included in her *Denktagebuch*, Arendt then begins to explore the question of the plurality of human beings in a more explicitly philosophical and political way. In fragment 21, dated August 1950, which was later published as the opening to the posthumous essay '*Was ist Politik?*', Arendt rethinks politics starting from the fundamental distinction between 'men', who are always in the plural, and 'Man', according to Arendt the object of both philosophical and theological inquiry. In the subsequent fragments, Arendt also reflects on the question of the semantic ambiguity of the Greek term Ἀρχή, which, at the same time, means 'beginning' and 'rulership', in Plato's *Statesman*.[27]

It is in a 1953 note included in her *Denktagebuch* that the word 'natalität' first appears in relation to the terms 'action', 'equality' and 'pluralität', and in contrast to the terms 'singularität', 'loneliness', 'mortalität'.[28] As the *Denktagebuch* editors suggest, this

---

25. Arendt, *The Human* Condition, pp. 177–8, 247.
26. Hannah Arendt, 'What Is Existenz Philosophy?', *Partisan Review*, vol. XIII, no. 1, Winter 1946, pp. 34–56.
27. Arendt, *Denktagebuch*, I, 34, pp. 26–8.
28. Ibid., XIX, 21, p. 461. As Jeffrey Champlin notes, this is the only passage in Arendt's *Denktagebuch* in which the word 'natality' is explicitly used. Champlin offers an analysis of this fragment, but he does not provide an overview of the concept in Arendt's thought diary. See Jeffrey Champlin, '"Poetry or Body Politic": Natality and the Space of Birth in Hannah Arendt's Thought Diary', in Roger Berkowitz and Ian Storey, eds, *Artifacts of Thinking: Reading Hannah Arendt's Denktagebuch*, Fordham University Press, New York, 2017, pp. 143–61. It is also worth noting that when Arendt first begins to employ the term 'natality' she does so in English, and she seems to translate it back from English into German as *Natalität*, instead of employing the word *Gebürtlichkeit*, which is the standard German translation for 'natality'. See Vatter, 'Natality and Biopolitics in Hannah Arendt', p. 139. Arendt seems to refer to the Latin etymology of the world 'natality', which comes

fragment might be considered a preparatory sketch for a series of
lectures Arendt delivered at Notre Dame in 1954.

One year later, Arendt refers to birth as an event of salvation.
After attending the premiere of Händel's *Messiah*, she writes in
her diary: 'The Alleluia is understandable only starting from
the text: "a child has been born unto us" ... every beginning is
a salvation, for love of the beginning, for love of salvation, God
created man in the world. Every new birth guarantees salvation
in the world, it is a promise of redemption for those who are no
longer a beginning.'[29] In a letter to Heinrich Blücher (her second
husband), in May 1952, Arendt further comments: 'For the first
time I appreciated the force of "a child has been born unto us".'[30]

The idea of the capacity for introducing a new beginning in
the world by virtue of human birth and the citation from Augustine's *De Civitate Dei* officially appear in the essay 'Ideology and
Terror', which will become the last chapter of the 1958 expanded
version of *The Origins of Totalitarianism*. In this essay, birth
is understood as new beginning and the possibility of acting
becomes a weapon of salvation against the blind automatism
imposed by totalitarian regimes.

> Total terror, the essence of totalitarian government, exists neither
> for nor against men. It is supposed to provide the forces of nature
> or history with an incomparable instrument to accelerate their
> movement. This movement ... can be slowed down and is slowed
> down almost inevitably by the freedom of man, which even
> totalitarian rulers cannot deny, for this freedom – irrelevant and
> arbitrary as they may deem it – is identical with the fact that men

from the term 'natalis': 'pertaining to birth or origin', from the past participle of the verb
nasci (*natu*), which means 'to be born'. As Alessandra Papa points out, '"natality" is a
demographic and statistical term that seems to have several meanings at the same time,
beyond the immediate evangelical suggestions. Semantically, the English word natality
refers both to the idea of fertility, and to the idea of ecumene, that is, of the inhabited
world.' Alessandra Papa, *Nati per incominciare. Vita e politica in Hannah Arendt*, Vita e
Pensiero, Milan, 2011, p. 6, my translation.

29. Arendt, *Denktagebuch*, IX, 12, p. 208, my translation.
30. Hannah Arendt and Heinrich Blücher, *Within Four Walls: The Correspondence
between Hannah Arendt and Heinrich Blücher 1936–1968*, Harcourt, New York, 2000,
p. 270.

are being born and that therefore each of them is a new beginning, begins, in a sense, the world anew.[31]

In the years from 1929 to 1958 (the year of the publication of *The Human Condition* and of the revised edition of *The Origins of Totalitarianism*) Arendt explores the centrality of the 'capacity of beginning' from a more political perspective.

In the first section of *The Human Condition*, after pointing out the three fundamental human activities of the *vita activa* (labour, work and action), Arendt claims

> Labor and work, as well as action, are ... rooted in natality in so far as they have the task to provide and preserve the world for, to foresee and reckon with, the constant influx of newcomers, who are born into the world as strangers. However, of the three, action has the closest connection with the human condition of natality; the new beginning inherent in birth can make itself felt in the world only because the newcomer possesses the capacity of beginning something new, that is, of acting. In this sense of initiative, an element of action, and therefore of natality, is inherent in all human activities. Moreover, since action is the political activity par excellence, natality, and not mortality, may be the central category of political, as distinguished from metaphysical thought.[32]

As for Arendt's latter claim, on the one hand we might say that she draws a traditional distinction between two different fields, dealing with distinct matters (political thought/action vs metaphysical thought/thinking); on the other hand, though, Arendt's work can help us rethink the so-called 'metaphysical' tradition, or even detect a more or less implicit critique of metaphysics in a quasi-Heideggerian fashion.

In the Preface to *Between Past and Future*, Arendt rethinks the question of the 'beginning' and its peculiar relation to the past in connection with the concepts of inheritance and

---

31. Hannah Arendt, *The Origins of Totalitarianism*, new edn with added prefaces, Harvest/Harcourt Brace Jovanovich, New York, 1973 (1951, 1958), p. 612.
32. Arendt, *The Human Condition*, pp. 8–9.

tradition.[33] In this context, the human capacity to begin is seen as the possibility of recovering and bringing into light again the 'lost treasures' in history that seemed to be drowned by the flow of time. For Arendt, thinkers, artists, intellectuals and historians are responsible for preserving these treasures. In Arendt's view, in the activities of thinking and judging, human beings insert themselves in the continuum of daily or ordinary time, interrupting its flow and allowing the 'opposite forces' of past and future to find a meeting point in the gap created by the withdrawal from activities that are performed in public. With this withdrawal, human beings are capable of isolating a sphere, a place 'sufficiently removed from past and future' that offers a position from which to judge the events of the world with an impartial glance.[34]

For Arendt, this space or gap is also removed from historical or biographical time (Arendt conceives of it as 'ageless') to the extent that it does not depend on a singular life spanning from birth to death. Though it constitutes a specific sphere from which to observe and judge the events occurring in the world, it remains, so to speak, untouched by them. By virtue of this distance, it is able to preserve the 'treasures' that, otherwise, would be drowned by the continuous flow of historical or biographical time. As Arendt remarks,

> this small track of non-time which the activity of thought beats within the time–space of mortal men and into which the trains of thought, of remembrance and anticipation, save whatever they touch from the ruin of historical and biographical time. This small non-time–space in the very heart of time ... cannot be inherited and handed down from the past; each new generation, indeed every new human being as he inserts himself between an infinite past and an infinite future, must discover and ploddingly pave it anew.[35]

---

33. Hannah Arendt, *Between Past and Future*, Viking Press, New York, 1968 (1961), pp. 3–15.
34. Ibid., p. 12.
35. Ibid., p. 13.

In these reflections on the importance of the past for the capacity of introducing a new beginning, as well as in her considerations on the figure of the historian/judge, Arendt seems to be influenced by Benjamin's *Theses on the Philosophy of History*, a manuscript that Arendt brought with her from Paris to New York in 1941. In Thesis II we read:

> the past carries with it a temporal index by which it is referred to redemption. There is a secret agreement between past generations and the present one. Our coming was expected on earth. Like every generation that preceded us, we have been endowed with a weak Messianic power, a power to which the past has a claim.[36]

When Arendt frames the 'gap between past and future' where the activities of thinking and judging are performed as 'non-time' or 'out of time', she does not have in mind a space of eternal quietness. Rather, recovering Kafka's parable 'HE', Arendt conceives of this gap as a battleground where the no-longer and the not-yet meet in the Now, the 'fighting present' where the thinking ego stands.[37] This region is not above or beyond the world and human time. As Arendt puts it,

> This timelessness, to be sure, is not eternity; it springs, as it were, from the clash of past and future, whereas eternity is the boundary concept that is unthinkable because it indicates the collapse of all temporal dimensions. The temporal dimension of the *nunc stans* experienced in the activity of thinking gathers the absent tenses, the not-yet and the not-more, together into presence.[38]

In this sense, the activities of thinking and judging are not really 'out of' time, but they produce a suspension, a rupture of time understood as a linear or a cyclic movement.[39]

---

36. Walter Benjamin, *Illuminations*, Schocken Books, New York, 1969, p. 254.
37. Hannah Arendt, *The Life of the Mind*, Harcourt Brace Jovanovich, New York, 1978, p. 207.
38. Ibid., p. 211.
39. See ibid., pp. 202–13.

The idea that the 'new beginning' retains a relationship with the past is central in *On Revolution*. For Arendt the concept of revolution must be able to mediate between the 'concern for stability' and the 'spirit of novelty', rejecting changes imposed by violence. The real revolution is always linked to birth, since it is able to introduce an element of 'absolute novelty' while preserving a relation to the past. Only in this way is it possible for Arendt to avoid the absolutist tendencies she denounces in the French and Russian revolutions.[40]

Reflections on the question of the beginning as the peculiar human capacity will accompany Arendt until the elaboration of her final and unfinished work, *The Life of the Mind*, published posthumously in 1978. In this text it is possible to detect the relevance of natality for the *vita contemplativa*, and specifically for the activities of willing and judging. Building on Augustine, Arendt makes a distinction between will understood as *liberum arbitrium*, a freedom of choice that arbitrates and decides between two given things, and will understood as the freedom and capacity to call something into being which did not exist before, which was not given.[41] The topic of the will is closely connected to that of freedom. Both refer to the typically human capacity of beginning something new.

Because of its attention to the particular, its capacity to generate general meanings from time to time, and its dependence on the plurality of human beings as earth-bounded creatures, the mental activity of judgement also seems to have a peculiar relationship with natality. It is perhaps not by chance that, as Simona Forti suggests, along with natality, Arendt's 'theory of judgement' is the other keystone of her political thought to which there remains only fragmentary textual allusions.[42]

40. Hannah Arendt, *On Revolution*, rev. edn, Penguin, London, 1990 (1963), p. 209.
41. Arendt, *The Life of the Mind*, pp. 158–217.
42. See Simona Forti, *Hannah Arendt tra filosofia e politica*, Mondadori, Milan, 2006. 'Judging' was to have been the third and last part of *The Life of the Mind*. This suggests

'While still a solitary business, Arendt remarks, judgement 'does not cut itself off from "all others". To be sure, it still goes on in isolation, but by the force of imagination it makes the others present and thus moves in a space that is potentially public, open to all sides.'[43] This capacity to 'enlarge' one's thought in order to include others' perspectives may be seen as a preparation for acting, to the extent that it creates the space where actions can be performed and welcomed. From this perspective, the figures of the actor and of the spectator and their respective activities blur or are seen as interrelated. On the other hand, the activity of the spectator/judge who retrospectively judges the course of the events (as Arendt did on the occasion of the Eichmann's trial) may be seen as a sort of action in itself, to the extent that, in the rare moments in which 'the stakes are on the table', it is able to 'tell right from wrong' and to preserve the seeds of a promise for the future.[44] In Benjamin's terms,

> Thinking involves not only the flow of thoughts, but their arrest as well. Where *thinking suddenly stops in a configuration pregnant with tensions*, it gives that configuration a shock, by which it crystallizes into a monad ... a Messianic cessation of happening, or, put differently, a revolutionary chance in the fight for the oppressed past.[45]

---

that Arendt had the intention of providing a more systematic account of this notion. Arendt addresses the topic of judgement in her 1964–65–66 and 1970 courses at the University of Chicago and the New School for Social Research, later published as *Lectures on Kant's Political Philosophy*, ed. with an interpretive essay by Ronald Beiner, University of Chicago Press, Chicago IL, 1982.

43. Arendt, *Lectures on Kant's Political Philosophy*, p. 43.

44. Arendt, *The Life of the Mind*, p. 193. In his interpretative essay in Arendt's *Lectures on Kant's Political Philosophy*, Ronald Beiner writes of 'two theories of judgment' in Arendt's work, one in which judgement is considered from the point of view of the *vita activa* and one where it is approached from the point of view of the life of the mind. According to Beiner, the emphasis shifts from the enlarged mentality of political agents to the spectatorship and retrospective judgement of historians and storytellers. However, this interpretation only works if we read *The Human Condition* and *The Life of the Mind* as separate from each other, instead of conceiving the latter as a continuum and rethinking of the former. See Arendt, *Lectures on Kant's Political Philosophy*, p. 90.

45. Benjamin, *Illuminations*, pp. 262–3, my emphasis.

Arendt and German *Existenzphilosophie*

The concept of natality runs throughout most of Arendt's work and becomes a central category of her political thought. I would now like to emphasize how the elaboration of this concept was conditioned by Arendt's philosophical studies in Germany in the mid- and late 1920s.

After studying with Heidegger in Marburg in 1924, Arendt completed her doctoral thesis in Heidelberg under the supervision of Karl Jaspers. As we have seen, it is in her thesis on *Love and Saint Augustine* that she starts to re-elaborate and challenge some aspects of her mentors' philosophy, Heidegger in particular. However, as the editors of Arendt's thesis point out, the link between her political thought and its roots in twentieth-century German *Existenzphilosophie* are to some extent, still overlooked, if not intentionally obscured.[46]

Arendt's thesis was published in English only posthumously in 1996, when a certain idea or image of Arendt as a political thinker far from 'metaphysical' or philosophical-existential concerns had been established. Even the scholars who worked with the Arendt Papers in the Library of Congress in Washington D.C., where the revisions of the 1929 manuscript are collected (for example, Elizabeth Young-Bruehl and Margaret Canovan), marginalized the thesis or framed it as a pre-political or even apolitical work.[47] Furthermore, not many political theorists approaching Arendt's thought were (or are) familiar with the work of a Christian thinker like St Augustine, or even with the philosophy of her mentors, Heidegger and Jaspers.

Crucially, there was a perceived need to emphasize the break between Arendt's pre- and post-Holocaust works, or her German and American works. In particular, it was considered that

---

46. See Arendt, *Love and Saint Augustine*, pp. 125–34. See also Forti, *Hannah Arendt tra filosofia e politica*, pp. xi–xii.
47. Arendt, *Love and Saint Augustine*, pp. 125–34.

Arendt's thought needed to be freed from Heidegger's influence.[48] This was, of course, due to Heidegger's political position – the fact that he became rector of the University of Freiburg in 1933 and joined the Nazi Party the same year. Arendt, on the contrary, was the Jew who had left Nazi Germany to escape first to Paris and then to find refuge in the United States. She was the political theorist of democracy and one of the first twentieth-century thinkers to reflect on totalitarianism. It is interesting in this regard that, as the editors of Arendt's thesis underline, her early biography of Rahel Varnhagen was accepted and received into the 'Arendt canon', as it could be included among the works anticipating Arendt's subsequent considerations of the questions of exile and assimilation, of the figures of the pariah and the parvenu, and of the problem of statelessness.[49]

Heidegger and other German philosophers contemporary with Arendt were taken to represent the latest version of the 'professional thinkers' of the Western philosophical tradition that overlooked the plurality of human beings and obscured the specificity of political action. Arendt herself contributed to this reading when she explicitly framed (Western) philosophy and politics in sharply distinct, if not antagonistic, terms.[50] On the one hand, in a letter to Scholem from 1963, Arendt recognizes this philosophical tradition as her origin: 'If I can be said to "have come from anywhere", it is from the tradition of German philosophy.'[51] On the other hand, in her interview with Günter Gaus, Arendt famously claims:

---

48. The editors mention, for example, the American political scientists Thomas Pangle, Luc Ferry and John Gunnell. They charge Arendt with undermining the rationalistic foundations of Western philosophy, as well as attacking American pragmatism and empiricism with German nihilism. Ibid., pp. 174–7.

49. Ibid., p. 127.

50. See for example Arendt, *The Human Condition*, p. 9, and Arendt, 'Philosophy and Politics', *Social Research*, vol. 57, no. 1, 1990, pp. 73–103, www.jstor.org/stable/40970579. Some feminist interpreters of Arendt, such as Cavarero, emphasize this separation and endorse this antagonistic reading to stress the originality of Arendt's thought and her detachment from a masculine metaphysical way of philosophizing.

51. Arendt, 'An Exchange of Letters between Gershom Scholem and Hannah Arendt',

I do not belong to the circle of the philosophers. My profession,
if one can speak of it at all, is political theory. I neither feel like a
philosopher, nor I do believe that I have been accepted in the circle
of philosophers... As you know, I studied philosophy, but this does
not mean that I stayed with it... I want to look at politics, so to
speak, with eyes unclouded by philosophy.[52]

As these passages suggest, Arendt does not reject her philosophical roots in Western and, more specifically, German
philosophy. However, she adopts an external position to look
at it and challenge some of its premisses. More recently, the
connection between Arendt and German *Existenzphilosophie* has
been explored by scholars such as Dana Villa, Jacques Taminiaux,
Seyla Benhabib and Simona Forti, with particular attention to
the philosophical exchange with Heidegger.[53] If all these authors
agree on Arendt's rootedness in twentieth-century German philosophy and uncover specifically her critique and re-elaboration of
Heidegger's thought combined with a reinterpretation of Aristo-
telian categories, they nonetheless suggest different analyses of
these connections.

Both Taminiaux and Villa insist on what we may call Arendt's
'polemical appropriation' of Heidegger's critique of metaphysics
and of some of the key concepts he outlines in *Being and Time*.
However, by framing almost all of Arendt's categories as a
polemical response to Heidegger, they end up presenting them as
a mere reversal, or even an expansion, of Heidegger's philosophy,
which risks obscuring the originality of Arendt's thought. In
contrast, Seyla Benhabib and Simona Forti frame the exchange
between the two philosophers as a 'dialogue', thus underlining

---

p. 246.
  52. Arendt, '"What Remains? The Language Remains"', pp. 1–2.
  53. Villa, *Arendt and Heidegger*; Jacques Taminiaux, *The Thracian Maid and the
Professional Thinker: Arendt and Heidegger*, SUNY Press, New York, 1997; Seyla Benhabib,
The Reluctant Modernism of Hannah Arendt, new edn with a new preface and an
appendix, Rowman & Littlefield, New York, 2003; Forti, *Hannah Arendt tra filosofia e
politica*.

the equal position Arendt and Heidegger now have in philosophical debates.

What is, for our context, the theoretical gain in retracing
the roots of Arendt's thought in the German tradition of
Existenzphilosophie? First, the originality of Arendt's categories,
and specifically the shift in perspective entailed by her focus
on birth and natality rather than death and mortality, can be
better grasped if we understand that these categories emerged
in dialogue with twentieth-century German philosophy. Indeed,
as we have seen, Arendt does not refer to a different tradition
of thought, but rather engages with classic thinkers of Western
philosophy.

Second, retracing Arendt's philosophical lineage in German
Existenzphilosophie allows one to grasp the dynamicity of her
categories or to put them into motion. Indeed, in approaching
Arendt's framework, what is often missed is the dialectical and
intimate relationship between the spheres and the activities that
she outlines, which do not stand in binary and rigid oppositions.
Arendt's interpreters usually focus on the content of each sphere,
the criteria used to place certain kind of activities in one or
the other, or suggest ways to challenge these very distinctions.
For example, Benhabib warns against what she calls Arendt's
'phenomenological essentialism', which in her view runs the risk
of becoming paralysing and exclusive, imprisoning agents and
activities in fixed roles and locations.[54] What is often overlooked
is *how* these spheres take shape, are modified and temporarily
displaced/articulated. As Villa points out,

> Unlike many of her critics, Arendt refused to reify the capacities and
> conditions of human existence into a transhistorical human 'nature'
> … It is not … simply a question of the relative status an activity has
> in the hierarchy of the vita activa; it is also a matter of the peculiar

---

54. Seyla Benhabib, 'Feminist Theory and Hannah Arendt's Concept of Public Space',
History of the Human Sciences, vol. 6, no. 2, 1993, pp. 97–114; p. 104.

historical reality the activity inhabits. Hence the possibility not only of a change in rank (the 'reversal' within the vita activa that helps define the entry into modernity), but of a dis-essencing or transformation of the capacities themselves.[55]

Although Arendt stresses that 'each human activity points to its location in the world', her categories cannot be conceived as static and given once and for all, we might say in a sort of metaphysical presence, so that certain kinds of activity and the corresponding human type find their proper and definitive place in one or the other sphere.[56] In this respect, it is interesting to consider Lewis and Sandra Hinchman's claim that 'almost all of Arendt's crucial terms are in fact "existentials" that seek to illuminate what it means to be-in-the-world and not "categories"', while Heidegger's *existentialia* are actually 'articulations of being'.[57] As applied to Heidegger, I agree with the Hinchmans' thesis, to the extent that Heidegger's main concern even in *Being and Time*, where we find the existential analytic of *Dasein*, is actually the *Seinsfrage*, the question of Being.[58] But with regard to Arendt, it is hard to completely embrace the Hinchmans' suggestion. Indeed, the distinctions Arendt proposes in, for example, *The Human Condition* and *The Life of the Mind* are actually *new* categories that can be used for a philosophical-political analysis.

What is interesting in the Hinchmans' reading is the connection they draw between politics as understood by Arendt – that is, not primarily as a given institution or organization (such as the nation-state), but as an *in-between* – and German

55. Villa, *Arendt and Heidegger*, p. 174.
56. Arendt, *The Human* Condition, p. 73.
57. Lewis P. and Sandra K. Hinchman. 'In Heidegger's Shadow: Hannah Arendt's Phenomenological Humanism', *Review of Politics*, vol. 46, no. 2, 1984, pp. 183–211, www.jstor.org/stable/1407108, p. 197.
58. The question of the meaning of Being is not a question for Arendt, who also criticizes Heidegger for using the term *Dasein* to speak of human beings. This way, he 'resolve[s] man into several modes of being that are phenomenologically demonstrable'. Arendt, 'What is Existenz Philosophy?', in *Essays in Understanding*, p. 178. Arendt not only avoids the word *Dasein*, but, in various contexts, she also emphasizes that the subject and the starting point of politics is not 'man' but 'men in the plural'. See for example Arendt, *Denktagebuch*, I, 21, p. 17.

Existenzphilosophie. In this sense, Lewis and Sandra Hinchman speak of 'Phenomenological Humanism' or 'Existentialism Politicized'. This connection becomes particularly evident when focusing on categories like 'natality' and 'mortality' that are closely attached to human existence.

In her essay 'What is Existenz Philosophy?', Arendt discusses how, starting from Kierkegaard, death, and/or the fear of death, becomes one of the central (if not *the* central) theme of existential philosophy and is seen as human beings' *principium individuationis*, to the extent that 'even though it is the most universal of all universals, nonetheless inevitably [death] strikes me alone'.[59] Even in Jaspers, death persists as one of the main 'boundary situations' that conditions human life (while birth is not mentioned). As Arendt shows in *The Life of the Mind*, this is not a new trope. Indeed, she highlights an essential 'affinity between death and philosophy' that, since Plato, runs throughout most of the Western philosophical tradition.[60]

What is important for us is that Arendt recovers some elements of the tradition of German *Existenzphilosophie*, and specifically of Heidegger's perspective, but simultaneously distances herself from it by putting the concept of birth at the centre of her reflection. Indeed, she embraces Heidegger's *dynamic* concept of human existence as *Ex-sistere*. In Arendt's view, human existence and, with it, the realm of politics unfold in a dialectic of darkness and unconcealment that recalls Heidegger's conception of disclosure (*Erschlossenheit*). However, by shifting the focus from the solitary relationship of *Dasein* with its own death to the relationship that every human being entertains with their birth, this movement can occur only in a plural sphere. In the section dedicated to Jaspers in 'What is Existenz Philosophy?' Arendt writes:

---

59. Arendt, 'What is Existenz Philosophy?', p. 178.
60. Arendt, *The Life of the Mind*, pp. 79–80.

Existenz itself is, by its very nature, never isolated. It exists only in communication and in awareness of others' existence. Our fellow men are not (as in Heidegger) an element of existence that is structurally necessary but at the same time an impediment to the Being of Self. Just the contrary: *existence can develop only in the shared life* [togetherness] *of human beings inhabiting a common world given to them all.*[61]

If the Heideggerian anticipation (*Vorlaufen*) of death reveals and preserves one's authentic self in solitude and silence, the Arendtian conception of birth is the place of visibility, of listening and of mutual recognition. For Arendt, to appear means to be seen by others. If Heidegger's appearance is inward, 'self-distorting' and informed by the anticipation of death intended as concealment and protection, for Arendt phenomena appear to others and are distorted by the plurality of glances witnessing them. For Heidegger the public realm (*die Öffentlichkeit*) remains that of the impersonal *Man* where *Dasein* is first and foremost absorbed. But for Arendt, the public realm or the realm of plurality is the only space where human beings can appear authentically, by means of actions and words.[62]

As Arendt's dissertation suggests, human beings' reciprocal disclosure and, with it, the public realm of politics unfold in a temporal dimension oriented by past and remembrance rather than future and anticipation. As Arendt puts it:

---

61. Arendt, 'What is Existenz Philosophy?', p. 186, my emphasis. In a 1953 *Denktagebuch* entry Arendt claims that 'to establish a science of politics one needs first to reconsider all philosophical statements on Man under the assumption that men, and not Man, inhabit the earth. The establishment of political science demands a philosophy for which *men exist only in the plural*. Its field is human plurality. Its religious source is the second creation myth – not Adam and rib, but: male and female created He them. In this realm of plurality, which is the political realm, one has to ask the old questions – what is love, what is friendship, what is solitude, what is acting, thinking, etc.' Arendt, *Denktagebuch*, XIII, 2, p. 295, my emphasis.

62. Although it is possible to reconstruct Arendt's categories as mirroring and overturning Heidegger's concepts, Arendt does not merely spatialize or externalize them as Villa often suggests. Indeed, for example, Arendt makes a crucial distinction between the social (that we might connect to Heidegger's 'Man' as described in §27 of *Being and Time*) and the political sphere which is absent in Heidegger. See Villa, *Arendt and Heidegger*, pp. 130, 136.

human existence consists in acting and behaving in some way or other, always in motion, and thus opposed in any way to eternal 'enduring within itself' (*permanere in se*) ... this precarious mode of existence is not nothing, it exists in relating back to its origin... Through remembrance man discovers this twofold 'before' of human existence... In this process of re-presenting, the past not only takes its place among other things present but is transformed into future possibility... The fact that the past is not forever lost and that remembrance can bring it back into the present is what gives memory its great power (*vis*) ... it is memory and not expectation (for instance, the expectation of death as in Heidegger approach) that gives unity and wholeness to human existence.[63]

According to Heidegger, *Dasein*'s temporality is oriented by the anticipation and repetition of a specific past which dis-closes a limited range of possibilities to be 'freely' chosen. In this respect, I disagree with Villa's claim that Arendt recovers Heidegger's concept of freedom. As Villa himself points out, Heidegger's *Dasein* can 'freely' make a decision among a range of possibilities already given. In this sense, Heidegger conceives of human freedom as non-sovereign because it is limited and oriented by one's specific location (the *Da-*) and one's own specific Being. Thus, differently from Arendt, he conceives of 'freedom' only in this sense of *liberum arbitrium* (i.e. the capacity to choose among a range of possibilities already given) and not as a capacity to 'call into being' something absolutely new, a concept that Arendt traces back to St Augustine.[64] In Arendt's perspective, this capacity is non-sovereign because it depends and is limited by the presence and actions of other human beings.

63. Arendt, *Love and Saint Augustine*, pp. 53–6. It is worth noting that in *Being and Time* Heidegger does not speak of *expectation* of death, but of *anticipation* (*Vo*̈*rlaufen*). As pointed out before, Arendt adds the line explicitly mentioning Heidegger when she revises her thesis for publication in English in the early 1960s, but the manuscript was published only posthumously in 1996. She may have revised her choice of terminology in the final version. See Martin Heidegger, *Being and Time*, trans John Macquarrie and Edward Robinson, Blackwell, Oxford, 1962 (1927), p. 306.
64. Villa, *Arendt and Heidegger*, pp. 114, 126, 132. See Hannah Arendt, 'What is Freedom?', in *Between Past and Future*, p. 167.

In Arendt, the 'return to the past' is not primordially closed, but it is the only way human beings can introduce a new beginning in the world by recalling their own having-been-originated. The event of this new beginning is radically contingent and depends on the plurality of human beings that confirm and take part in it. In this way, it unfolds in a potentially infinite network of actions and reactions that keep it open to unpredictable consequences.

9

How to incorporate colonialism into Marx's *Capital*

MORTEZA SAMANPOUR

The theoretical necessity of incorporating an account of colonialism into the structure of Marx's *Capital* is embedded within the wider process of intellectual 'decolonialization' that has traversed the humanities and social sciences, globally, in recent decades. As a transdisciplinary critique of the historical present, philosophy as critical theory is not untouched by the reverberations of this wave. That colonial perspectives have increasingly become culturally untenable, across the world, is not the achievement solely of significant strands of postcolonial studies; it is also rooted in objective social processes of global accumulation. From a materialist perspective, forms of thought are to be considered in conjunction with the development of abstract social forms of value. The rise of globalization and financialization since the 1980s intricately interwove new social spaces and temporalities into the fabric of global capital, establishing mutual interrelations among circuits of accumulation across the world market, whilst differentiating them from one another. This unification through differentiation has endowed global capitalist relations of production with an extraordinary heterogeneity of form, marked by profound social inequalities reminiscent of colonial times. Almost all societies now live in the same historical present of capitalist modernity, coevally, in a way that was previously denied to them during the colonial era. However, this contemporaneity is internally fractured via the disjunctions between the equally present but differentiated times that are thereby conjoined. One thing that is problematized within this objective process is 'our' conception of historical time. If in the twentieth century it was fascism and world war that threw into crisis progressivist teleological conceptions of historical time (as noted by Ernst Bloch, Walter Benjamin and Theodor W. Adorno), today it is the global-colonial facets of capitalism that render the Enlightenment providential fantasy of progress obsolete.[1]

This essay investigates the plural and uneven social temporalities of capital from the standpoint of the enduring legacies of colonialism in the present. By critically engaging with temporal and Hegelian-informed readings of *Capital*, I posit the hypothesis that colonialism is a geopolitically mediated mode of temporal domination rooted in real abstraction. Marx's critique of value as the historically specific abstract social form of wealth contains crucial political elements that need be revitalized against its depoliticization by value-form analysis.[2] It is from this political conception of social form that I approach colonialism. *Capital* treats colonial processes of accumulation through coerced forms

---

1. See Antonio Y. Vázquez-Arroyo, 'Universal History Disavowed: On Critical Theory and Postcolonialism, *Postcolonial Studies*, vol. 11, no. 4, 2008, pp. 451–73. On the concept of the contemporary, see Peter Osborne, *Crisis as Form*, Verso, London and New York, 2023, 'Part I. History as a Project of Crisis', pp. 3–38; Osborne, *The Postconceptual Condition: Critical Essays*, Verso, London and New York, 2018, 'Part I: Time of the Present', pp. 3–58; and Osborne, *Anywhere or Not at All: Philosophy of Contemporary Art*, Verso, London and New York, 2013, 'The Fiction of the Contemporary', pp. 15–35. On the heterogeneity of contemporary capitalism, see Sandro Mezzadra and Brett Neilson, *The Politics of Operation: Excavating Contemporary Capitalism*, Duke University Press, Durham NC and London, 2019; Arif Dirlik, *Global Modernity: Modernity in the Age of Global Capitalism*, Routledge, London and New York, 2007.
2. 'Value-form analysis' is employed here in the broad sense of the term, referring to both the *Neue Marx-Lektüre*/New Reading of Marx, developed originally by Adorno's students in the mid-1960s, and the current theoretical frameworks that are influenced by this tradition. I consider Reuten and Arthur's 'systematic dialectic' and the work of Bonefeld, Heinrich and Postone to occupy a common discursive field unified by a set of basic principles and problems. For an overview of this field, see Ingo Elbe, 'Between Marx, Marxism, and Marxisms: Ways of Reading Marx's Theory', *Viewpoint Magazine*, 2013, available at viewpointmag.com.

of unwaged labour only as the historical presupposition for the emergence of capital, in the chapter on 'So-Called Primitive Accumulation'. To conceptualize colonialism as the *result* of fully industrialized capital, we must push *Capital* beyond its own methodological boundaries. This requires dispelling established modes of thinking about capitalist relations embodied in concepts of 'society', 'the permanence of so-called primitive accumulation', and 'formal subsumption'. I aim to cast doubt on the critical effectivity of these concepts for grasping the pluralized temporalities of contemporary capital, and a multilinear conception of historical time more generally. As an alternative to these, I propose a conceptual constellation comprising the endogenously related categories of the world market, reproduction and real abstraction. Their critical unification produces a conception of historical temporalities that is philosophically more adequate to the historical experiences of colonialism, one that is internally differentiated through the *social relationality* of disjunctive processes of global accumulation. In my use of Marx, colonialism is a mode of subjection integral to the historical reproduction of abstract-temporal forms of value through the world market.

No such thing as society: world market and world history

Marx often employs what would later be referred to as a 'sociological' concept of society to name the philosophical idea of a total social process unified by the all-embracing character of capital, which he describes as 'capable of determining the form of society as a whole'.[3] Within the framework of value-form analysis, Marxian categories are treated as expressions of historically determined social relations of production, constituting the social

---

3. Karl Marx, *Capital: A Critique of Political Economy, Volume I*, trans. Ben Fowkes, Penguin, Harmondsworth, 1976, p. 1023.

mediation of capitalist social life in its entirety. *Capital* is thus interpreted not merely as a contribution to economics but as a critical social theory of the capitalist mode of production. Hence the critique of political economy, its subtitle, is conceived by critical theorists as a 'critique of society'.[4] However, the question remains: what precisely constitutes society?

Within the critical theory of the Frankfurt School, society is often approached through the dialectical formula of the 'necessity but impossibility' of the concept – both in its actuality and as an object of knowledge encompassing the totality of social relations marked by open historical temporalities. In his brief essay 'Society', Adorno criticizes the concept of society for its tendency to misrepresent a dynamic social process as a fixed, reified totality, while simultaneously affirming its necessity for the question of social mediation, especially when critically deployed in opposition to positivistic currents within sociology.[5] What I want to suggest here is that the notion of society is illusory not only for epistemological reasons but also because it is confined to the spatio-temporalities of the nation-state, implicitly reproducing the bourgeois and colonial imaginary of the nation as an isolated and self-sufficient entity. If we are to maintain the negation and affirmation of the whole – an inherently problematic task requiring critical investigations – it is more appropriate to employ the Marxian category of the world market as the medium for capital circulation and globally universal social mediation.[6]

4. See Michael Heinrich, *An Introduction to the Three Volumes of Karl Marx's Capital*, Monthly Review Press, New York, 2012; Riccardo Bellofiore and Tommaso Redolfi Riva, 'The *Neue Marx-Lektüre*: Putting the Critique of Political Economy Back into the Critique of Society', *Radical Philosophy* 189, January/February 2015, pp. 24–36; Werner Bonefeld, '*Kapital* and its Subtitle: A Note on the Meaning of Critique', *Capital & Class*, vol. 26, no. 3, 2001, pp. 53–63.
5. Theodor W. Adorno, 'Society', trans. Fredric Jameson, *Salmagundi* 10/11, Fall 1969–Winter 1970, pp. 144–53. For further details, see Theodor W. Adorno, 'Aspects of Hegel's Philosophy', *Hegel: Three Studies*, MIT Press, Cambridge MA and London, 1993 (1963), pp. 1–52, 27; Peter Osborne, 'Adorno and Marx', in Peter E. Gordon, Espen Hammer and Max Pensky, eds, *A Companion to Adorno*, Wiley Blackwell, Hoboken, 2020, pp. 303–20, 309.
6. Sandro Mezzadra, 'Into the World Market: Karl Marx and the Theoretical Foundation of Internationalism', in Anne Garland Mahler and Paolo Capuzzo, eds, *The*

The surprisingly undertheorized category of world market represents neither simply a scalar extension of the nation-state, external to allegedly self-enclosed national markets, nor a mere mechanical aggregation of them. Unlike the empirical and ideological category of 'foreign trade' in classical political economy, the world market is conceived by Marx in historical-ontological terms as being 'directly given in the concept of capital itself'.[7] As an inherently global social form, capital forges mutual interconnections among societies, weaving their fate together through all-round material dependence, thus mediating social reproduction in an increasingly world-historical manner. As the *Communist Manifesto* declared of the globalizing tendency of capital to subordinate ever more territories and temporalities: 'It must nestle everywhere, settle everywhere, establish connections everywhere.'[8] The concept of the world market (*Weltmarkt*) is yet to be fully interpreted as the materialist appropriation of the philosophical concept of world history (*Weltgeschichte*). Its actual historical genesis and existence, marked by the discovery of the Americas and subsequent colonization, constitutes the material basis for the philosophical transition from universal history to world history in the late eighteenth century, a shift from a mere aggregate collection of facts to a mode of historiography aimed at gasping the inner connections between causes and effects, unified into a general historical narrative. 'World history has not always existed', Marx writes in the *Grundrisse*; 'history as

---

Comintern and the Global South; Global Designs/Local Encounters, Routledge, London and New York, 2023, pp. 47–67. See also Oliver Nachtwey and and Tobias ten Brink, 'Lost in Transition: The German World-Market Debate in the 1970s', *Historical Materialism* 16, 2008, pp. 37–70. For Claudia von Braunmühl's insightful critique of an internalist concept of the state as the 'political form of capitalist society', see 'On the Analysis of the Bourgeois Nation State within the World Market Context', in John Hollaway and Sol Picciotto, eds, *State and Capital: A Marxist Debate*, Edward Arnold, London, 1978, pp. 160–77.

7. Karl Marx, *Grundrisse: Foundations of the Critique of Political Economy*, trans. Martin Nicolaus, Penguin, Harmondsworth, 1973, p. 408.

8. Karl Marx and Friedrich Engels, *The Communist Manifesto*, trans. Samuel Moore, Pluto Press, London, 2008, p. 38.

world history [is] a result.'⁹ Two historically specific ontological principles, distinctive only to the capitalist mode of production, provide the conditions of possibility for construing world history: capital as a totalizing social form, tending to subordinate total social process to its own reproduction, and its intrinsically global sociality that systematically establishes mutual relations of dependency, albeit in an asymmetrical and uneven manner. In contemporary capitalism, this mode of social mediation reaches historically unprecedented levels through the growing socialization and interdependencies of globalized and financialized capital. Integrated into global capital, the historical temporalities of local, national and regional social spaces are increasingly over-determined by larger processes of capital reproduction. Marx's description of the 'connection of the *individual with all*' and the '*independence of this connection from the individual*', outlining the alienated structure of the world market, is arguably more actual today than ever before.[10] Colonialism becomes intelligible only from the standpoint of the world market – that is, the world-historical field of capital's action.

Beyond the permanence of so-called primitive accumulation

Colonial circuits of accumulation, mediated by the world market and based on coerced modes of surplus-extraction from unwaged labour, go beyond the object and methodological assumptions of *Capital* as the critique of the 'fundamental form' of capital's 'inner workings' in its 'ideal average'.[11] Although *Capital* largely

---

9. *Grundrisse*, p. 109. See also Reinhart Koselleck, 'From "Historia Universalis" to "World History"', trans. Marie Louise Krogh as the Appendix to her PhD thesis, 'Temporalities and Territories: The Geopolitical Imaginary of German Philosophies of History', CRMEP, Kingston University London, 2020, pp. 181–6; Reinhart Koselleck, *Futures Past: On the Semantics of Historical Time*, Columbia University Press, New York, 2004, pp. 237–8; Chenxi Tang, 'Writing World History: The Formation of Colonial Thinking at the Threshold of Modernity', in Raymond Vervliet and Annemarie Estor, eds, *Methods for the Study of Literature as Cultural Memory*, Brill, Leiden, 2000, pp. 175–85.
10. *Grundrisse*, p. 161.
11. *Capital, Volume I*, p. 710, and *Capital: A Critique of Political Economy, Volume III*,

abstracts from the category of world market for methodological reasons, treating 'the whole world of trade as one nation', its rejection of 'methodological nationalism' lays the fundamental groundwork for reinterpreting Marx within the context of global histories of social stratification.[12] As early as 1845, Marx consistently presents the world market as *internal* to the very concept of capital – both as the historical presupposition for the emergence of capital and as the result of its logic of expanded reproduction. The international sphere of commodity, money and capital circulation, historically established by merchant capital as pre-capitalist capital, must be of sufficient character – that is, 'already available' – in order for capital to get its grips on global social life and assert its dominance as the prevailing social form.[13] The historical genesis of capital in England, expounded in *Capital*'s pivotal chapter on 'So-Called Primitive Accumulation', involves not only the violent separation of labour from the means of life, a prerequisite for the establishment of generalized wage-labour, but also 'a whole series of forcible methods' on a global scale, including international debt, trade wars and colonialism. Among these, colonial practices are described as 'the chief moments of primitive accumulation', contributing to the *capital* side of the genesis of the capital–wage-labour relationship in the metropolis.[14] The discovery of the Americas and the extraction of gold and silver as world money from Peru and Mexico, the transatlantic slave trade and 'the conversion of Africa into a preserve for commercial hunting of blackskins', along with the 'plantation-colonies set up exclusively for the export trade, such as the West Indies', are the globally epoch-making practices that

trans. David Fernbach, Penguin, Harmondsworth, 1981, p. 970, respectively.
    12. *Capital, Volume I*, p. 727 n2.
    13. *Grundrisse*, p. 505. See also Marx and Engels, *The German Ideology*, in Karl Marx and Frederick Engels, *Collected Works* (hereafter *MECW*), vol. 5, Lawrence & Wishart, London, 1976, pp. 49–51.
    14. *Capital, Volume I*, pp. 928 and 915, respectively.

constituted the world-historical social revolution of capital in its infancy.[15] In evocative terms,

> The treasures captured outside Europe by undisguised looting, enslavement and murder flowed back to the mother country and were turned into capital there.[16]

Colonial surplus extraction, incorporated either as commodity-capital or money-capital into the circuits of metropolitan capitals, thus played a crucial role in generating the initial wealth needed to set the entire process in motion. However, beyond this contribution to the historical birth of capital, how do we grasp colonialism as posited by and within fully industrialized capital?

The historical genesis of capital's presuppositions is internally related to the self-positing of these presuppositions. Once the historical presuppositions are brought into being by violence – on the one side the owners of money capital, and on the other the proletarianized wage labourers – capital acquires a self-sufficient life form. It posits its own presuppositions through the silent compulsion of exchange relations and competition, immanently. The 'conditions of its becoming' are sublated into the 'results of its presence'; the causes become effects.[17] Nonetheless, in this dialectical narrative it is not clear how and why colonialism is actively posited as the *result* of capital's existence. For instance, the historically unprecedented expansion and transformation of the transatlantic slave trade and plantations from the 1780s onwards – known as 'second slavery'– was driven by the requirements of already industrialized capital itself, rather than being the precondition of its arising. Far from being a historical residue from a dead and bygone past, second slavery was capitalistic to the core, based on what is described in *Capital* as a 'calculated

---

15. Ibid., pp. 915 and 917, respectively.
16. Ibid., p. 918.
17. *Grundrisse*, p. 459.

and calculating system'.[18] Setting slavery aside, colonialism as a
whole persisted juridically until the symbolic year of 1945. Such
historical experiences, increasingly elucidated via global critical
historiography, compel our 'philosophizing beyond philosophy'
to develop a conceptual framework capable of expounding how
fully developed metropolitan capital historically posited the
differentiated circuits of colonial accumulation based on its own
reproductive requirements.

The problem of understanding colonialism, as posited by
capital's existence, cannot be solved by embracing the fashion-
able notion of the 'permanence of primitive accumulation', which
is loosely invoked in discussions of contemporary capitalism
to capture various forms of accumulation not mediated by the
valorization process of productive capital through the exploitation of labour-power. It encapsulates a broad spectrum of social
processes: global practices of expropriation, imperialist wars,
commodification of social reproduction, and the financialized appropriation of value are all considered manifestations
of today's ongoing process of originary accumulation, not
temporally bounded to the historical emergence of capitalism.
While there is no doubt about the historical actuality of these
processes and the necessity of their conceptualization, I remain
unconvinced that the 'permanence of primitive accumulation', as
articulated under the umbrella of 'accumulation by dispossession'
by David Harvey, is adequately equipped for such a critical task.[19]
To put it provocatively, 'so-called primitive accumulation' is not
strictly a *category* akin to expropriation, surplus-value, fictitious

18. *Capital, Volume I*, p. 435. On the capitalist character of accumulation via unfree,
unwaged forms of labour-power, see Jairus Banaji, *Theory as History: Essays on Modes of
Production and Exploitation*, Brill, Leiden, 2010. On second slavery, see Dale W. Tomich,
Through the Prism of Slavery: Labor, Capital, and World Economy, Rowman & Littlefield,
Lanham MD, 2004, especially pp. 56–75. Dale W. Tomich 'The Second Slavery and World
Capitalism: A Perspective for Historical Inquiry', *International Review of Social History*, vol.
63, no. 3, December 2018, pp. 477–501.
19. David Harvey, 'Accumulation by Dispossession', in *The New Imperialism*, Oxford
University Press, Oxford, 2003, pp. 137–82.

capital, and so on.[20] Instead, it represents a historical discussion – a genealogical analysis of capital's prehistory, wherein the results of the process in which the object is born are sublated into the historical-ontological conditions of its present life-process. As such, it demonstrates how the historical presuppositions of capital are established through a multiplicity of violent practices and transformed into objective social relations, internalized by individual and collective human subjectivities. As Foucault wrote in *Discipline and Punish*, genealogy is not simply 'a history of the past in terms of the present' but 'a history of the present'.[21] What often goes unnoticed in the literature around the last part of *Capital* is the crucial use of the adjective 'so-called' in its title, conveying the negative and ironic sense that Marx intended regarding the mythical historical narratives of bourgeois political economy on the genesis of capitalism, particularly Adam Smith's notion of 'previous' or 'primitive' accumulation:

> Long, long ago there were two sorts of people; one, the diligent, intelligent and above all frugal elite; the other, lazy rascals, spending their substance, and more, in riotous living... Thus it came to pass that the former sort accumulated wealth, and the latter sort finally had nothing to sell except their own skins. And from this original sin dates the poverty of the great majority who, despite all their labour, have up to now nothing to sell but themselves, and the wealth of the few that increases constantly, although they have long ceased to work.[22]

To deconstruct the bourgeois version of the Adam and Eve story, Marx offers an alternative, counter-narrative on the prehistory of capitalism, marked by 'one of the most extraordinary

---

20. On 'primitive accumulation' as a 'misleading and erroneous concept', see Ian Angus, 'The Meaning of "So-Called Primitive Accumulation"', *Monthly Review*, vol. 74, no. 11, April 2023, www.monthlyreview.org.
21. Michel Foucault, *Discipline and Punish: The Birth of the Prison*, trans. Alan Sheridan, Vintage Books, New York, 2012, p. 31; 'Nietzsche, Genealogy, History', in *Language, Counter-Memory, Practice: Selected Essays and Interviews by Michel Foucault*, ed. Donald F. Bouchard, Cornell University Press, New York, 1977, pp. 130–64.
22. *Capital, Volume I*, p. 873.

relations of treachery, bribery, massacre, and meanness'.[23] It illus-
trates that capital historically assumes the dominant social form
not out of social necessity but through constitutive violence.
Capital has a historical birth, and therefore a death. The adjective 'so-called' is indispensable for grasping the critical thrust
of the genealogical aspect of *Capital* – a crucial moment that
underpins the entirety of Marx's historical-ontological critique.[24]
If we approach it from this standpoint, rather than adhering to a
theory of primitive accumulation, we require alternative concepts
to capture historical experiences of colonial accumulation. So,
if not the permanence of primitive accumulation, what category
allows us to grasp colonialism?

Formal subsumption: sounds like Marxism, acts like postcolonialism

Marx's category of formal subsumption delineates the process
whereby capital encounters pre-existing labouring practices
inherited from prior historical epochs, subsequently incorporating them into the capitalist logic of accumulation. Capital 'takes
over an existing labour process developed by different and more
archaic modes of production' and gets its grip on 'an *available,
established labour process*'.[25] Recently, formal subsumption has
been expanded and redefined within the materialist critiques of
Eurocentrism, seeking to distil an uneven and plural conception
of historical temporalities based on capital's synchronization of
'non-capitalist' relations received from the past.[26] Within this

---

23. Ibid., p. 917.
24. Werner Bonefeld, *Critical Theory and the Critique of Political Economy: On
Subversion and Negative Reason*, Bloomsbury, London and New York, 2014, pp. 79–100.
25. *Capital, Volume I*, p. 1021.
26. Massimiliano Tomba, 'On Subsumption as Form and the Use of Asynchronies', in
Karen Benezra, ed., *Accumulation and Subjectivity*, State University of New York Press,
New York, 2022, pp. 27–44; Harry Harootunian, 'Piercing the Present with the Past:
Reflections on Massimiliano Tomba's *Marx's Temporalities*', *Historical Materialism*, vol. 23,
no. 4, 2015, pp. 60–74. For an overview of this literature, see Filippo Menozzi, 'Marxism

Blochian-informed framework of the synchronicity of the non-synchronous, unwaged forms of colonial labour such as slavery are interpreted as reconfigured by capital and located alongside capitalist relations. This gives rise to what Massimiliano Tomba describes as 'pluralities of temporal layers', as opposed to 'a succession of stages'.[27] However, formal subsumption alone fails fully to expound the historical processes of colonialism or the contemporary dynamics of capital expansion. Dissociated from the social mediation of the world market (the interwoven circuits of valorization based on differentials of subsumption), the literature on formal subsumption tends to focus on the cultural singularities of local and national social spaces. Just as the slave plantations were differentiated and subordinated to the reproduction of industrialized capital in the metropolis, so too are Walmart's suppliers in the south-western Guangdong Province in China socially mediated by their integration into the reproduction of global capital across the world.[28]

The recent revival of the concept of formal subsumption functions as a critique of the post-Operaist inclination to generalize real subsumption via the thesis of the 'total subsumption of society'. In the section entitled 'Real Subsumption and the World Market', for example, Hardt and Negri's *Empire* posits that once all pre-existing modes of production are encompassed by the world market and become capitalist at the level of general social production, the 'stage' of real subsumption supposedly begins:

> At a certain point, as capitalist expansion reaches its limit, the processes of formal subsumption can no longer play the central role... Through the real subsumption, the integration of labor into

in Plural Times: Decolonizing Subsumption', *Rethinking Marxism*, vol. 33, no. 1, 2021, pp. 111–33.
27. Massimiliano Tomba, *Marx's Temporalities*, Brill, Leiden, 2013, p. 152.
28. Richard Appelbaum and Nelson Lichtenstein, 'A New World of Retail Supremacy: Supply Chains and Workers' Chains in the Age of Wal-Mart', *International Labor and Working-Class History* 70, 2006, pp. 106–25.

capital becomes more intensive than extensive and society is ever more completely fashioned by capital.[29]

The 'passage from formal subsumption to real subsumption' is thus predicated upon 'a fully realized world market', marking the historical moment when 'the entire realm of reproduction ... is subsumed under capitalist rule'.[30] While this brief exposition oversimplifies the arguments put forth by Hardt and Negri, the central problem with this narrative is its portrayal of subsumption, the *form* or *mode* of capital's command over labour, as a historical *stage*. This implicitly perpetuates a developmentalist conception of capital's historical temporalities, characterized by the linear progression of subsumption forms. Marx, however, viewed formal subsumption as 'the general form of every capitalist process of production', implying its ongoing nature rather than confining it to specific historical stages. While real subsumption 'entails' formal subsumption, 'the converse does not necessarily obtain'.[31] Various forms of subsumption, therefore, denote multiple methods by which capital extracts surplus-value and exercises its power for valorization. Formal subsumption appropriates surplus labour-time by extending 'the duration of the labour process as far as possible' and making it more continuous by supervision and discipline. This is its '*sole* manner of producing surplus-value'.[32] Real subsumption, on the other hand, increases the productive capacities of labour, thereby relatively reducing the necessary labour-time (equivalent to the value of labour-power) through social cooperation, division of labour and the technological employment of machinery. Moreover, distinct forms of subsumption are presented in *Capital* as mutually conditioning, and simultaneously contemporaneous

29. Michael Hardt and Antoni Negri, *Empire*, Harvard University Press, Cambridge MA and London, 2000, p. 255.
30. Ibid., pp. 255 and 364, respectively.
31. *Capital, Volume I*, p. 1019.
32. Ibid., pp. 1010 and 1021, respectively.

with one another. The introduction of machinery, for instance, does not diachronically surpass absolute surplus-value but *presupposes* synchronically the intensification and the extension of the working day: 'methods of producing relative surplus-value are, at the same time, methods of producing absolute surplus-value'.[33] The real subsumption of labour in the metropolis is also presented in historical-empirical terms as being conditioned by 'the new world-market relations created by large-scale industry', namely the reconfiguration of coerced modes of colonial surplus extraction.[34] Viewed from this standpoint, Negri's narrative appears historicist.[35]

If 'real subsumption of society' is criticized for its underlying historicism, its theoretical counterpart, recent uses of formal subsumption are susceptible to charges of culturalism, wherein capital's contingent encounter with pre-existing social times in local spaces constitutes the basis of multilinear and heterogenous temporalities. The framework of formal subsumption adopts a methodologically internalist standpoint, perceiving capital as merely 'adapting' to specific social conditions. Consequently, capitalist relations of production assume different forms and historical trajectories in each distinct social space, engendering the 'multiplicity of possible lines of development', as Harootunian remarks.[36] In this manner, the temporal-social differentials *actively* posited by the reproduction of dominant social capitals through the world market are displaced by the

33. Ibid., p. 646. See also ibid., pp. 411 and 526–33.
34. *Capital, Volume I*, p. 573.
35. This is so especially given its methodological grounding in the evolutionist conception of historical time found in the *Grundrisse* but abandoned altogether in Marx's *1861–63 Manuscripts*. On the crucial discoveries of the *Manuscripts*, see Michael Heinrich, '*Capital* After MEGA: Discontinuities, Interruptions, and New Beginnings', *Crisis & Critique*, vol. 3, no. 3, 2016, pp. 93–138; Michael Heinrich, 'The "Fragment on Machines": A Marxian Misconception in the *Grundrisse*', in Riccardo Bellofiore, Guido Starosta and Peter D. Thomas, eds, *In Marx's Laboratory: Critical Interpretations of the Grundrisse*, Brill, Leiden, 2013, pp. 197–213, 202.
36. Harry Harootunian, *Marx after Marx: History and Time in the Expansion of Capitalism*, Columbia University Press, New York, 2015, p. 53.

multiplicity of trajectories stemming from the singularities of 'non-capitalist' relations, which are passively given to capital. It is true that capital possesses an extraordinary capacity for determinate negation, dissolving certain pre-existing relations and appropriating others in accordance with the requirements of its own life process. Nevertheless, formal subsumption falls short in fully accounting for the social temporalities of colonial circuits of accumulation as mediated by world-market relations. This should not be interpreted as diminishing the historical-ontological significance of 'free gifts of history' to capital but rather as stressing the active and global element in pluralized social temporalities. The contemporary reconstruction of formal subsumption appears to parallel Dipesh Chakrabarty's thesis on the 'two histories of capital', where local historical differences (History 1) are subordinated to the universal and abstract logic of value (History 2).[37] The project to critically expand formal subsumption, as outlined in Harootunian's *Marx after Marx*, may sound Marxian in its theoretical underpinnings, but in practice it aligns more closely with a postcolonial perspective. Hence the culturalist account of 'capitalism's compulsion to produce un-evenness as an unyielding condition of its law of accumulation'.[38] Harootunian's solution to this problem – the concept of formal subsumption – is insufficient because the problem itself is not articulated adequately, as that of interdependent circuits of accumulation within the global reproduction process of capital, shaped by their asymmetrical dependencies. It is this limita-tion that leads us to the concept of reproduction, developed in *Capital, Volume II*: the metamorphoses of abstract forms of value from commodity- to productive- and money-capital within an

37. Dipesh Chakrabarty, *Provincializing Europe: Postcolonial Thought and Historical Difference*, Princeton University Press, Princeton NJ, 2000, pp. 47–71.
38. Harootunian, *Marx after Marx*, p. 70. On culturalism, see Peter Osborne's review of Harootunian, 'Marx after Marx after Marx after Marx', *Radical Philosophy* 200, November/December 2016, pp. 47–51.

individual circuit of accumulation are structurally conditioned by the reproduction of other capitals.[39] It was from this standpoint of reproduction that Marx wrote: 'the veiled slavery of the wage-labourers in Europe needed the unqualified slavery of the New World as its pedestal.'[40]

Reproduction

At its core, the category of reproduction captures the ongoing vitality of capital's life process, expanding itself and persisting through crises and social struggles. Its full conceptualization emerges for the first time in the *1861–63 Manuscripts*, incorporated later into *Capital, Volume II*.[41] Crucially, social reproduction feminism expanded the concept of reproduction to encompass diverse practices that sustain and secure capital's existence, within the terms of its logic. Gendered relations are perceived as functionally deployed for the reproduction of labour-power within the 'social factory', and subsequently for the reproduction of capital itself. Modern patriarchy may be logically contingent to, but historically necessary for, the life process of capital. Social reproduction theory offers a historical ontology of capital's constitutive relations that overcomes the duality of 'logic' versus 'history', without explicitly acknowledging its theoretical breakthroughs in these terms.[42] Drawing from the critical insights of

---

39. Karl Marx, *Capital: A Critique of Political Economy, Volume II*, trans. David Fernbach, Penguin, Harmondsworth, 1978, pp. 427–600.
40. *Capital, Volume I*, p. 925.
41. Enrique Dussel, *Towards an Unknown Marx: A Commentary on the Manuscripts of 1861–63*, Routledge, London and New York, 2001 (1988); Roberto Fineschi, 'Reproduction', in Riccardo Bellofiore and Tommaso Redolfi Riva, eds, *Marx: Key Concepts*, Edward Elgar, Cheltenham, 2024, pp. 145–55; Étienne Balibar, 'Reproductions', *Rethinking Marxism*, vol. 34, no. 2, 2022, pp. 142–61; Amy De'Ath, 'Reproduction', in Jeff Diamanti, Andrew Pendakis and Imre Szeman, eds, *The Bloomsbury Companion to Marx*, Bloomsbury Academic, London, 2019, pp. 395–404.
42. See, among others, Tithi Bhattacharya, ed., *Social Reproduction Theory: Remapping Class, Recentring Oppression*, Pluto, London, 2017; Endnotes, 'The Logic of Gender: On the Separation of Spheres and the Process of Abjection', *Endnotes 3: Gender, Class, and Other Misfortunes*, September 2013, endnotes.org.uk.

social reproduction feminism, we need to inquire into how and why unwaged forms of colonial exploitation sustain the global reproduction of capital.

The concretization of capital as 'abstraction in action' through the introduction of capital circulation in *Capital, Volume II* reveals that the value-form acquires its full unity only as the processual-cyclical social form that restlessly reproduces itself through metamorphoses of 'forms of existence of value-in-process'.[43] Viewed from the standpoint of this processual historical ontology, the social relations between the movement of individual capitals enter the scene:

> the circuits of individual capitals are interlinked, they presuppose one another and condition one another, and it is precisely by being interlinked in this way that they constitute the movement of the total social capital [*gesellschaftliche Gesamtkapital*].[44]

Total social capital is not merely the mechanical sum of individual capitals but rather the dialectical unification of reciprocal dependencies between intertwined circuits of individual capitals. The emphasis here lies not so much on the adjective 'total (*gesamt*)' as on the 'social', denoting the sense of a social whole constituted by 'a system of synchronic dependencies', as pointed out by Balibar.[45] In the case of colonialism, these synchronic dependencies assume the specifically asymmetrical form whereby colonial circuits based on unwaged labour are subordinated to

---

43. *Capital, Volume II*, p. 185, and *MECW*, vol. 30, p. 13, respectively.
44. *Capital, Volume II*, p. 429. Both translations of *gesellschaftliche Gesamtkapital*, 'aggregate social capital' and 'total social capital', are problematic. The adjective 'aggregate' implies a simple mathematical total of individual capitals without the unification that is derived from their mutual relations – the precise opposite of what Marx wants to convey. On the other hand, 'total social capital' implies the Hegelian concept of 'totality' with all the negative connotations it has for Marx: the self-enclosed, completed and fixed type of whole – as opposed to a processual, open-ended and heterogenous-dynamic one. The term can be oddly but more precisely translated as 'collected social capital', as in *Gesamtausgabe* ('collected edition').
45. Étienne Balibar, 'On Reproduction', in Louis Althusser and Étienne Balibar, eds, *Reading Capital*, Verso, London, 1979, pp. 254–72, 258.

the reproduction of the capital–wage-labour relationship in the metropolis.

Many argue that the schemas of reproduction in *Capital, Volume II* aim to refute 'Smith's dogma', which holds that the value of a commodity, and thus that of total social product, is wholly resolved into 'revenues': wages, profit and rent.[46] Smith's 'wealth of society' is exclusively composed of the value-added within the valorization of individual capitals plus the sum total of wages, leaving no room for the value created by the past labours objectified in constant capital. Beyond this economic reading, schemas of reproduction can be interpreted as a critique of the bourgeois vision of the reproduction process, portraying it as a 'self-enclosed' entity devoid of social interdependencies beyond national frontiers. This social-relational ontology of reproduction allows the formal possibility to grasp the internally related but differentiated modes of accumulation within the global reproduction process, driven by the process of 'real abstraction' – a concept never used by Marx but which gained popularity following the publication of Alfred Sohn-Rethel's *Intellectual and Manual Labour.*[47]

Real abstraction and exploitation

The contemporary reception of Marx's treatment of abstraction involves two distinct but related moments: epistemological and practical. The first concerns the social constitution of abstract and universal conceptual forms of thought, which are the

---

46. *Capital, Volume II*, pp. 435–67. See, for instance, Fred Moseley, 'Marx's Reproduction Schemes and Smith's Dogma', in Christopher J. Arthur and Geert Reuten, eds, *The Circulation of Capital: Essays on Volume Two of Marx's Capital*, St. Martin's Press, New York, 1998, pp. 59–86; Michael Heinrich, 'Capital in General and the Structure of Marx's Capital: New Insights from Marx's *Economic Manuscripts of 1861–63*', *Capital & Class*, vol. 13, no. 2, 1989, pp. 63–79.
47. Alfred Sohn-Rethel, *Intellectual and Manual Labour: A Critique of Epistemology*, trans. Martin Sohn-Rethel, Brill, Leiden, 2021. For further details, see Alberto Toscano, 'The Open Secret of Real Abstraction', *Rethinking Marxism*, vol. 20, no. 2, 2008, pp. 273–87.

conditions of possibility for grasping the abstract culture of capitalist modernity. Sohn-Rethel's materialist epistemology, circumscribed by circulationist tendencies, traces the origin of Ancient Greek philosophy to the coinage of money. According to this narrative, the historical genesis of what Kantian philosophy presents as given *a priori* categories of the understanding lies in the 'social synthesis' of exchange relations, ideally reflected into 'intellectual form'.[48] The second moment relates to the social-ontological nature of real abstraction, encompassing modes of subjection to abstract forms of value, as highlighted in the *Grundrisse*: 'individuals are now ruled by abstractions'.[49] My primary focus here lies on the political dimensions of Marx's discourse on abstraction, particularly concerning the relationship between what Moishe Postone calls 'abstract social domination' and class despotism.[50] As Peter Osborne rightly observes, the '*imposition* of the law of value ... is as much a political as an "economic" form'.[51]

In *Capital*'s opening pages, abstraction emerges as historically specific to generalized exchange relations, signifying a purely social attribute achieved by negating qualitative differences of concrete use-values and equating them with 'merely congealed quantities of homogenous human labour'.[52] As Marx notes:

> Equality in the full sense between different kinds of labour can be arrived at only if we abstract from their real inequality, if we reduce them to the characteristic they have in common, that ... of human labour in the abstract.[53]

48. Sohn-Rethel, *Intellectual and Manual Labour*, p. 51. On the positive necessity of cognitive abstraction, see Peter Osborne, 'The Reproach of Abstraction', *Radical Philosophy* 127, September/October 2004, pp. 21–8, p. 22.
49. *Grundrisse*, p. 163.
50. Moishe Postone, *Time, Labor, and Social Domination: A Reinterpretation of Marx's Critical Theory*, Cambridge University Press, Cambridge, 1993, especially pp. 123–225.
51. Peter Osborne, 'Marx and the Philosophy of Time', *Radical Philosophy* 147, January/February 2008, pp. 15–22, 20.
52. *Capital, Volume I*, p. 128.
53. Ibid., p. 166.

However, expressions such as 'they have in common' or 'As crystals of this social substance, which is *common* to them all' can obscure the social-relational structure of value, implying that an isolated commodity inherently possesses the 'common substance', merely shared with other commodities. As Michael Heinrich points out, in the second edition of *Capital* the adjective 'common' is not *gemeinsam* (as in the first edition), suggesting a shared feature intrinsic to each, but *gemeinschaftlich* or 'communal'.[54] This philological analysis reinforces the philosophical argument that abstract form of value arises from the form-determinations of social relations:

> Outside their relation to each other – outside the relation, in which they count as equal – neither coat nor linen possess value objectivity.[55]

Marx's contribution to post-Kantian philosophy of abstraction involves conceiving an abstraction that is neither empirical nor logical, nor is it generic, derived from a common denominator. Instead, it is historical-ontological and social-relational. The 'sublime objectivity' of value is 'ideal', not empirically visible, yet objective:

> Not an atom of matter enters into the objectivity of commodities as values; in this it is the direct opposite of the coarsely sensuous objectivity of commodities as physical objects ... their objective character as values is therefore *purely social*.[56]

The theory of the value-form constitutes a spectral-historical ontology that registers the contradictions and antagonisms inherent in subjection to abstract social forms: the subsumption of the sensuous under the super-sensuous, use-value under

54. Michael Heinrich, *How to Read Marx's Capital: Commentary and Explanations on the Beginning Chapters*, Monthly Review Press, New York, 2021, p. 70.
55. Karl Marx, 'Additions and Revisions' [*Ergänzungen und Veränderungen*], *MEGA* II/6, cited in Werner Bonefeld, 'Abstract Labour: Against Its Nature and on Its Time', *Capital & Class*, vol. 34, no. 2, 2010, pp. 257–76, 266.
56. *Capital, Volume I*, p. 138, my emphasis.

exchange-value, and the labouring process under the valorization process. The former is relegated to a mere 'bearer' for the latter, a pure means to an end, with crucial consequences for labour and nature alike.

The groundbreaking discovery of Marx's critique of the political economy lies in the articulation of value as the historically specific *social form* of wealth. This rests, first, on abstract labour and the process of real abstraction, and, second, on the exploitation of labour-power. However, these two internally related discoveries have become bifurcated into two one-sided modes of critical thinking about capital. Either class relations are dissociated from social mediations of value and the 'impersonal domination' imposed by market imperatives, or capital is perceived in a reified self-sufficient form that has no bearing on the exploitation of living labour. This is most evident in value-form analysis that primarily focuses on capital's mute compulsion, highlighting how it immanently posits its own presuppositions and exerts an impersonal domination over all social classes. This approach has faced valid critique, including from its own theorists, for neglecting class relations as premissed on the separation of the labourer from her means of life, thus offering an overly abstract conception of real abstraction.[57] Indeed, capital reproduces itself through the objectivity of exchange practices, compelling the 'personification' of economic categories to reproduce capitalist relations. However, the process of reproduction does not occur at a metaphysical level above the agents of social production, but *in and through* social antagonism and crises.

Without going into the endless debates on the relationship between exchange and production, it suffices to note that abstract labour is posited in advance during the valorization

57. Werner Bonefeld, 'On Postone's Courageous but Unsuccessful Attempt to Banish the Class Antagonism from the Critique of Political Economy', *Historical Materialism*, vol. 12, no. 3, 2004, pp. 103–24; Christopher Arthur, 'Subject and Counter-Subject', *Historical Materialism*, vol. 12, no. 3, 2004, pp. 93–102.

process but realized *retrospectively* by and through exchange
relations. Heinrich aptly calls this 'retroactive socialization'.[58]
Similarly, Chris Arthur has argued that the real abstraction
of exchange relations is the view from the standpoint of the
result, whilst the abstract form of value-positing labour is that
of process/activity. Just as exchange-value negates the specifici-
ties of use-value and is indifferent to it except as its bearer,
capital is similarly formally indifferent to concrete labour other
than as the bearer of abstract labour: 'living labour is treated
as abstract prior to exchange precisely because it is treated as
abstract in exchange'.[59] In the sphere of exchange, value is a
ghost, a 'phantom-like objectivity', but it becomes a vampire
seeking the blood of living labour in production.[60] Driven by
logically infinite accumulation, the life-process of capital appropriates the life of living labour as variable capital for its own
purpose of valorization. Abstract labour (real abstraction) and
exploitation are thus internally related to one another within
the antagonistic relationship between capital and labour. How
labour-power is violently put into motion for the maximization
of surplus extraction is itself mediated by, and in turn mediates,
the abstract social temporalities imposed by the world market.
As the world market undergoes greater levels of socialization in
contemporary capitalism through logistics and financialization,
the mechanisms of competition intensify, leading to a greater
autonomization of capital and a strengthened grip on global
life processes. The intensification of capital's social power has
exerted a pervasive influence over the valorization processes,

---

58. Heinrich, *How to Read Marx's Capital*, pp. 160–67. On the dichotomy between circulation and production, see Christopher J. Arthur, 'The Practical Truth of Abstract Labour', in Riccardo Bellofiore, Guido Starosta and Peter D. Thomas, eds, *In Marx's Laboratory*, Brill, Leiden, 2013, pp. 99–120.
59. Christopher J. Arthur, *The New Dialectic and Marx's 'Capital'*, Brill, Leiden, 2004, p. 46.
60. Riccardo Bellofiore, 'A Ghost Turning into a Vampire: The Concept of Capital and Living Labour', in Riccardo Bellofiore and Roberto Fineschi, eds, *Re-reading Marx: New Perspectives after the Critical Edition*, Palgrave Macmillan, Basingstoke, 2009, pp. 178–95.

particularly for those situated at the lower end of global value chains, forcing them to adjust their relations of production in accordance with the imperatives of global demands, forms and rhythms of consumption, as well as globally determined average prices.[61]

Marx's perspective on abstract domination and class despotism as parts of a unified process allows us to consider the most fundamental social genesis of coercive modes of colonial exploitation in terms of real abstraction. In my interpretation, the identity of the non-identical products of labour and their homogenizing reduction to abstract labour measured by average socially necessary labour-time results in *differentiated* social times within valorization processes. The impersonal domination of value historically required interpersonal and, in its most expanded form, geopolitical modes of oppression.

Colonialism and abstract social temporalities

Temporal readings of *Capital* have proliferated since 1989, particularly in the quest for a Marxian framework to address the uneven temporalities of global capitalist relations. The unifying principle among these diverse interpretations is encapsulated by Tomba's *Marx's Temporalities*: '*Capital* is a treatise on time, not only on stolen time, but also on its transformation and ontologization.'[62] At its fundamental historical-ontological level, value is a temporal social relation constituted by abstract labour-time and measured by the homogeneous and identical moments of the mechanical clock-time. Postone's *Time, Labor, and Social Domination* stands as one of the pioneering critical

---

61. Søren Mau, *Mute Compulsion: A Marxist Theory of the Economic Power of Capital*, Verso, London and New York, 2023, pp. 273–96.
62. Tomba, *Marx's Temporalities*, p. 137. Massimiliano Tomba, 'Time' in Beverley Skeggs, Sara R. Farris, Alberto Toscano and Svenja Bromberg, eds, *The SAGE Handbook of Marxism*, SAGE, London, 2021, pp. 491–596.

works articulating the radical novelty of *Capital* with respect
to an abstract form of time. What determines value-positing
labour-time is not the time spent in production, but rather 'the
labour-time required to produce any use-value under the conditions of production normal for a given society'.[63] The temporal
abstraction occurs through the reduction of individual labour-
times to a general temporal norm objectively established within
the market, to which production agents must conform to attain
the average profit. The decisive lesson learned from Postone
is that the historically specific mode of *temporal domination*,
stemming from the process of real abstraction, operates behind
the back of producers.[64] In this context the social relations
between commodities impose a field of temporal constraints,
shaping what is to be produced, under what conditions, and how
much time is allocated to conform to the abstract imperatives of
the value-form. In a way similar to the rise of telegraph and the
improvement of means of circulation via steamship and railroad,
today's logistics and digitized information and communication technologies intensify the abstract power of capital in an
unprecedented manner. The temporal unity of socially necessary
labour-time is thus acquired only at the level of the world market
as the 'universal sphere' of value constituted by 'abstract universal labour', measured by 'the average unit of universal labour'.[65]
Marx's lexicon of universality, however, does not entail social
homogenization but rather geopolitical heterogenization derived
from the striving in common of individual and social capitals
for conforming to, and diverging from, the abstract prevailing
temporality. Tomba draws our attention to Marx's distinction
between 'individual value' and 'social value' within the discussion
of relative surplus-value in *Capital, Volume I*: dominant capitals

63. *Capital, Volume I*, p. 129.
64. Postone, *Time, Labor, and Social Domination*, pp. 123–85.
65. *Capital, Volume I*, pp. 222, 209 and 702, respectively.

can deviate from the abstract-temporal norm of socially average necessary labour-time by virtue of employing new machinery, thereby accumulating 'extra surplus-value'.[66] The dominant temporality of an individual capital tends to necessitate the subordinate temporality of other capitals, creating a temporal disjunction that leads to extra profit for those capitals gaining a competitive edge. Increasing productivity, though crucial, is only one aspect of the value's magnitude; enforcing discipline to intensify the production process is another. *Socially necessary labour-time is composed of a multiple set of social times and determined by a wide range of circumstances.* This includes both the subjective temporality of the social skills, knowledge, productivity and intensity of labour-power that 'must possess the average skill, dexterity and speed prevalent in that trade' and that of the objective means of production that must conform to the 'socially predominant' level, in order to achieve the average rate of profit.[67] Since the ultimate purpose of valorization is surplus labour-time, one can lower production costs by depressing wages, resulting in a commodity whose cost price falls below its value. This indirect compliance with abstract temporal imperatives involves the 'forcible reduction of the wage of labour beneath its value', altering the temporality of the wage-form by reducing the time needed to produce the equivalent value of commodities consumed in social reproduction.[68] Consequently, under the compulsion of value, there are plural methods of diverging from the temporal norm of socially necessary labour-time, which are not merely juxtaposed within the world market but endogenously interconnected through synchronization and differentiation.

---

66. Ibid., pp. 434–6; Massimiliano Tomba, 'Differentials of Surplus-Value', *The Commoner* 12, 2007, pp. 23–37.
67. *Capital, Volume I*, p. 303; Stavros Tombazos, *Time in Marx: The Categories of Time in Marx's Capital*, Brill, Leiden, 2013, p. 34.
68. *Capital, Volume I*, pp. 747–8.

Colonialism contributed at the most basic temporal level to the reproduction of dominant capital by producing commodities with less than the average socially necessary labour-time in the metropolis. It was primarily the social temporalities of unwaged forms of labour that reduced the costs of valorization *relative to the metropolis*. While this formulation invites further investigation into the interrelationship between exploitation, value and prices, nonetheless, the temporal dialectics of the 'free' wage and unfree unwaged labour within the reproduction process is clear. Amidst the generalization of wage-labour and the remarkable surge in the productive forces of metropolitan social capital, a distinct set of temporal requirements emerged, finding fulfilment through the expansion and reconfiguration of colonial accumulation, including slave plantations and the grotesque mass movement of enslaved Africans across the Atlantic.

Rendered inexpensive through value-positing (unwaged) labour, colonial commodities are systematically integrated into both the variable and the constant components of metropolitan capital, thereby diminishing the socially necessary labour-time for the reproduction of wage-labourers and the objective conditions of valorization. Viewed from the standpoint of reproduction, the double character of labour implies here that the concrete labour of wage-labourers transferred the value of constant capital, previously posited by the abstract labour of slaves, to metropolitan commodities. This results in the manufacturing of commodities in the metropolis attuned to the abstract temporal imperatives dictated by the world market, thereby enabling dominant capital to explore a range of possibilities, such as accelerating turnover-time and the expansion of future-oriented credit forms of value, which were heavily involved in colonial business.[69] In *Capital, Volume III*, colonial

69. Alexander Anievas and Kerem Nişancıoğlu, *How the West Came to Rule: The Geopolitical Origins of Capitalism*, Pluto, London, 2015, pp. 162–8.

accumulation is also depicted as a countervailing tendency to the tendency of the rate of profit to fall. The 'capital invested in the colonies', notably 'through the use of slaves and coolies', could 'yield higher rates of profit', thereby upholding the rate of the profit in 'its country of origin'.[70]

Put briefly, the reproduction of capital *as a whole* was sustained and secured via colonialism. The abstract-temporal compulsion of value shaped the social conditions under which circuits of colonial accumulation were temporally differentiated based on coerced modes of exploitation and subordinated to the reproduction of the capital–wage-labour relationship. In confronting the afterlives of colonialism within the historical present, it becomes evident that unravelling the intricate web of abstraction, domination and geopolitical violence is not just an intellectual pursuit, but a practical imperative for shaping a future in which time is liberated from the command of capital.

---

70. *Capital, Volume III*, p. 345.

10

The guilt of reification: Adorno's critique of sociological categories

LOUIS HARTNOLL

Though a minor episode in the history of the Institute for Social Research, Max Horkheimer's extended letter to Henryk Grossman of 20 January 1943, discussing and criticizing the latter's manuscript 'The Evolutionist Revolt against Classical Economics', contains some paradigmatic statements regarding a reading of the work of Karl Marx. Taking to task what he believed to be an 'intellectual-historical approach', Horkheimer charged Grossman with rendering Marx indistinguishable from a run-of-the-mill 'progressive positivist' or 'narrow-minded empiricist' and for reducing him to merely 'another link in the long chain of ever more astute political economists'.[1] Whether or not this is a fair characterization of Grossman's position, Horkheimer would propose the counterinterpretation that Marx's primary achievement was better understood as being 'as universally anti-sociological as it could possibly be'.[2] Articulated at a point in which *Dialectic of Enlightenment* was already well in train – at that moment, that is, when Horkheimer and Theodor W.

---

1. Max Horkheimer, letter to Henryk Grossman, 20 January 1943, in Max Horkheimer, *Gesammelte Schriften, Band 17: Briefwechsel 1941–1948*, ed. Gunzelin Schmid Noerr, Fischer Verlag, Frankfurt am Main, 1996, pp. 398–415, here p. 401. Unless otherwise stated, all translations from German are my own.
2. Ibid.

Adorno's close intellectual collaboration marked their supposed
turn away from classical Marxian concerns – this image of Marx
as a critical, non-positivist and anti-empiricist thinker further
underscores a certain Marxian approach to sociology.[3] This
approach, I will here argue with respect to Adorno's oeuvre, involves a twentieth-century retranslation of the subtitle of *Capital*
as a philosophical 'critique of sociological categories'.[4] From this
standpoint, in revisiting Adorno's interventions into sociology
from the 1930s through to the 1960s, whether as an awkward
and semi-reluctant researcher or in his facilitating role as director of the Institute, we cannot view him as straightforwardly
offering a competing sociological counter-model, as if he were
but another link in the chain of ever more astute sociologists.
Whilst this latter interpretative possibility may be open to us,
it is rendered inherently problematic by the fact that Adorno's
unorthodox commitment to sociology was simultaneously a
dialectical commitment to the critical value of its fundamental
untenability – at least, in its dominant bourgeois variant. Or, as
Werner Bonefeld succinctly puts it, there is no 'sociologist by the
name of Adorno'.[5]

---

3. Following Helmut Dubiel, the Institute's development is often framed in terms of
a sequence of programmes that drew it away from its original political and theoretical
commitments until, in the 1940s, it sought 'the conscious abandonment of the Marxist
theoretical tradition'. Helmut Dubiel, *Theory and Politics: Studies in the Development
of Critical Theory*, trans. Benjamin Gregg, MIT Press, Cambridge MA, 2016, p. 93. For a
refutation of Dubiel's claim that '[t]he programmatic concept of critique and dialectic
is, after 1937, no longer conceived in terms of *Critique of Political Economy*' (ibid.,
pp. 92–3), see Nico Bobka and Dirk Braunstein, 'Adorno and the Critique of Political
Economy', trans. Lars Fischer, in Werner Bonefeld and Chris O'Kane, eds, *Adorno and
Marx: Negative Dialectics and the Critique of Political Economy*, Bloomsbury, London,
2022, pp. 35–54. For a reading of Adorno's relation to Marx and Marxism in the context
of the philosophical interpretation of sociology, see Peter Osborne, 'Adorno and Marx',
in Peter E. Gordon, Espen Hammer and Max Pensky, eds, *A Companion to Adorno*, Wiley
Blackwell, Hoboken NJ, 2020, pp. 303–19.
4. Theodor W. Adorno, 'On the Logic of the Social Science', in Theodor W. Adorno
et al., *The Positivist Dispute in German Sociology*, trans. Glyn Adey and David Frisby,
Heinemann Educational Books, London, 1976, pp. 105–22, here p. 114. See also Hans-
Georg Backhaus, *Dialektik der Wertform. Untersuchungen zur marxschen Ökonomiekritik*,
ça ira Verlag, Freiburg, 2018, p. 75.
5. Werner Bonefeld, 'Economic Objectivity and Negative Dialectics: On Class and
Struggle', in Bonefeld and O'Kane, *Adorno and Marx*, pp. 99–120, here p. 102.

Commenting on this project, Helmut Reichelt indicates that
Adorno's critique of sociological categories draws from a dual
inheritance of Marx and G.W.F. Hegel, thereby positing a notion
of critique understood in a twofold sense. The first extends
Marx's mature critique of political economy, taking it to be the
dialectical dispelling of a discipline's central concepts as bound
up in a politically complicit scientific representation of the social
relations of production. In this regard, Reichelt writes:

> Like Horkheimer, Adorno saw very precisely that what Marx
> meant with the concept of critique was not only a critique of
> science, but he also grasped critique as a principle of presentation
> [*Darstellungsprinzip*], as a critique of categories and their dialectical
> development. This dialectic – in which, as Adorno himself suggests,
> the critique of categories has to unfold the 'incomprehensible'
> (that is, the objective abstraction) in its immanent dynamic – is
> simultaneously the methodologically sophisticated demonstration of
> the unity of this actual, real system.[6]

The second notion of critique turns instead on a critique
of what 'would have to be thematized under the heading of
'phenomenal knowledge [*erscheinendes Wissen*]'. This, Reichelt
continues, is to examine 'how social objectivity is experienced by
humans themselves', how a subject is confronted by an abstraction that they encounter 'as an object (in money and all the other
categories connected to it)'. Though the money-form was more
properly a concern of Alfred Sohn-Rethel than it was Adorno,
this second notion is useful here for stressing an element of the
critique of sociological categories that must critique sociology
'as a form of knowledge', a form that constructs and presents
a notion of social objectivity itself.[7] To this dual critique, we
might add the following claim taken from Adorno's 'Reflections

---

6. Helmut Reichelt, *Neue Marx-Lektüre. Zur Kritik sozialwissenschaftlicher Logik*, ça ira
Verlag, Freiburg, 2020, p. 34. Though Reichelt does not note this, often when Adorno
speaks of 'comprehending the incomprehensible' or some variation thereon he is
commenting on the work of Émile Durkheim.
    7. Ibid.

on Class Theory', drafted just a year earlier than Horkhemer's aforementioned letter, as a compressed methodological maxim: 'Nothing helps', Adorno writes, 'but to turn the truth of the sociological concepts against the untruth that produced them.'[8]

This essay is an attempt to examine one instance of this critique, centred on the category of reification and one of its closest sociological cognates, Émile Durkheim's concept of the social fact. Whilst Adorno's reception of Durkheim is multifaceted and for the most part misunderstood, there is one line of argument I want to draw out and expand upon for the purposes of sharpening his account of and confrontation with post-war sociology and sociological positivism: the critique of Durkheim's treatment of social process as if it were a reified thing. Although the criticism might be assumed in advance to be relatively straightforward, a mere 'tick-box exercise' in the mechanical and uncharitable Marxian dismissal of Durkheim,[9] Adorno's account rather turns on several theoretical and political ambiguities, ambiguities that ensure that Durkheim is conversely figured as an enduring theoretical resource for social analysis and critique.

I begin with a reconstruction of Adorno's concept of reification as outlined in *Negative Dialectics* and elsewhere. With recourse to Marx's extended mature project, and *pace* the interpretation offered by Gillian Rose, I argue that reification in Adorno underscores not the discrepancy between use-value and exchange-value, as well as the exchange of equivalents, but the social and relational forms of value that objectively arise from the exchange process. This concept of reification is supplemented by a second philosophical source, the work of Hegel. Arguing that this element in Adorno's thought should not be minimized,

8. Theodor W. Adorno, 'Reflections on Class Theory', trans. Rodney Livingstone, in Rolf Tiedemann, ed., *Can One Live After Auschwitz? A Philosophical Reader*, Stanford University Press, Stanford CA, 2003 (1942), pp. 93–110, here p. 102.
9. Hans-Peter Müller, 'Interview by Gregor Fitzi and Nicola Marcucci with Hans-Peter Müller on the reception of Émile Durkheim in Germany', *Journal of Classical Sociology*, vol. 17, no. 4, 2017, pp. 399–422, here p. 402.

I attempt to demonstrate the pertinence of *The Phenomenology of Spirit* for combating reified thought in the positive sciences.

I then recount Durkheim's concept and theory of the social fact as advanced in his early plea for the sociological discipline, *The Rules of Sociological Method*. Here I delineate both the fundamental coordinates of this base sociological object and his account for their evidence through social constraint. Drawing on Adorno's essays, interventions, lectures and, albeit cautiously, seminar protocols, I then take the concept of reification as a leitmotif to reconstruct his mature encounter with Durkheim. Doing so, I suggest, demonstrates that Adorno finds in the concept of the social fact a correct but deficient notion of reification, a recognition, to paraphrase Marx, that social relations between individuals assume the phantasmagoric form of relations between things, though with the intonation inverted.

Finally, I go on to show how this framework is redeployed as part of Adorno's confrontation with Karl Popper and others as part of the now-infamous 'positivism dispute'. At the level of self-conception, the question of reification was one of the principal dividing lines that separated the disputants, or, as Adorno writes, the 'dialectical critique of positivism finds its most important point of attack in reification'.[10] Viewed from the perspective of his critique of sociological categories, the positivism dispute appears less concerned with narrow epistemological issues, less concerned with arbitrating among competing sociologies, as it were, than with spelling out how post-war sociology is bound up in a political problematic. From this I argue that some of the stakes involved in this dispute might be better understood if Adorno's criticisms are viewed as offering a particular reading of internal developments within sociological positivism itself. For whilst Adorno characterizes both Durkheim and Popper as

10. Theodor W. Adorno, 'Introduction', in *The Positivist Dispute in German Sociology*, pp. 1–67, here p. 63.

positivists, much to the chagrin of their defenders, the charges
levelled against them are not equivalent. Comparing the two
critiques brings to the forefront how, over the course of the
twentieth century, sociological positivism was to undergo a
theoretical impoverishment. Durkheim is mobilized because his
sociological theory sketched a 'more serious' alternative approach
to those sociologists who lacked even the faintest hint of, to use
Adorno's phraseology, the 'guilt of reification'.[11]

Adorno and the reified social

Though it was, as Rose summarizes in her study of the subject,
'the centrifuge of all his major works and of his many shorter
articles' from 1932 onwards,[12] Adorno's concept of reification
is most cogently and forcefully articulated in a few passages
of *Negative Dialectics*. There, its backdrop is 'the ideological
accompaniment of the emancipation of the bourgeois I', the
philosophical subjectivism that protests the 'priority of the
object'.[13] According to his historico-philosophical sketch, such
protestation is driven by the reactionary theoretical suspicion
that the subject may not be as powerful as assumed, a suspicion
that emerges from 'a misdirected opposition to the status quo,
from opposition to its thingness'.[14] Adorno rereads Marx's theory
of reification as a commentary on the history of bourgeois philosophy, a reading in which the chapter on the fetish character
of the commodity is not only an exposition of part of the basic
logic of capital, but simultaneously inherits and formulates
a critique of 'classic German philosophy'.[15] Given the replete

11. Adorno, 'Introduction', p. 12.
12. Gillian Rose, *The Melancholy Science: An Introduction to the Thought of Theodor W. Adorno*, Verso, London, 2014, p. 55.
13. Theodor W. Adorno, *Negative Dialectics*, trans. E.B. Ashton, Continuum, New York, 2007, p. 189.
14. Ibid.
15. Ibid., p. 190.

philosophical coordinates of Marx's mature project, Adorno unfortunately remains characteristically vague in specifying just which of Marx's statements he is referring to, leaving open to interpretation which elements are constitutive of his concept. As such, whilst an indicative reference is made to the chapter on the fetishism of the commodity, the passages in *Negative Dialectics* contain no direct quotation from or coded reference to the *locus classicus* of the theory of reification in Marx, which in the original reads:

> the commodity-form, and the value-relation of the products of labour within which it appears, have absolutely no connection with the physical nature of the commodity and the material [*dinglich*] relations arising out of this. It is nothing but the definite social relation between men themselves which assumes [*annimmt*] here, for them, the phantasmagoric form of a relation between things [*Dingen*].[16]

This widely cited remark from *Capital* compresses at least two lines of argument. The first, textually restricted argument presents a moment in the opening analysis of the commodity, now subject to extensive Marxological reconstruction. The second, which I want to concentrate on, rearticulates an idea that Marx had variously tested and reformulated in his extended mature project. Turning to the first notebook of the *Grundrisse*, 'The Chapter on Money', Marx describes the mutual co-dependence of all individuals as 'their social connection'.[17] In the capitalist mode of production, an individual's activity is rendered 'social' in so far as it is expressed as exchange-value or, at this point in his analysis, as money. An individual's capacity to define and shape the activity of others is thereby determined by their possession of

---

16. Karl Marx, *Capital: A Critique of Political Economy, Volume I*, trans. Ben Fowkes, Penguin, London, 1976, translation amended. For a brief commentary on Fowkes's translation of *phantasmagorische Form* as 'fantastic form' rather than 'phantasmagoric form', the latter of which I have opted for here, see Rose, *The Melancholy Science*, pp. 40ff.
17. Karl Marx, *Grundrisse: Foundations of the Critique of Political Economy (Raw Draft)*, trans. Martin Nicolaus, Penguin, London, 1993, p. 156.

exchange-value or money. Evocatively formulated, 'The individual carries his social power, as well as his bond with society, in his pocket.'[18] Here Marx articulates what Rose characterizes as 'the germ of commodity fetishism'[19] – though it must be noted and in distinction from her reconstruction, Marx's stress is not on the discrepancy between use-value and exchange-value but on the conditions of exchange as presented and confronted in the value form. Marx writes:

> The social character of activity, as well as the social form of the product, and the share of individuals in production here appear as something alien and objective, confronting the individuals, not as their relation to one another, but as their subordination to relations which subsist independently of them and which arise out of collisions between mutually indifferent individuals. The general exchange of activities and products, which has become a vital condition for each individual – their mutual interconnection – here appears as something alien to them, autonomous, as a thing. In exchange-value, the social connection between persons is transformed into a social relation between things; personal capacity into objective wealth.[20]

Shortly thereafter, in the chapter on the commodity in *A Contribution to the Critique of Political Economy*, this line returns as part of the burgeoning discussion of the double character of labour. In these passages, Marx is specifically concerned with establishing the relation of labour time to exchange-value and, further, how an individual's labour becomes specifically social labour. In the course of the exposition, Marx contends that

> it is a characteristic feature of labour which posits exchange-value that it causes the social relations of individuals to represent themselves, as it were, in the perverted [*verkehrt*] form of a social relation between things. The labour of different persons is equated and treated as universal labour only by bringing one use value into relation with another one in the guise of exchange-value. Although

---

18. Ibid., p. 157.
19. Rose, *The Melancholy Science*, p. 40.
20. Marx, *Grundrisse*, p. 157, translation amended.

it is thus correct to say that exchange-value is a relation between persons, it is however necessary to add that it is a relation hidden beneath a material veil [*dinglicher Hülle*].[21]

Then, strikingly extending this through his analysis of money in the same chapter,

A social relation of production appears as something existing apart from individual human beings, and the distinctive relations into which they enter in the course of production in society appear as the specific properties of a thing – it is this perverted appearance, this prosaically real, and by no means imaginary, mystification that is characteristic of all social forms of labour positing exchange value. This perverted appearance manifests itself merely in a more striking manner in money than it does in commodities.[22]

Whilst it is not my concern here to draw out the strict conse-quences of this unfolding line of argument for the development of Marx's thought, I want to argue that it is not, as Rose inter-prets it, the transformation of a use-value as a product of labour into a commodity, but the *social* and *relational* characteristics and appearance that exchange-value adopts, its form-determinant aspects, that are consequential, not only for Marx's claim in *Capital*, but also for Adorno's mature concept of reification.[23]

As Adorno unfolds his reading of Marx, he proposes to read exchange and the exchange process speculatively, suggesting that

21. Karl Marx, *A Contribution to the Critique of Political Economy*, trans. Victor Schnittke, in Karl Marx and Frederick Engels, *Collected Works* [hereafter *MECW*], Volume 29: *Marx: 1857–1861*, Lawrence & Wishart, London, 1987, pp. 257–417, here pp. 275–6, translation amended.

22. Ibid., p. 289. Marx later goes on to comment on these passages in Karl Marx, *Economic Manuscripts of 1861–63*, trans. Emile Burns, Renate Simpson and Jack Cohen, *MECW*, Volume 32: *Marx: 1861–1863*, Lawrence & Wishart, London, 1989, pp. 317ff. My thanks to Morteza Samanpour for impressing upon me the importance of the *1861–63 Manuscripts* for Marx's *Capital* project.

23. Rose's interpretation imports aspects that are neither textually nor conceptually justified. Whilst it leads to a theoretically richer account of Adorno's notions of identity and exchange – enabling us, as part of a growing chorus, to recognize the buried importance of Marx to Adorno's mature philosophical project – by recasting Adorno's concept of reification as the philosophical extrapolation of Marx's theory of value and exchange (rather than the narrower presentation of exchange-value, the commodity form and the form of social relations), it too hastily conflates reification with the more important and original notions of identity and exchange, and downplays its formal and phenomenological aspects.

they possess a 'real objectivity' as a structuring and systematic social force and yet are simultaneously 'objectively untrue' because they betray the principle of equality upon which they are based.[24] Importantly, however, the contradiction between these two poles results in the 'distortion in the commodity form',[25] a contradiction mirrored in the commodity's appearance as an 'extremely obvious, trivial thing' and which Marx's analysis reveals as a complex and secretive 'sensuous suprasensory thing'.[26] That exchange is 'a law of nature' is only true, Adorno argues, 'in a sardonic sense': lawful at the level of the fundamental structural logic of capital, natural at the level of its presentation, and sardonic at the level of their combination. Whilst for Adorno, then, 'reification itself is the reflection-form [Reflexionsform] of false objectivity', its formal appearance is not to be confused with the conditions of its genesis and thus not to be taken as primary.

> The cause of human suffering, meanwhile, will be glossed over rather than denounced in the lament over reification. The trouble is with the conditions that condemn mankind to impotence and apathy and would yet be changeable by human action; it is not primarily with people and with the way conditions appear to people. Against the possibility of total catastrophe, reification is an epiphenomenon; even more so is the alienation coupled with reification, the subjective state of consciousness that corresponds to it.[27]

Returning to the remark that Marx's exposition of the commodity form is simultaneously a commentary on classic German philosophy helps underscore another major resource for Adorno's concept of reification, the work of Hegel. Beyond *Negative Dialectics*, clues for this inheritance are to be found in Adorno's essay 'The Experiential Content of Hegel's Philosophy', wherein he outlines a Hegelian concept of reification via the critique of

---

24. Adorno, *Negative Dialectics*, p. 190.
25. Ibid., translation amended.
26. Marx, *Capital, Volume I*, p. 163, translation amended.
27. Adorno, *Negative Dialectics*, translations amended.

a false notion of objectivity operative in positivist science, the claim that what is 'true' in science is that which corresponds to its own criteria. On this reading, Immanuel Kant's delimitation of philosophical knowledge in the *Critique of Pure Reason* returns as the limitations of consciousness to be criticized and overcome in the progression of the *Phenomenology*. Hegel, according to Adorno, confronts the rigidity and inadequacy of the structure of positive scientific consciousness in those moments in which consciousness reflects on these limitations, reflects, as moments in which the shape of consciousness transforms, on the ways in which it has distorted its object. This 'contradiction between scientific spirit and the critique of science' is, in Hegel, 'the motor of philosophical activity'.[28] On Adorno's reading, the *Phenomenology* thereby marshals an objection to

> that rational science, which imagines itself to be the basis of truth's legitimacy, trims objects down to size and processes them until they fit into the institutionalised, 'positive' disciplines, and does so in the service of its own ordering concepts and their immanent practicability and lack of contradiction.[29]

Hegel's notion of reification, as Adorno reconstructs it, exposes how science is theoretically inimical to its own pursuits, having little to do 'with the life of things' themselves, little, that is, with the attempt to think the object itself. Despite its self-image – prominent, for instance, in the debates over value freedom and value neutrality – positive science is confined by its unacknowledged subjectivism, unreflectively stuck at the early shapes of consciousness sketched in the *Phenomenomology*.[30] In

28. Theodor W. Adorno, 'The Experiential Content of Hegel's Philosophy', in *Hegel: Three Studies*, trans. Shierry Weber Nicholsen, MIT Press, Cambridge MA, 1993, pp. 53–88, here p. 73.

29. Ibid.

30. In this, Adorno concurs with Herbert Marcuse: 'The first three sections of the *Phenomenology* are a critique of positivism and, even more, of reification.' Herbert Marcuse, *Reason and Revolution: Hegel and the Rise of Social Theory*, 2nd edn, Routledge, London and New York, 2000, p. 112. It is this statement of Marcuse's that Rose claims 'may be the source of the mistaken belief that Hegel used the word. This widespread

a sense, then, Hegel anticipates and criticizes 'the institution of positivist science, which increasingly presents itself the world over as the sole legitimate form of knowledge'.[31] Such a notion of reification in Hegel offers us a critique of false or abstract objectivity, of the '*naiveté* that confuses facts and figures, the plaster model of the world, with its foundation'.[32] And it is owing to the social actuality of this problem, the problem of positive social science's dominance in the post-war period, that it is Hegel who offers an occasion for returning to the concept of reification that we find in Marx.

Pursuing an interpretation of these all-too-loaded and all-too-brief passages, we must recognize that neither the Hegelian nor the Marxian element should be jettisoned or minimized. While Adorno finds Marx essential for thinking the genesis of reification, remembering Adorno's famous description of historical materialism as the 'anamnesis of the genesis',[33] Hegel demonstrates where it becomes epistemologically operative. The inclusion of Hegel is not simply the result of a 'misattribution', but a central part of Adorno's critique of sociological categories, one that would seek to construct and theorize a notion of reification that furthers its diagnostic force. Without Marx, the Hegelian critique of science lacks a politics; without Hegel, the

---

misattribution has contributed to the debasement of the term.' Rose, *The Melancholy Science*, p. 38. In his defence, Marcuse makes no claims that the term *Verdinglichung* appears or originates in Hegel, instead consistently underscoring that he is interpreting the notion from a Marxian standpoint.

31. Adorno, 'The Experiential Content of Hegel's Philosophy', p. 73.

32. Ibid., pp. 73–4.

33. This oft-quoted remark appears in a set of notes taken by Adorno from a conversation about Sohn-Rethel's 'Historical Materialist Theory of Knowledge' (1965), stressing the conservative dimension of the philosophical practice of generating concepts and categories: 'The confrontation of the categories with one another does not, however, take place in their purity, but with the object [*am Objekt*]. The constitution of the categories, the reflection of the exchange abstraction as philosophy, demands the abandonment (the forgetting) of their social genesis, or of genesis altogether. Historical materialism is [the] anamnesis of the genesis.' Theodor W. Adorno, 'Notizen von einem Gespräch zwischen Th. W. Adorno und Alfred Sohn-Rethel', in Alfred Sohn-Rethel, *Schriften IV. Geistige und körperliche Arbeit. Theoretische Schriften 1947–1990. Teilband 1*, ed Carl Freytag, Oliver Schlaudt and Françoise Willmann), ça ira Verlag, Freiburg, 2018, pp. 129–33, here p. 131.

Marxian notion recalls and critiques a genesis but occludes the full extent of its consequences. Or, to state it alternatively, if the issue of reification underpins the 1950s' and 1960s' confrontation with positivism, Adorno requires Marx for it to be socio-political and Hegel for it to be socio-epistemological.

Durkheim, a theory bewitched

Any fundamental claim about the method of a science and, indeed, about its disciplinary legitimacy, coherence and independence, *The Rules of Sociological Method* suggests, first requires a thoroughgoing definition and exposition of its object. As Durkheim therein conceived it, for sociology this involves an account of those 'facts termed "social"'.[34] As is well known, the opening chapters of this book make a case for the existence of the social fact as a unique scientific object by arguing that such an object cannot be accounted for by the existing sciences, foremost biology, psychology and economics. This definite class of facts, he argues, do not reside in the individual, though they exert themselves in and through individuals:

> they consist of manners of acting, thinking and feeling external to the individual, which are invested with a coercive power by virtue of which they exercise control over him. Consequently, since they consist of representations and actions, they cannot be confused with organic phenomena, nor with psychical phenomena, which have no existence save in and through the individual consciousness. Thus they constitute a new species and to them must be exclusively assigned the term *social*.[35]

Durkheim elaborates this claim by advancing two interlocking lines of argument. The first identifies where, if neither in the

34. Émile Durkheim, *The Rules of Sociological Method and Selected Texts on Sociology and Its Methodology*, 2nd edn, trans. W.D. Halls, ed. Steven Lukes, Palgrave Macmillan, Basingstoke, 2013, p. 20.
35. Ibid., p. 21.

individual nor in physical material, the social fact resides – what, in other words, it has as its 'substratum'[36] – and concludes that it must be society, understood as a collective of individuals in association, that constitutes this foundation. Moreover, in order for it to cohere as a definite entity – in order, that is, for this association to be constitutive over and above a mere agglomeration of individuals – any given society must present a degree of consistency, regularity and universality such that the same behaviours are exhibited by different individuals in different contexts and situations.[37] Within this structure, social facts acquire 'a shape, a tangible form peculiar to them and constitute a reality *sui generis* vastly distinct from the individual facts which manifest that reality'.[38] Society is thus a 'condition of the group repeated in individuals because it imposes itself upon them', of which the most important factor for the association's cohesion is not necessarily the physical proximity or density of this association, but the strength of its moral bond.[39] The second line of argument looks to the available evidence for the existence of social facts – how, that is, they can be identified. Towards this end, Durkheim argues that social facts are made known to us through the experience of an external coercive force, the *contrainte sociale*, that they exercise over the individual.[40] Such a force shapes those

36. Ibid.
37. A similar claim had already been advanced in Émile Durkheim, *The Division of Labour in Society*, 2nd edn, trans. W.D. Halls, ed. Steven Lukes, Palgrave Macmillan, Basingstoke, 2013, pp. 273–4.
38. Durkheim, *The Rules of Sociological Method*, pp. 23–4.
39. Ibid., p. 25.
40. On more than one occasion Adorno links Durkheim's concept of social constraint to that aspect of 'logical compulsion' required by Hegel's philosophy of objective spirit, to those 'positive realities ... defended in the *Philosophy of Right* ... the realities that today we would term coercive situations'. Theodor W. Adorno, 'Aspects of Hegel's Philosophy', *Hegel: Three Studies*, pp. 1–51, here p. 20; Adorno, *Lectures on Negative Dialectics: Fragments of a Lecture Course 1965/1966*, trans. Rodney Livingstone, ed. Rolf Tiedemann, Polity Press, Cambridge, 2008, p. 16. Cf. Axel Honneth, 'Hegel and Durkheim: Contours of an Elective Affinity', in Nicola Marcucci, ed., *Durkheim and Critique*, pp. 19–41, Palgrave Macmillan, Cham, 2021. This work is part of Honneth's broader project of reviving a non-Marxist theory of the division of labour for the theory of modern democracy. In this regard, see Axel Honneth, *Die arbeitende Souveräne. Eine normative Theorie der Arbeit*, Suhrkamp Verlag, Frankfurt am Main, 2023.

harder and softer behavioural norms, moral conventions, beliefs, opinions and collective practices that constitute the social fabric and is directly confronted, in the form of predetermined social or institutionalized sanctions, when an individual acts against or violates these standards. If a social fact has become sufficiently general, a subtler, indirect variant of this constraint may also be uncovered 'by ascertaining how widespread it is within the group'. Although he takes this to be mostly a variation on direct constraint, this second, indirect social constraint, 'as with that exerted by an economic organisation', is harder to immediately and individually detect.[41]

In these lines of argument, Durkheim not only renders constraint the way in which social facts can be traced and evidenced, but also makes it 'intrinsically a characteristic' of them.[42] It is this intrinsic bond between social fact and social constraint that inadvertently makes Durkheim's work an important reference for the critical theory of society. It will express, to use Adorno's words, 'the cruelty [*Härte*] with which the world repeatedly confronts me',[43] that location 'where we feel the friction, where we come up against an obstacle, where our own impulses are subjected to controls that are stronger than we are'.[44] In this, Durkheim constructs a notion of social experience 'on the model of what hurts',[45] on the experience of the individual's 'nullity [*Nichtigkeit*] in the face of the power of society'.[46] It is, to continue this thread, where one confronts society as the 'compulsion' of the unintelligible,[47]

41. Durkheim, *The Rules of Sociological* Method, p.25.
42. Ibid., p. 21.
43. Theodor W. Adorno, *Nachgelassene Schriften. Abteilung VI: Vorlesungen. Band 1: Erkenntnistheorie*, ed. Karel Markus, Suhrkamp Verlag, Frankfurt am Main, 2018, p. 186.
44. Theodor W. Adorno, *Philosophy and Sociology*, trans. Nicholas Walker, ed. Dirk Braunstein, Polity Press, Cambridge, 2022, p. 56.
45. Theodor W. Adorno, 'Einleitung zu Emile Durkheim "Soziologie und Philosophie"', *Gesammelte Schriften. Band 8: Soziologische Schriften I*, pp. 245–79, here p. 250.
46. Gerhard Beuter, '29. May 1956. Protokoll', in *Die Frankfurter Seminare Theodor W. Adornos. Band 1: Wintersemester 1949/50–Sommersemester 1957*, ed. Dirk Braunstein, De Gruyter, Berlin, 2021, 410–13, here p. 410.
47. Adorno, *Philosophy and Sociology*, p. 66.

of 'that which absolutely cannot be absorbed by the individual, something incommensurable and impenetrable'.[48] However, Durkheim's peculiar emphasis on the 'thingness [*Dinghaftigkeit*]' of social facts at once both sought 'to arrest the decay of collective consciousness threatened by the conflict of capital and labour' and legitimated this conflict in a 'pure science of facts'.[49] Though Adorno detects in this something of an authoritarian impulse – in the attempt to withdraw this experience and its underlying conditions from the scrutiny of critical reason – Durkheim is judged to have accurately, albeit mystifyingly, described the form of appearance of social relations under capital.

In other early works, such as *The Division of Labour in Society* and *Suicide*, Durkheim does indeed appear to recognize, describe and protest the corrosive aspects of capital through his exposition of the generalized experience of anomie and social unintegration, for instance. From the results of these studies, Durkheim not only develops an account and image of modernity and the various ills it causes, but also demonstrates how sociology, as *Ordnungswissenschaft*, gains its practical and interventionist imperatives. Much like in Auguste Comte, Durkheim operates with a notion of the objectivity of social laws and maintains that the comprehension of these laws allows, in contrast to Henri de Saint-Simon and Marx, for the peaceful resolution of social antagonism and conflict.[50] But by concerning himself primarily

---

48. Adorno, 'Einleitung zu Durkheim', p. 250.
49. Ibid., pp. 248 and 250, respectively. Though not a direct reference to Durkheim, Adorno would state elsewhere: 'We believe that the concept of the fact is accordingly so suspect because we persistently see that individual facts are, in real life, of such a kind that they help to obscure capitalism.' Theodor W. Adorno in Max Horkheimer and Theodor W. Adorno, '[Diskussion über die Differenz zwischen Positivismus und materialistischer Dialektik (15 February 1939)]', in Max Horkheimer, *Gesammelte Schriften. Band 12: Nachgelassene Schriften 1931–1949*, ed. Gunzelin Schmid Noerr, Fischer Verlag, Frankfurt am Main, 1985, pp. 476–83, here p. 477.
50. Alfred Müller, '15. Mai 1956. Protokoll', in *Die Frankfurter Seminare Theodor W. Adornos. Band 1*, pp. 405–9, here pp. 405–6. See also Adorno, 'Introduction to the Positivist Dispute', p. 34.

with observing, describing and classifying the existence of
moral and social facts, these studies fail to adequately recognize
and reflect on their historical presuppositions, leading him to
propose 'cures' to the 'sickness' of the 'social body' that are at
best a mere amelioration of a much graver condition.[51] That is,
the normative character of Durkheim's objective social laws is
articulated with a view to subjective intervention, not, as they
are in Marx, to their dissolution.[52]

Within this framework, Durkheim advances an ambiguous
account of a latent problem. Although he had been alert enough
to integrate, without properly naming it, a notion of reification
into his social theory, he simultaneously neglected the theoretical implications, which were a 'blind spot, a formula to which
his work is bewitched'.[53] Durkheim failed, that is, to adequately
reflect on its mechanisms, absolutizing it and allowing it to
furnish the criteria for sociology's procedures, even inadvertently
elevating it to the level of scientific norm.[54] Social control is a
feature Durkheim builds into his theory of the social itself. He
would not, Adorno suggests, have been able to properly recognize
a society without coercion.[55] Rather, what interests Durkheim
in these mechanisms of coercion and compulsion is not their
prescription by definite historical social relations but their
demonstration of fixed limits through which the regularity of
social laws is expressed.[56]

To speak of a notion of reification in Durkheim is, therefore,
neither to claim that his sociological theory expresses a particular
allegiance to a reading of Hegel or Marx,[57] nor to suggest that his

51. For just one particularly emotive instance of the corporeal analogy, see Durkheim, *The Division of Labour*, p. 28.
52. Müller, '15. Mai 1956. Protokoll', p. 406.
53. Adorno, 'Einleitung zu Durkheim', p. 250.
54. Adorno, *Philosophy and Sociology*, pp. 57, 67.
55. Gerhard Brandt, '12. Juni 1956. Protokoll', in *Die Frankfurter Seminare Theodor W. Adornos. Band 1*, pp. 417–22, here p. 421.
56. Beuter, '29. May 1956. Protokoll', pp. 411ff.
57. There are two moments in which Durkheim reflects on Marx and Marxism: initially, in the 1890s, around the time he was preparing both a lecture course on Marx and the

theory anticipates, by nearly three decades, certain arguments contained in Georg Lukács's *History and Class Consciousness*. Rather, it is to claim that the outlines of the notion can be detected in Durkheim's work. Although this will not be sufficiently developed or theoretically rich enough to offer a third source for Adorno's concept, it would offer something of a sociological countermodel to the Weberian and Simmelian one at the centre of Lukács's account and it would allow Adorno to sharpen some of the central elements of his theory.[58] In a sense, then, Durkheim stumbles into a quasi-Marxian, but ultimately deficient analysis of reification. Where this analysis furthers the standard Marxian account is where it allows us to think the double-sidedness of Marx's original claim that social relations between individuals assume the phantasmagoric form of a relation between things. Such a notion of reification cannot, of course, be a true description of the fetishism of the commodity form, but only of social relations themselves, of their thing-like quality. Alternatively restated, because Durkheim emphasizes the thing-like quality of social relations, his work provides a conceptual resource that complements the Marxian theory of reification. It allows the thinking of the appearance of social relations *themselves* as things.[59] This rearticulates the standard Marxian phrase on reification but with the intonation inverted. As Adorno claims:

---

first edition of *The Rules*; and then in the 1920s, with the publication of his *Le socialisme*. For the most part, these minor writings have less to do with Marx himself than with Marxists or readers of Marx (Antonio Labriola and Gaston Richard), the notion of socialism (principally in Saint-Simon) and socialists (Saverio Merlino). For these writings, see Émile Durkheim, *Durkheim on Politics and the State*, trans. W.D. Halls, ed. Anthony Giddens, Stanford University Press, Stanford CA, 1986, pp. 97–153; and Émile Durkheim, *Socialism and Saint-Simon*, trans. Charlotte Sattler, ed. Alvin W. Gouldner, Routledge, Abingdon, 2010. Though there is a case to be made for the overlap between Hegel and Durkheim, there are no significant commentaries on Hegel in Durkheim's oeuvre.

58. For an account of Adorno's criticisms of Lukács, see Timothy Hall, 'Reification, Materialism, and Praxis: Adorno's Critique of Lukács', *Telos* 155, Summer 2011, pp. 61–82, and Konstantinos Kavoulakos, 'Lukács' Theory of Reification and the Tradition of Critical Theory', in Michael J. Thompson, ed., *The Palgrave Handbook of Critical Theory*, Palgrave Macmillan, New York, 2017, pp. 67–85.

59. Cf. Simon Jarvis, *Adorno: A Critical Introduction*, Polity Press, Cambridge, 1998, pp. 45ff.

In other words, if I may appeal to an old and famous formulation, in the world that we inhabit, with its prevailing structure of exchange, the relations between human beings are reflected back to us as if these relations were really properties of things, and the objective reason why the world appears to us in a thing-like way lies precisely in the reified character of our own experience. Thus Durkheim's *chosisme* expresses a correct consciousness of the reification of the world; it precisely and adequately reproduces the ossified character of the world we encounter, and of positivism as a whole, insofar as it makes use of intrinsically reified methods, is tailor-made to suit the world as it is.[60]

On Adorno's account, therefore, Durkheim is not wrong to assert that social facts appear as things, to seek evidence of their existence in social constraint, and to make these aspects central to his sociological theory. However, by transforming this analysis into the basic object of sociology, by establishing the rules and methods for which sociology is to proceed, in failing to identify the proper socio-historical cause of his concepts, and in misrecognizing the consequent significance and implications of his theory, Durkheim inadvertently confuses appearance with social objectivity. Indeed, Durkheim makes a disciplinary programme of his deficiencies, transforming reified social relations into the object and ground concept of sociology and producing an apology for this state. With this, the 'reification of society, a reification which always contains an element of mere appearance, is accepted as an absolute'.[61] This acceptance is what, ultimately, motivates Adorno's conclusion that

Durkheim's concept of *faits sociaux* is utterly aporetic. He transposes that negativity, in which, for the individual, the social is the opaque and painfully foreign, into a methodological maxim: 'you should not comprehend'. With a positivistic scholarly attitude, he duplicates the enduring myth of society as fate.[62]

60. Adorno, *Philosophy and Sociology*, pp. 66–7.
61. Adorno, *Introduction to Sociology*, p. 37.
62. Theodor W. Adorno, 'Notiz über sozialwissenschaftliche Objektivität', *Gesammelte*

The positive in the positivism dispute

In the post-war period, Adorno's critique of sociological categories reached its apogee in the positivism dispute. Though regularly maligned as an ill-fated clash between Adorno and Popper, or, with more precision, as a clash between them and a shadowy 'third man',[63] the dispute remains interesting for readers of Adorno, not least because it offers a sociological counterpart to his critique of the philosophically positive in *Negative Dialectics*, and also because it presents one of the few explicit examples of what is taken to be his critique of political economy.[64]

Later reflecting on the 'scientific-practical consequences' of the dispute, Adorno would describe the separation of sociology from 'critical social theory' as running the risk of leaving empirical research entirely to the former. Not only would this ignore that the Institute had, 'for more than 30 years, qualified itself on the basis of empirical investigations'; it would also ensure that '[e]mpirical research would become the sole prerogative of the empiricists'.[65] For Adorno, it could not 'be emphasized expressly enough' that the dispute was not 'about empirical research or its cessation, but about its interpretation, about the status assigned to it within sociology'. Thus, what was at stake, in Adorno's view, was

> not a yes or no to the empirical, but the interpretation of the empirical itself, particularly of the so-called empirical methods. Just as dialectics, empiricism was once philosophy. If we instead admit this, the word 'philosophy', a word held against us as if it were an opprobrium, loses its horror and exposes itself as both a condition

Schriften. Band 8: Soziologische Schriften I, ed. Rolf Tiedemann, Suhrkamp Verlag, Frankfurt am Main, 1972, pp. 238–44, here p. 240.

63. Ralf Dahrendorf, 'Remarks on the Discussion of the Papers by Karl R. Popper and Theodor W. Adorno', in Adorno et al., *The Positivist Dispute in German Sociology*, pp. 123–30, here p. 125.

64. Dirk Braunstein, *Adorno's Critique of Political Economy*, trans. Adam Baltner, Brill, Leiden, 2023, p. 3.

65. Theodor W. Adorno, 'Gesellschaftstheorie und empirische Forschung', *Gesammelte Schriften. Band 8: Soziologische Schriften I*, pp. 538–46, here pp. 538–9.

and goal of a science that strives to be more than mere technique and that will not bow to technocratic domination.[66]

How, though, did these interpretations of the empirical differ and what were the substantial issues that motivated the disagreement? To answer this, we need to briefly introduce a further element, which Adorno alternatively describes as positivism's 'innermost contradiction' and 'the focal point of the controversy': positivist sociology's subjective tendencies. In the attempt to abstract the subject from sociological process, positivism mistakenly 'adheres to an objectivity which is most external to its sentiments and purged of all subjective projections'. As Hegel had already argued, such rigidity does not escape the various issues or contradictions associated with the inclusion of the subjective within social science, but, in insisting over and again on objectivity and marshalling this as part of its rightful claim to scientific authority, it 'simply becomes all the more entangled in the particularity of mere subjective, instrumental reason'.[67]

Adorno saw this as playing out in two senses. The first in that positivist sociology 'operates with catalogues of hypotheses or schemata imposed upon the material', that it 'tends to accept such categories as simply given, and probably untransformable'. And the second in that it 'takes as its starting point opinions, modes of behaviour and the self-understanding of individual subjects and of society', believing that what must be examined is 'the average consciousness or unconsciousness of societalized and socially acting subjects, and not the medium in which they move'. On both fronts, positive sociology eschews any kind of claim to the objectivity of structure in which the empirical persists

66. Ibid., pp. 545–6.
67. Adorno, 'Introduction to the Positivist Dispute', pp. 5, 8. Though not here central, it has not gone unnoticed that Adorno compares these subjective tendencies in sociology to those in subjective economics. See Hans-Georg Backhaus, 'Between Philosophy and Science: Marxian Social Economy as Critical Theory', trans. Gordon Finlayson and Ulrich Haase, in Werner Bonefeld, Richard Gunn and Kosmas Psychopedis, eds, Open Marxism, Volume One: Dialectics and History, Pluto Press, London, 1992, pp. 54–92.

and forgoes that such structure provides the 'condition and the content of the social facts' it examines. By treating empirical material as the factual and limiting its investigation accordingly, such sociology thereby indexes as true a partial perspective of social reality and pre-emptively abandons 'the emphatic idea of objectivity' that critical theory holds as essential.[68] In place of this idea, it codifies as objective processes associated with 'the regularity of repeated occurrences',[69] the statistically average, and the 'law of large numbers',[70] or testable and demonstrable hypotheses that subsequently allow for prediction and prognosis.[71] Such an account both dismisses and approximates a notion of social law, of the lawlike structure of society.

The resemblance of Adorno's critique here to his reading of Durkheim is neither formal nor coincidental. Instead, it demonstrates how he subtly figures the historical advancement and prevalence of post-war sociological positivism as both a definite continuity and a discontinuity with its precursors – or, seen in reverse, how Durkheim deviates from the positivist tradition that follows in his wake.[72] Indeed, the contrast between the two bodies of work and their critique is instructive for clarifying how post-war sociology broadly represents something of a qualitative regression internally to positivism. This is how we are to make sense of the observation that, although Adorno inveighs against sociological positivism for abandoning the emphatic notion of objectivity in the assumption that the regular is the lawful,

68. Adorno, 'Introduction to the Positivist Dispute', pp. 7–8.
69. Theodor W. Adorno, 'Marx and the Basic Categories of Sociological Theory: From a Seminar Transcript in the Summer Semester of 1962', trans. Verena Erlenbusch-Anderson and Chris O'Kane, in Bonefeld and O'Kane, eds, *Adorno and Marx*, pp. 241–51, here p. 241.
70. Adorno, 'Introduction to the Positivist Dispute', p. 42, and Adorno, 'Sociology and Empirical Research', in Adorno et al., *The Positivist Dispute in German Sociology*, pp. 68–86, here p. 77.
71. Jürgen Habermas, 'The Analytical Theory of Science and Dialectics: A Postscript to the Controversy between Popper and Adorno', in Adorno, et al., *The Positivist Dispute in German Sociology*, pp. 131–62, here pp. 136ff.
72. Durkheim, that is, developed a rather 'unusual theory for a positivist'. Beuter, '29. May 1956. Protokoll', p. 410.

he simultaneously argues that Durkheim 'had good reason for associating the statistical laws, to which he also adhered, with the *contrainte sociale* and even for recognizing in the latter the criterion of society's general law-like nature'.[73] Again, what is valuable in this conceptual schema is precisely its inbuilt ambiguity, paradoxes and contradictions. For all its shortcomings and oversights, or, better, owing to its particular shortcomings and oversights, Durkheim's sociology 'is superior to the main current of positivism' of the post-war period, a current 'that has today achieved near total dominance'.[74]

Understood as part of a critique of sociological categories, Adorno's encounter with Durkheim leverages the deficient truth of the discipline's concepts against the untrue conditions it masks in scientistic replication. It drives one of these concepts, that of the social fact, to the point of its critical inflection. This will receive its most significant, though not comprehensive, philosophical treatment in his unfinished magnum opus, *Aesthetic Theory*. However, when viewed within the context of Adorno's interventions into sociology, Durkheim's concept helps underscore and subvert a complicity the discipline sustains. By integrating compulsion into his sociological framework and base object, by claiming this compulsion 'to be the essence of the social as such', Durkheim gives expression, however limited and incomplete, to 'the guilt of reification', a guilt to which contemporary sociology naively pleads its innocence.

73. Adorno, 'Sociology and Empirical Social Research', p. 75.
74. Adorno, 'Einleitung zu Durkheim', p. 250.

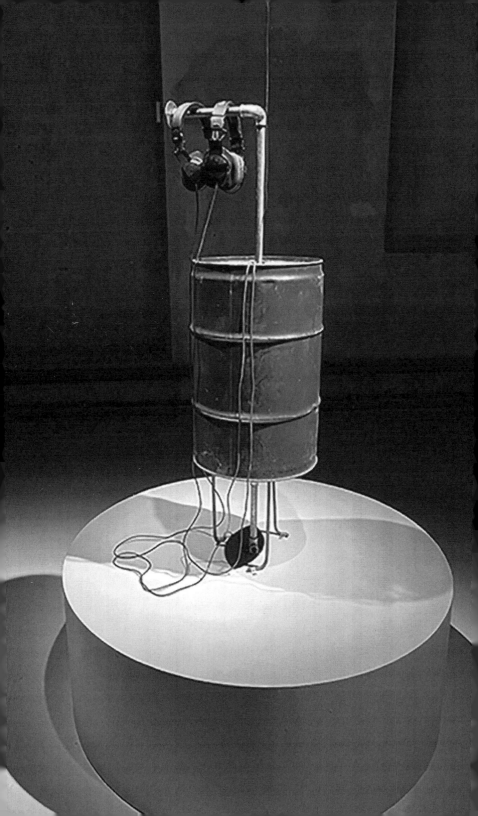

PANEL

DERRIDA'S *ARCHIVE FEVER*,
THIRTY YEARS ON

Introduction

SIMON WORTHAM

Before its publication, Derrida's *Mal d'archive/Archive Fever*
was first presented as a lecture thirty years ago, in 1994, at
the Courtauld Institute in London under a title that, perhaps
tellingly, was almost immediately to be modified. It featured as
part of a conference on 'The Question of Archives' organized
by René Major and Elisabeth Roudinesco and sponsored by the
Freud Museum and the International Society for the History
of Psychiatry and Psychoanalysis. In recalling this text thirty
years later,[1] we should start by remembering what the book
tries to tell us about remembrance itself, not least in respect of
psychoanalysis.

The history of psychoanalysis, Derrida notes, is not just a
history of events and discoveries found in archival records which
might subsequently be construed as an exterior deposit and secondary support to psychoanalysis itself. Rather, psychoanalysis is
itself, over time, a thinking of the archive – or, put differently, it
is *archive-thinking*. The archive is thus not an empty receptacle, a
strong box into which psychoanalysis is deposited after the fact,
since for psychoanalysis there is no archive that precedes its own

---

1. This panel took place at the Zaha Hadid Foundation, in Clerkenwell, London, on 15
February 2024.

achivo-analysis or 'archive-fever'. The psychoanalytic archive is at the same time the psychoanalysis of the archive. Where the archive is concerned, there is little prospect of neat detachment from the 'object' of psychoanalytic thought.

In *Archive Fever*, the death drive is found at – or as – the foundation of the Freudian archive. This drive is the discovery which prevents psychoanalysis from becoming, as Freud pretended to worry, merely wasted paper and ink. As Derrida reminds us, however, it is the death drive that encourages the destruction of memory and that therefore threatens to ruin the archive as monumental deposit. If the novelty of the death drive is invoked by Freud as the principal reason for conserving the findings of psychoanalysis, then the deposit works against itself, in principle, driven by a febrile amnesia, feverishly incinerating what is consigned to archivable memory in a way that flouts the economic principle of the archive as a reckonable accumulation, founded stably on some exterior substrate.

For Derrida, the concept of the archive is deconstructable. The archive takes place through a situation of domiciliation. Typically, this opens an institutional trajectory leading from the private to the public, but, as Derrida points out, not necessarily from the secret to the non-secret, since the archived text always keeps something in reserve beyond the merely informational or evidential. The archive is formed via domiciliary acts of consigning, but while this aims to produce a coherent corpus in which each artefact or element translates itself in terms of a unified or ideal arrangement, nevertheless such activity observes a double economy. Every archive is at once conservative and institutive, wanting to reflect and defend the givenness of that which it inherits while engaging in highly artificial processes and acts of selection in order to do so. Indeed, since it must make its own law, the archive is as radically inventive as it is conservative.

For Derrida, the archivization of psychoanalysis is complexly shaped by the technologies of communication and recording available in Freud's time. Since the question of the archive is found at the origin of the history of psychoanalysis, these technologies cannot be thought to lie merely on the outside of psychoanalysis or to come along afterwards. Rather, the technical conditions of archivization produce as much as record the event (and advent) of psychoanalysis. The entire terrain of the psychoanalytic archive would be transformed, Derrida insists, had Freud and his followers enjoyed access to electronic media, electronic devices and communications characterizing the era of computers, faxes and email. (Written in the mid-1990s, this vocabularly has inevitably dated, and one wonders what Derrida might have made of Instagram – not least the etymology of its neological name: Insta-gram.) Writing technologies do not determine merely the conservational recording of psychoanalysis, but instead produce the very institution of its archivable event.

Derrida does not subscribe to a simple idea of the archive as a violation of the event itself, something that amortizes its original importance. Indeed, the question of psychoanalysis *as* archive already entails a thinking of the event to come. Turning attention to Yosef Hayim Yerushalmi's *Freud's Moses: Judaism Terminable and Interminable*, Derrida makes an event of the book by showing how it resists its own archivable status or value as a work of scholarship. This happens at the point that Yerushalmi departs from the classical norms and conventions of scholarly writing in order to apostrophize inventively according to a complex fiction which hails Freud's spectre, only to register the futility of asking of it whether psychoanalysis might be called a Jewish science. This may never be knowable, Yerushalmi speculates, and would in any case depend on future work, including decisions still to come concerning the very definition of 'Jewish' and 'science'. Thus, the relationship of such a science to its own archive begins by coming (back) from an unpredictably spectral future, from the *l'avenir* of a complexly unreconciled history.

All of this means that any event commemorating *Archive Fever* 'thirty years on' is already problematic, to the extent that the usual work of memorialization does not readily observe the double law of the archive itself. The title of our panel, *'Archive Fever – Thirty Years On'* points, first, to the thirty years that have passed since 1994, but there is also, surely, a lasting hint of the thirty years to come: not just the thirty years ahead of us, between now and the middle of the twenty-first century, but perhaps also the thirty years since 1994 that may be said to await us still.

11

Archive Fever afterthought

ISABELLE ALFANDARY

On 5 June 1994, at the Courtauld Institute in London, Derrida
gave a lecture originally entitled 'The Concept of Archive: A
Freudian Impression', now better known as *Mal d'archive/Archive
Fever*. In what follows, I would like to return to certain aspects
of this text, which was a landmark in Derrida's thinking, in an
attempt to make its unaltered topicality heard and to measure
certain after-effects.

Archive Fever has the effect of a subtle rhapsody between
questions, a knot of threads that intertwine like a dreamlike
constellation: the death drive, time, Judaism, psychoanalysis – to
name but the few most important.

Archive Fever is first and foremost a reflection on psychoanalysis – a 'certain psychoanalysis' as Derrida calls it, Freudian
psychoanalysis – but it is also a text that Derrida devotes to
Freud, more than thirty years after 'Freud and the Scene of
Writing', first published in French in 1967 in *Writing and Difference*. In *Archive Fever*, Derrida concludes that the meaning of
Freud's contribution consists in a new way of thinking about the
archive.[1] He understands Freudian psychoanalysis as a 'theory

1. Jacques Derrida, *Archive Fever*, trans. Eric Prenowitz, Chicago University Press,
Chicago IL, 1998 pp. 4, 10.

of the archive' and 'a science of the archive'. This new science
of the archive throws the economy of the historical archive into
turmoil, upsetting the philosophical concept of the archive and
even disturbing the concept of science.

By giving a new consistency to the archive, psychoanalysis
allows us to glimpse – and forces us to confront – the violent
contradiction it conceals. Without the hypothesis of the
mnemic trace, from which Freud deduced the hypotheis of
the unconscious, and without the theory of differred action
(*Nachträglichkeit*), thinking about the archive would literally and
figuratively remain a dead letter. The archive has an astounding
effect on the categories of metaphysics.

Freud is thinking afresh – or, as I will come back to later,
almost afresh – about the 'archontic principle', a metaphysical
principle if ever there was one. Derrida recalls that the Greek
word *arkheion* designates 'initially a house, a domicile, an
address, the residence of the superior magistrates, the *archons*,
those who commanded'.[2] Who were the archons? They were
the guardians of the archive, who not only ensured its physical
preservation, but were also endowed with the power to interpret
it. It was the interpretation of the fundamental law contained
in the archive that gave them power over the city. The archive is
originally political: it is the archive that institutes the polis, and
constitutes power as such.

Against what Derrida calls the 'archontic' conception of the
archive, the psychoanalytic archive inaugurates a new conception
of temporality, a new 'philosophy of time', to use psychoanalyst
Jean Laplanche's expression.[3] From now on, we have to reckon
with the differred action, what Freud called *Nachträglichkeit*, and
which he discovered in one of his first cases, that of Emma. In

---

2. Ibid., p. 2.
3. Jean Laplanche, *Problématiques VI: L'après-coup*, PUF, Paris, 2006, p. 24, my
translation.

his first theory of trauma, Freud discovered that 'the memory of the scene (which will prove traumatic) exerts a deferred action'.[4] The concept of deferred action, which applies to trauma, paves the way for a renewed conception of memory, inseparable from a particular way of thinking about writing, inscription and reinscription, and the translation of traces. In a letter to Fliess dated 6 December 1896, Freud writes:

> You know that I work with the hypothesis that our psychic mechanism is generated by stratification, the available material of memory traces being reordered from time to time according to new relationships, a rewriting. What is essentially new in my theory, then, is the assertion that memory is not present in a single way, but multiple, deposited in various kinds of signs... I want to emphasize that the inscriptions that follow one another present the psychic production of successive periods of life. It is at the boundary between two of these periods that the translation of psychic material must take place.[5]

The Freudian 'logic of the after-the-fact' disrupts the thought of metaphysical time and questions the very concept of memory:

> Is it not true that the logic of the after-the-fact (Nachtäglichkeit), which is not only at the heart of psychoanalysis, but even, literally, the sinews of all 'deferred' obedience, turns out to disrupt, disturb, entangle forever the reassuring distinction between the two terms of this alternative, as between the past and the future, that is to say, between the three actual presents, which would be the past present, the present present, and the future present? In any case, there would be no future without repetition.[6]

Psychoanalysis is a power of deconstruction: its thinking about the archive disrupts the stable, homogeneous metaphysical categories of time, its line, its arrow, its unity. But there is more. At the same time, psychoanalysis is discovering the violence

4. Ibid., p. 54.
5. *The Complete Letters of Sigmund Freud to Wilhelm Fliess (1887–1904)*, Harvard University Press, Cambridge MA and London, 1985, p. 207.
6. Derrida, *Archive Fever*, pp. 80, 83.

inherent in any archive, the death drive it conceals. As Derrida notes, the archive is anything but memory:

> Because the archive, if this word or this figure can be stabilized so as to take on a signification, will never be either memory or anamnesis as spontaneous, alive and internal experience. On the contrary: the archive takes place at the place of originary and structural breakdown of the said memory.[7]

In so far as it implies an outside and a technique of repetition, the archive is threatened by the logic of repetition, or even the repetition compulsion, another Freudian name for the death drive. The archive is always and *a priori* working against itself. In its very structure, it is a failure to remember, a hypomnesis. Archive fever is the archive put to death by the archive itself. This is one of the meanings of the expression 'archive fever' (*mal d'archive*) that gives the book its title.

The archive as Derrida thinks of it in relation to psychoanalysis is not just about the anamnesis of the past, far from it:

> In an enigmatic sense, which will clarify itself *perhaps* (perhaps, because nothing should be sure here, for essential reasons), the question of the archive is not, we repeat, a question of the past. It is not the question of a concept dealing with the past that might *already* be at our disposal or not at our disposal, *an archivable concept of the archive.* It is a question of the future, the question of the future itself, the question of a response, of a promise and of a responsibility for tomorrow. The archive: if we want to know what that will have meant, we will only know in times to come.[8]

The archive raises the question of the future of the past, the law of necessity and the indeterminacy of the future. This question was addressed by Freud in an article that we might call testamentary, since it appeared in 1938 and deals with the end of the cure: 'Analysis Terminable and Interminable'.[9] On several

---

7. Ibid., p. 11.
8. Ibid., p. 36.
9. Sigmund Freud, 'Analysis Terminable and Interminable', in *The Standard Edition of*

occasions in this text, Freud uses the term *Schicksaal* (fate).
According to Freud, what happens at the end of the treatment
leaves open and undecidable the question of the future of the
drive, of the individual's exposure to the future. Not only does
Freud consider that it is never certain that analysis can liquidate
a drive conflict durably or definitively, but one can know nothing
about the ways in which a patient exposed to the vicissitudes
of life will see his/her neurosis flare up or not. What Freud
conceives as 'the subsequent destiny of a cure' remains opaque,
suspended in the unknown fate of the infantile archive – the
so-called unconscious – whose facets cannot all have been
worked on, facets that always threaten to resurface and show
their pathogenic force. In this late and relatively pessimistic
essay, Freud oscillates between two terms that are also found
in Derridean thinking on the archive: 'root' and 'destiny': terms
that denote Freud's concern with the psychic determinism
that psychoanalysis seeks to analyse and dissolve if necessary.
Reading Freud's text, it would be an understatement to say that
the psyche – that is, the infantile archive – is without guarantee.

One instance of Derrida's archive constantly present in *Archive
Fever* is that of filiation, a filiation which is almost exclusively
from father to son, from grandfather to grandson. For once,
Derrida dedicates his lecture to 'his sons', twice mentioning
his father's first name, Hayim, and each of his grandfathers',
Moses and Abraham. Although he notes what he calls at the end
of *Archive Fever* 'patriarchal logic',[10] he does not fundamentally
seem to distance himself from it, with the sole exception of the
mention of Anna, Freud's daughter.

Archive Fever is shaped by the question of the father as *arkhe*,
as 'commandment' and 'commencement', to use the two initial

the Complete Psychological Works of Sigmund Freud, Volume XXIII: *Moses and Monotheism,
an Outline of Psycho-Analysis and Other Works*, Hogarth Press, London, 1964, pp. 211–53.
   10. Derrida, *Archive Fever*, p. 95.

parts of Derrida's definition of the archive. The question of
the archive is the question of inheritance, of a transmission,
a succession that falls to the son whether he likes it or not,
whether he is aware of it or not. *Archive Fever* is hence haunted by
spectres and doubles – fathers and sons, fathers and brothers –
punctuated by scenes of interpellation and interlocution beyond
death. The spectres include: the dead father of the Freudian
horde in *Totem and Taboo*, as well as Hamlet's murdered father,
who returns to exhort revenge on his son in Shakespeare's play;
the spectre of Freud himself, whom Yosef Hayim Yerushalmi,
an American historian, addresses in his monologue, to obtain
from him the admission of the Jewish character of the science
of psychoanalysis; the spectre of Gradiva, with whom Jensen's
character Hanold converses; and the secret dialogue *in absentia*
that Derrida maintains with Freud himself throughout *Archive
Fever*, obliquely, through interposed exegesis and commentaries.
One of Derrida's doubles is Yerushalmi, who can in many ways
be seen as Derrida's *doppelgänger*, heir to Freudism and Judaism
in the same and different ways. Derrida dedicates his lecture to
him. Yerushalmi was invited to the conference, but was unable
to present his paper, which was read *in absentia*.

In any case, 'the structure of the archive is *spectral*', writes
Derrida. *Archive Fever* could have been entitled *Spectres de Freud*,
if the title had not already been taken. Indeed, Derrida notes
that Freud, like Marx, put his 'scientific positivism ... at the
service of his declared hauntedness and unavowed fear'. Far from
turning away from spectres and telepathy, delirium and hal-
lucinations, Freud sought to account for them: 'Courageously, in
as scientific, critical, and positive a fashion as possible.'[11] Derrida
returns to the Freudian commentary on Jensen's short story, and
to Freud's own story of a doctor who, having lost a patient, saw

---

11. Ibid., pp. 84–5.

her return to his practice some years later – the doctor, it turned out, being Freud himself. (It was in fact the patient's sister, but for a moment Freud tells himself that it is true 'that the dead can come back'.

By declaring 'truth' spectral in a Freudian context, Derrida is not unaware that he is echoing deconstruction – 'his' deconstruction, if I dare call it that – for which *Of Grammatology* laid the foundation stone, and which Freud's name spectrally saturates by its absence. The alliance of words ('spectral truth') has the effect, for the reader, of a joint effraction and repetition: if the formula is striking, the idea belongs to the archive of Derridean thought thus revisited.[12] Speaking of Freud and to Freud, Derrida speaks of himself and to himself. In his lecture, he is seized by the logic of the archive, which works underground. *Archive Fever* is the occasion for a recapitulation: of the double movement of repetition, the compulsion to repeat, and the retranslation of Derrida's thought from the repression of writing. In this respect, the archive is not just another metonymy for the names of *différance* (trace, hymen, parergon, etc.). The Freudian concept of the archive repeats and upsets, 'impresses' in every sense of the word, confuses and leaves its mark on Derridean deconstruction.

Archive fever is the metaphysical fever that psychoanalysis helps to highlight and criticize, but it is also the fever from which it *ultimately* suffers as well as itself. According to Derrida, Freud, who was passionate about archaeology, had an absolute dream of the archive. 'It is the nearly ecstatic instant Freud dreams of, when the very success of the dig must sign the effacement of the archivist: *the origin then speaks by itself.* The *arkhe* appears in the nude, without archive.'[13] Freud is not immune to the metaphysical dream itself, the dream of pure *phone* to the exclusion of

---

12. Ibid., p. 87.
13. Ibid., p. 92.

all writing, in the erasure of all trace. The archive is also the site of psychoanalysis's most formidable and unexpected complicity with metaphysics: 'Because when the stones begin talking to set things straight in Freud's excavational reverie, it is as if the archaeologist had succeeded in putting the archivist out of work. And the translator too, of course. Yet these stones are archives, and everyone knows that archives do not speak.'[14]

No one is immune. The fever of the archive that Derrida elaborates throughout his lecture is a fever that can be understood not only as the fever of the drive for death, aggression and destruction that eats away at the archive, but also as the fever of the burning desire for origin.

> It is to burn with a passion. It is never to rest, interminably, from searching for the archive right where it slips away. It is to run after the archive, even if there's too much of it, right where something in it anarchives itself. It is to have a compulsive, repetitive, and nostalgic desire for the archive, an irrepressible desire to return to the origin, a homesickness, a nostalgia for the return to the most archaic place of absolute commencement.[15]

Against all odds, Derrida supports the Freudian thesis of *The Man Moses and the Monotheist Religion*, that of the murder of the founder of monotheism by his people, even if historiography rejects it, for the One, writes Derrida, implies violence: 'As soon as there is the One, there is murder, wounding, trau-matism. *L'Un se garde de l'autre.* The One guards against/keeps some of the other.'[16] The question of the One, or, to put it another way, the question of 'more than one', is the question of deconstruction, and undoubtedly also of psychoanalysis. The logic of the One is a mortifying logic, a logic that necessarily turns against itself, against the other:

---

14. Ibid., pp. 109–10.
15. Ibid., p. 93.
16. Ibid., p. 78.

At once, at the same time, but in a same time that is out of joint, the One forgets to remember itself to itself, it keeps and erases the archive of this injustice that it is. Of this violence that it does. *L'Un se fait violence.* The One makes itself violence. It violates and does violence to itself but it also institutes itself as violence. It becomes what it is, the very violence that it does to itself. Self-determination as violence. *L'Un se garde de l'autre pour se faire violence (because* it makes itself violence and *so as* to make itself violence).[17]

Archive Fever is a book about Freud, but it's also a book about Judaism, about the intertwining of psychoanalysis and Judaism, which Yerushalmi repeatedly refers to as 'Jewish science'. Does the Jewish people have a privileged, chosen relationship with the archive as Yerushalmi argues? A people of the Abrahamic covenant, renewed in the very body in the ritual of circumcision, a people of the Book, of the Philippson Biblie, which Freud's father, Jakob, notoriously gave his son on his 35th birthday, signing and recording the Jewish obligation to remember: Yizkor. The archive is inseparable from an obligation ('obligation of the archive'); it is literally a ligature ('ob-ligation'), reminiscent of the episode of Isaac's ligation that Derrida commented on at length in *The Gift of Death*. Derrida does not, however, follow Yerushalmi in assigning Israel alone 'the duty to remember'.[18]

Thinking about this justice, I wonder, trembling, if they are just, the sentences which reserve for Israel *both* the future *and* the past *as such, both* hope ('the anticipation of a specific hope for the future') *and* the duty of memory ('the injunction to remember'), assignation which would be felt by Israel *alone,* Israel as a *people* and Israel in its *totality* ('only in Israel and nowhere else ... as a religious imperative to an entire people'...). Like the question of the proper name, the question of exemplarity, which I put aside earlier, here situates the place of all violences. Because if it is just to remember the future and

---

17. Ibid.
18. Ibid., pp. 78, 77.

the injunction to remember, namely the archontic injunction to
guard and to gather the archive, it is no less just to remember
the others, the other others and the others in oneself, and that
the other peoples could say the same thing in another way.
And that *tout autre est tout autre,* as we can say in French: every
other is every other other, is altogether other.[19]

The archive is a power of dissemination, a 'disseminating
fission from which the archontic principle and the concept of
the archive and the concept in general suffer, from the principle on'.[20] In so far as it inscribes repetition in the future, it
is potentially mortifying: 'If repetition is thus inscribed at the
heart of the future to come, one must also import there, *in the
same stroke*, the death drive, the violence of forgetting, *super-
repression* (suppression and repression), the anarchive, in short,
the possibility of putting to death the very thing, whatever
its name.'[21] The archive is inseparable from its risk, the risk
of forgetting, but even more so from the risk of violence and
death it carries. In any case, there can be no future without
repetition, without a repetition that cannot but be understood
as a compulsion to repeat, as a death drive.

What is at stake in the archive is the indeterminacy of the
event, of the arriving as well as the returning:

and it gives vertigo while giving the only condition on which
the future to come remains what it is: it is to come. The
condition on which the future remains to come is not only
that it not be known, but that it not be *knowable as such*. Its
determination should no longer come under the order of
knowledge or of a horizon of preknowledge but rather a coming
or an event which one *allows* or *incites* to come (without *seeing*
anything come) in an experience which is heterogeneous to
all taking note, as to any horizon of waiting as such: that is to
say, to all stabilizable theorems as such. It is a question of this
performative to come whose archive no longer has any relation

---

19. Ibid., p. 77.
20. Ibid., pp. 84–5.
21. Ibid., p. 79.

to the record of what is, to the record of the presence of what is or will have been *actually* present. I call this *the messianic,* and I distinguish it radically from all messianism.[22]

This is why the archive is inseparable from the questions of responsibility that Derrida addressed in the early 1990s, from the question of secrecy as well as that of hospitality. The seminar *Répondre – du secret,* published this year in France, echoes in many pages the lecture that we are celebrating today.

Discreetly, *Archive Fever* raises the question of Jewish heritage – including Derrida's relationship with his 'own' Judaism – and the posterity of Judaism after what the American historian Raul Hilberg called 'the destruction of the European Jews'. We know that Hitler's regime not only destroyed in autos-da-fé the sacred books of Judaism, and those written by Jewish authors, but also wished to preserve the relics of the decimated communities, relics such as those still on display today in Prague's Jewish Museum, next to one of Europe's oldest Jewish cemeteries. The title of the book by the American Jewish historian and Marrano specialist Yerushalmi, which Derrida repeats several times, echoes the famous Freudian article mentioned earlier: *Judaism Terminable and Interminable.*[23] Derrida notes: 'But Yerushalmi clearly marks that if Judaism is terminable, Jewishness is interminable. It can survive Judaism. It can survive it as a heritage, which is to say, in a sense, *not without archive,* even if this archive should remain without substrate and without actuality.'[24] How can we understand this double negation? 'The Marrano hypothesis', as the contemporary French philosopher Marc Goldschmit calls it, haunts *Archive Fever,* doubling and embodying the becoming of the archive.[25]

22. Ibid., p. 75.
23. Yosef Hayim Yerushalmi, *Freud's Moses: Judaism Terminable and Interminable,* Yale University Press, New Haven CT, 1993.
24. Ibid., p. 75.
25. Marc Goldschmit, *L'hypothèse du marrane: Le théâtre judéo-chrétien de la pensée politique,* Éditions du Félin, Paris, 2014.

One does not necessarily have to be Jewish to be a
Marrano. The archive elaborated by the discoverer of the unconscious is, above all, an archive insignificant to the subject
himself, the Marrano of the unconscious archive.

> If we call a Marrano, by figure of speech, anyone who
> remains faithful to a secret he has not chosen, even where
> he lives, with the inhabitant or the occupier, with the first
> or the second arrival, even where he stays without saying
> *no*, but without identifying himself with belonging, well, in
> the night without contrary where the radical absence of any
> historical witness keeps him, in the dominant culture which
> by definition has the calendar, this secret keeps the Marrano
> even before the latter keeps it. ...
> By the luck of this anachrony, Marranos in any case,
> Marranos that we are, whether we want to be, whether we
> want to be or not, and having an incalculable number of
> ages, hours and years, of untimely stories, at once greater
> and smaller than each other, still waiting for each other,
> we would be ceaselessly younger and older, in a final word,
> infinitely finite.[26]

The unconscious that Freud discovers is not only individual: as he explains in *Man Moses,* it is not limited to the
subject's own infantile trauma, but is also transindividual
and transgenerational. The science founded by Freud is
intended to be the science of this 'mysterious transmission',
the science of the archive as understood by Derrida in
Archive Fever.

In the *Prière d'insérer* accompanying the book, Derrida
asks: 'Why re-elaborate a concept of archive today? In one
and the same configuration, at once technical and political,
ethical and legal?' The archive or archives? – the historians
and archivists with whom I work keep reminding me that
they are to be understood in the plural – are more than

---

26. Jacques Derrida, *Apories*, Galilée, Paris, 1996, pp. 140–41, my translation.

ever to be elaborated, consulted and questioned, at a time when democracy is on the verge of yielding to the attacks of the most hateful and insane ideologies, and revisionism is seeking to gain the upper hand over the work of facts and historians. The topicality of *Archive Fever* is intact, even more burning today than it was thirty years ago.

12

Ceasefire now

ERIC PRENOWITZ

> Without even the memory of a translation, once the
> intense work of translation has succeeded.[1]

So I read or reread *Archive Fever*, more or less, in my own way,
in honour of this event, thirty years after, which is to say, you
might conclude, that I had not read it since... Yes, that's what
I seem to be saying, that I had not read it since the day, which
was anything but a day, thirty years ago, when I made my way
through it that first and in some sense only time. I will try here
to describe my complicated relation to this book, to the reading
or translation of this book, but I have to say from the start that
I have a spectral sense of having been the first – and worse, or
perhaps better, in some sense, the only – reader of *Archive Fever*.
Now this spectral and clearly preposterous feeling has a flip side,
which is that I also feel as if I will have been the last person to
read, to have read this book.

---

1. Jacques Derrida, *Archive Fever*, trans. Eric Prenowitz, Chicago University Press,
Chicago IL, p. 93.

An/amnesis

This sense that I have not read the book since having translated
it may not be strictly speaking true, but it is not false either; it
is perhaps what Freud would call a 'historical fiction'. I have not
picked it up also, I suspect, because I never put it down. As if I
have never stopped reading and rereading this text for the past
thirty years. Because one of the things I realized in reading it
recently, one of the things I received and thought for the first
time, was that somehow I had myself become a strange spectral
archive of the text. Though I think with envy of the actors,
perhaps not too far from here, who are said to have reconstituted
Shakespeare's texts from memory for the publication of the
'bad' quartos. But never forget: 'The bad *pharmakon* can always
parasitize the good *pharmakon*.'[2] I recall that there is also a
practice of rememoration as mental archivization, mneme and
anamnesis, in *Fahrenheit 451*, a cold war parable about censorship,
technology... and archive fever. No, if I am an archive, it is the
fever that predominates. I am mostly an archive of oblivion, as
the French word *oubli* is sometimes translated into English, a
translation that is inept in a number of ways, but that I nonetheless like in so far as it preserves and even accentuates the plosive
-*ble* or the -*oble*, a thing that I feel only just consents to enter
into language from the abyss.

If I do have a sense of having been the first reader of this text,
it is a complicated sense that goes beyond the actual historical
fact that I probably was indeed the first reader, something that
is in itself very odd: as if the author of a text could never be
in addition its reader, or in any case its first reader. I suppose
this lines up with Derrida's critique of the auto-affection of
s'entendre parler, hearing oneself speak, we might here say *se lire*

---

2. Jacques Derrida, 'The Rhetoric of Drugs', trans. Michael Israel, in *Points...*, Stanford
University Press, Stanford CA, 1995, p. 234.

écrire: reading oneself write, while writing, as if reading and
writing happened simultaneously, inseparably, if not read-writing
oneself. Of course, Derrida will have none of it, as for example
in *Speech and Phenomena*, when he points out, with Husserl, that
the 'absolute proximity' between signifier and signified that the
latter imagines to pertain in speech is 'broken when, instead
of hearing myself speak, I see myself write or gesture [*au lieu
de m'entendre parler, je me vois écrire ou signifier par gestes*]', and
then contra Husserl, that there can be no such proximity even
in speech.[3] At the very least, this supports the idea that reading
is not necessarily congruent, synonymous or simultaneous with
writing, inseparable from writing – and that in some sense
Derrida could not have been the first reader of the text he wrote.

Derrida said to me at one point, during the process of
translation or shortly after, something to the effect that he had
more than one mode of writing, suggesting that he felt this
piece belonged to a second category, relatively loosely composed
compared with some of his more traditionally philosophical
texts. This was my impression, in any case, and it made me think
of the astonishing way he wrote his seminars, each week a two-
hour monologue with very little ad lib read from the printout of
what he had typed into his computer in the preceding days, as I
understood it; a kind of hybrid 'oral' writing that was destined
not for publication, but to be read aloud, a script to be acted,
professed, by the *ex cathedra* character of the professor. On the
other hand, there's the equally astonishing way his apparently
extemporaneous performances in interviews seem to come out
fully formed, practically typeset, proof-read and camera-ready,
even when he is clearly inventing something new or unexpected.
I hesitate, nonetheless, to relate this anecdote not just because it

---

3. Jacques Derrida, *Speech and Phenomena*, Northwestern University Press, Evanston
IL, 1973, p. 80 [*La Voix et le phénomène*, Presses Universitaires de France, Paris, 1967, p.
90].

may be fiction or projection, but because it might seem to lend
some authorial authority to an idea that is as widespread as it is
false: that Derrida or Derrida's work made a 'turn', in fact several
'turns' in chronological, historical, biographical time. The odd
thing, though it is hardly reassuring, is that the two dominant
discourses on purported Derridian turns contradict each other,
and arguably go some way to cancelling each other out: on the
one hand, Derrida's only serious, properly philosophical work
was his early work, after which he gave in to impressionistic
purple prose, but on the other, it was only in the 1990s that he
seriously engaged with ethical, if still not properly political,
concerns. Suffice it to say that while it's indisputable that there
are important, vital changes in and across Derrida's work, these
two tales of turns are 'at least wrong'.

At the same time, Derrida of course also deconstructs the
border or the opposition between reading and writing, and in
this sense any writing is also a reading; there are only different
mixes of reading and writing. A corollary to this is that while a
text may always already be read, it is also always unread – that is,
it always also remains readable, to (be) read.

I do recall Derrida asking me at one point what I thought of
the text, and my distinct feeling at the time, despite the fact that I
was incapable of responding in any coherent manner (for obvious
reasons, but also for perhaps less obvious reasons I'll return to in
a second), was that while he was no doubt asking me this to be
courteous, and maybe with some genuine curiosity, it also seemed
to me, and it is impossible to know where to draw the line, that
he wanted to hear my reaction in a more disarming or disarmed
way, as if I would be able to see or read it, thanks to my structural
position as first reader, better than he. This took place, in my
memory, at the Théâtre du Soleil, so all bets are off, it is certainly
a 'reconstruction', whatever that is, or an oneiric projection on the
screen of a screen memory, I would even say 'wishful thinking', a

phrase that makes 'wish fulfilment' come across differently too. But it left me with the impression that he really was hoping to learn in that moment what it was he had written.

I also remember the time, perhaps the same time, I am not sure, when he asked me whether I had read the text before translating it. My feeling is that he may well have wanted simply to confirm that I had read it before translating it, but there was maybe a hint of surprise in his voice, as if he had surmised, from something I had said or not said, that I might have translated it blind, so to speak, that for me the translating in fact preceded the reading; that I translated first and read later, or perhaps that they happened simultaneously or coterminously, the one in the other or through the other. Or maybe that I translated it without reading it at all, if I can put it that way. Now I felt I could not confess all these things at once, on the spot, as I would have had to do, so I nodded and smiled and said that yes of course I had read first. Or maybe it was just something he was curious to know, maybe it was a kind of informal research project of his – he certainly had lots of translators – and it would make sense to think that translation was not just a vital part of his thinking, the way translation is one of his privileged metaphors, if it's a metaphor, for deconstruction, but that he was also interested in the mundane practice of translation: how it happens or plays out, how it thinks of itself, or does not, as the case may be, as it goes.

I was a student of Hélène Cixous, and I will return to her in a second, as I always do, to say something I think is important: a shout, actually, a shout-out to Hélène Cixous! I had more or less translated a few texts of hers when she asked me one day in 1994, it must have been, if I would like to translate a text that was not yet called *Mal d'archive*, by Jacques Derrida. The text did not even exist, I think, because what ensued was a kind of comical *chassé-croisé* with Derrida across Paris over several months – he would give me the latest instalment and I would give him back the previous one in English – with a series of meetings in locations including the bar at the *Lutétia*, the *Théâtre du Soleil* and Cixous's living room.

So while I am not sure even today that I have really read *Archive Fever*, this may be the only thing I will ever have read, this and a few texts by Cixous that I have translated. Translating is a paradigm of reading. And, as Derrida points out, there is no line between literacy and illiteracy: a text worthy of the name teaches you how to read it *as you're reading it*, however paradoxical and impossible that sounds.

Now in the guise of a reading or a translation, a couple of shout-outs, perhaps call-outs as the case may be, and it's not exactly the same thing.

Shouts and calls

Thirty years on?! I want to shout: But what's wrong with you people?! Why haven't you read Derrida??! It's the most important thinking thing that has ever been done; it changes everything about our lives and our politics and our minds and our relations. And we are still hearing that it is obscure or it is just wordplay? And not only on the Internet, but scholars for goodness' sake are still saying it's this or it's that, a little game, some self-indulgent navel-gazing, cautious reformism, fence-sitting or a dangerous nihilism?

There is an amusing essay in which Roland Barthes vents about people chucking adjectives at music – he calls adjectives the 'poorest of linguistic categories' and in effect describes 'predication', or its 'most facile and trivial form', the epithet, as an impotent phallocratic 'bulwark' against the threat of castration.[4] There is indeed something about Derrida's work that

---

4. Roland Barthes, 'The Grain of the Voice', trans. Stephen Heath, in *Image Music Text*, Hill & Wang, New York, 1977, p. 179.

provokes or reveals not just an intellectual but a kind of sexual poverty in many of those who probably need it the most, the self-obsessed speculative miserliness of a masculine libidinal economy that is not just threatened by the idea that this unruly object will deprive it of its most precious attribute, but more fundamentally by the prospect it offers of an entirely different economy that does not even recognize the zero-sum rules of phallocratic subjectivity. In fact, what Barthes proposes as a 'little parlour game' ('talk about a piece of music without using a single adjective'[5]) could serve, *mutatis mutandis*, as a rather telling description of what's big about deconstruction. Take Derrida's much-cited but little-heeded declaration that 'All sentences of the type "deconstruction is X" or "deconstruction is not X" *a priori* miss the point, which is to say that they are at least false',[6] which suggests that predication itself is an ideological presupposition to be deconstructed, while the 'at least' actually does some deconstruction here, refusing a binary right/wrong opposition by gesturing at something it can't quite say with (binary) language ('even wronger than wrong').

So what are we waiting for? These last thirty years for almost nothing are a massive symptom of a massive failure in the human capacity to transform itself. There is no excuse and not a minute to waste.

So, without waiting, here's a first deconstructive postulate or insight, in under a minute, that we'll need shortly: *Nothing is pure!* In other words, there is never a pure, homogeneous, self-identical inside; there's always outside on the inside and vice versa. There are no atoms, there is complexity, there is impurity, all the way down. One consequence with regard to the archive is what Derrida calls our 'technological condition': technology is not

5. Ibid.
6. Jacques Derrida, 'Letter to a Japanese Friend', trans. David Wood and Andrew Benjamin, in Peggy Kamus and Elizabeth Rottenberg, eds, *Psyche: Inventions of the Other*, vol. II, Stanford University Press, Stanford CA, 2008, p. 5.

some dead, machine-like thing that is outside or added on to our living, organic, natural inside bodies: we are originally, in every atom, organic-technological mixtures. In particular, our internal, living memory is also a kind of mechanical archival technology, an outside on the inside. This is one of Derrida's main points in *Archive Fever*: he speaks of a '*domestic outside*', and a '*prosthesis of the inside*',[7] and it links back to some of his earliest work.

But first my second shout, my second shout-out that is also a call-out: *Archive Fever* is wonderful and important, but what about Derrida's books on Cixous? The second of these, *Geneses, Genealogies, Genres and Genius*, published in 2003, is literally also about archives: its subtitle is *The Secrets of the Archive*. It is in many ways a follow-up or a sequel to *Archive Fever*. And, in any case, Derrida's books on Cixous are arguably the most beautiful and extraordinary and profound books he wrote, and so they are among the most beautiful and extraordinary and profound books anyone wrote. Let me cite a single, literal reprise in *Geneses* of *mal d'archive*. Derrida is reflecting on the gift by Cixous to the French National Library of her archives, what Derrida calls her 'archivable corpus'. He wants both to offer a reading of the genius of the work and to point out that it cannot be circumscribed: it is open to the future, yet to be read. In this context, Derrida formulates a paradoxical law of archivization:

> the belonging of an element to an ensemble never excludes the inclusion of that ensemble itself (the bigger thing) in the element it is supposed to contain (the smaller thing). The smaller thing is big with the bigger thing, the small is bigger than the bigger.

He goes on: 'Jonas is bigger than the Whale, and the corpus remains immeasurably vaster than the library that is supposed to archive it. This too is *mal d'archive*.'[8]

7. Derrida, *Archive Fever*, p. 19.
8. Jacques Derrida, *Geneses, Genealogies, Genres and Genius: The Secrets of the Archive*, trans. Beverley Bie Brahic, Edinburgh University Press, Edinburgh, 2006, pp. 71–2

Ceasefever

There are many things in *Archive Fever*, but one we must not
neglect today is Derrida's own very forceful call-out of Y.H.
Yerushalmi concerning a certain reflection on 'Israel', if I can put
it that way. It is a deeply political, ethical and philosophical call-
out that has a strange, sad, perhaps predictable topicality today,
thirty years later. In *Archive Fever* Derrida reads Yerushalmi's
book *Freud's Moses*, and he points out a last atom of something
like essentialism: a very sophisticated, erudite atom admittedly,
but an atom of – let's maybe not call it Jewish supremacy, but –
Jewish singularity at the least. Derrida calls Yerushalmi out for
insisting on something hard, something small, maybe, but hard
– and by 'hard' I mean something that does not end in a question
mark, but sits as a stable, unambiguous predicate affixed to the
'Jewish' subject.

Derrida refuses forcefully to admit this attempt to impose an
incontestable or invariable definition, to mark in a univocal way
an identity. It has everything to do with the archive, of course,
and there's a kind of overdetermined irony in that Yerushalmi
wants to box into a fixed Jewish identity an engaged commitment to the past and an openness to the future that sounds,
at least, a lot like what Derrida wants to assign or leave to the
archive in general.

There is a crucial and a fascinating complication, however,
which has to do with translation and identity. Near the end
of the Foreword, which is to say about two-thirds through the
book, Derrida quotes Yerushalmi as follows: 'Only in Israel and
nowhere else is the injunction to remember felt as a religious
imperative to an entire people.'[9] In other words Jews, Judaism or
Jewishness have a unique relation to the past, a unique obligation

---

(*Genèses, généalogies, genres et le génie: Les secrets de l'archive*, Galilée, Paris, 2003, p. 84),
translation modified.
   9. Derrida, *Archive Fever*, p. 76.

to archive, no doubt, and to recall the past, unique to them and no others. Derrida responds with a question: 'How can one not tremble before this sentence? I wonder if it is just. Who could ever be assured, by what archive, that it is just, this sentence?'[10] A few pages earlier, Derrida had quoted Yerushalmi saying something similar about a uniquely Jewish relation to the future: 'the anticipation of a specific hope for the future'.[11] These are the essentialist atoms in Yerushalmi's view, this singular relation to the past and the future, the proprietary property of 'Israel', the defining characteristics that belong to it alone. Further on, Derrida continues:

> I wonder, trembling, if they are just, the sentences which reserve for Israel *both* the future *and* the past *as such*, *both* hope ('the anticipation of a specific hope for the future') *and* the duty of memory ('the injunction to remember'), assignation which would be felt by Israel *alone*, Israel as a *people* and Israel in its *totality* ('only in Israel and nowhere else' 'as a religious imperative to an entire people').[12]

What Derrida is criticizing here is a certain kind of identity politics, in effect, the assignation of essential attributes exclusively to one group over all others.

Now this is partly a question of words, of the definition of words. If 'Israel' were an open, universal label used simply to designate anyone who shared these attributes, that would be fine. Derrida says: 'Unless, in the logic of this election, one were to call by the *unique* name of Israel all the places and all the peoples who would be ready to recognize themselves in this anticipation and in this injunction.'[13] But this, of course, is not what Yerushalmi had in mind: he was confident he knew what the Israeli people and places were, who was in and who was out.

10. Ibid.
11. Ibid., p. 73.
12. Ibid., p. 77.
13. Ibid.

Then Derrida says this lovely thing: that one must care not only for the past or the archive, and for the future, but also for the 'other': other people, people who are not oneself or members of one's own group:

> if it is just to remember the future and the injunction to remember … it is no less just to remember the others, the other others and the others in oneself, and that the other peoples could say the same thing – in another way.[14]

Note this phrase, 'the same thing – in another way': you might think it means having one's cake and eating it too, but it is critically important here, a question of translation and the untranslatable, and what we might call impure differences, as we'll see in a second.

Derrida then proposes an idiomatic expression in French to express this complicated, double relation to the other: *tout autre est tout autre*. This means that every other person is totally other, totally different from me, with a radical difference that I must respect and that I cannot dominate or domesticate – I would translate this into psychoanalytic terms as 'desire', a relation to the other as fundamentally different to and non-reappropriable by me. On the other hand, this expression also means that every other person is the equivalent to every other person, *tout autre est tout autre*, that people are all fundamentally the same – and this I would translate as 'identification', when I see myself in you and can thus internalize or incorporate you in me. Freud strove to keep these two relations separate, at least at the critical – that is, the (hetero-)normative – moments of his theory. In Derrida's condensed, idiomatic expression, they can never be entirely disentangled.

Derrida then boils his critique of essentialism down to a critique of what he calls the 'One', with a capital O: the One

---

14. Ibid.

as a rigidly defined and pure identity, a unique and totalizing assemblage. This is not a good thing, in Derrida's book: 'As soon as there is the One, there is murder, wounding, traumatism.'[15] It is hard not to think of Israel/Palestine. And he goes on to propose several further idiomatic expressions to formulate in a pithy manner the destructive and self-destructive paradox of the constitution of any essentialist One. For example *l'Un se fait violence*,[16] a phrase that means both that the One does violence to itself, and that it constitutes itself as violence – aimed at the other.

What happens next is surprising: after Derrida writes that 'Only in French can this be said and thus archived in such an *economical* fashion',[17] there is a footnote that complicates this passage in an important way. In the note, Derrida recounts that after he had delivered his lecture, Geoff Bennington pointed out to him that this insistence on the idiomatic singularity of these French phrases seemed to contradict his more general critique of essentialist identity. 'Only in French', Derrida says on page 78, about his economical idiomatic expressions, and you might think this is not entirely different from Yerushalmi saying, on page 76, as quoted by Derrida, 'only in Israel'. This is significant because Derrida recognizes the apparent contradiction of his position, and thus it is the occasion for him to make the case for deconstructive non-essentialist differences, even non-essentialist uniquenesses – one could say, non-proprietary identities.

You might think that Derrida's radical anti-essentialism would leave him unable to make any distinctions at all: if there's no essential trait of Jewishness, then we might as well retire the term. And the same for any other identity-marker. And yet while demystifying binary oppositions, deconstruction leaves us with

15. Ibid., p. 78.
16. Ibid.
17. Ibid.

a whole world of differences between different combinations or superpositions of binary opposites. There is never a simple, pure inside, but there are very different mixes of inside and outside. So the fact that none is pure does not mean they are all the same; quite the contrary. Derrida suggests in effect that we think of Jewishness as a kind of idiomatic singularity, which he models in and as the text: untranslatable, I should know, yet translatable, untranslatably French, and yet by the same token strange to itself, somehow more French and less French. But there is no reason we cannot call this 'French', so long as we understand there is no essential truth there.

It is a question of the relation to the past, of distinguishing between 'the most detestable revisionisms' and 'the most legitimate, necessary, and courageous rewritings of history'.[18] And of the relation to the future. Not only to demand ceasefires in the face of all the relentless archive fevers and the 'great holocaustic tragedies of our modern history and historiography',[19] but to deconstruct every essentialist, every ethno-national-essentialist, sovereignty. Thanks to translation, idioms always cohabitate, two in one or one in two, identification and desire, equality and difference, like two nations in a single state, or two states in a shared land. There are no other futures.

---

18. Ibid., p. 90.
19. Ibid.

13

Forgiving archives

NAOMI WALTHAM-SMITH

As I speak about the silences of the archive, in mid-February 2024, few archives remain undamaged in Gaza. Many have been completely destroyed.[1] How does Derrida's *Mal d'archive/Archive Fever* speak to this conjuncture and to the future in which the traces of the Gazan archive will be read – in which, moreover, it will be necessary to continue reckoning with the destruction wrought by colonialism and by slavery on the archive? To begin to address why thirty years after its publication, *Mal d'archive* – with its insistence that the archive cannot be disentangled from *mal*, from harm, evil, malady, delirium – might still resonate today, and in thirty years to come, I want to pose a slightly different, at first blush tangential question: is it possible to read the Derridean archive *without Mal d'archive*? That is, without taking into account its thought of the archive? In a roundabout way to addressing the silences of the archive, I want to take as my starting point the stakes if we risk forgetting *Mal d'archive* when reading the Derridean archive today, or, conversely, if we fold into our way of reading, a Derridean concept of the archive,

---

1. Librarians and Archivists with Palestine, 'Israeli Damage to Archives, Libraries, and Museums in Gaza' October 2023–January 2024: A Preliminary Report', 1 February 2024, https://librarianswithpalestine.org/wp-content/uploads/2024/02/LAP-Gaza-Report-2024.pdf.

thereby making the archive in a way complicit with the conditions of its analysis.

In *Mal d'archive* Derrida argues against forgetting the archive: 'if this content concerns in fact historiography, there is', he suggests, 'no good method or epistemology' to justify bracketing it off.[2] Including what is archived in the reading of the archive provides a minimal 'stability'.

> To want to speak about psychoanalysis, to claim to do the history of psychoanalysis from a purely psychoanalytic point of view, purified of all psychoanalysis, to the point of believing one could erase the traces of any Freudian impression, is like claiming the right to speak without knowing what one's speaking about, without even wanting to hear anything about it. (*MA* 88/54–5)

Ten years after Derrida's death, Geoffrey Bennington writes over this passage, adhering to Derrida's rule of thumb that 'this structure is not only valid for the history of psychoanalysis [but] at least for all the so-called social or human sciences' (*MA* 88/55). According to this generalizability, Bennington substitutes the word 'deconstruction' for 'psychoanalysis', noting that the Derridean archive on this account poses incalculably even greater challenges for intellectual history than the Freudian one.[3] This, then, is the central point that he wants to make at a point twenty years after Derrida went into the archive: that one cannot read the archive without having taken into account *in the very reading* the ways in which that archive has transformed the concept of archive and its structure, hence remaking the very object of historical analysis. Upping the ante – and thus giving a demonstration of this imperative to read Derrida from within the horizon of deconstruction – Bennington suggests that

---

2. Jacques Derrida, *Mal d'archive: une impression freudienne*, Galilée, Paris, 1995, p. 88; *Archive Fever*, trans. Eric Prenowitz, Chicago University Press, Chicago IL, 1996, p. 54. Hereafter cited in the text as *MA*.

3. Geoffrey Bennington, 'Derrida's Archive', *Theory, Culture & Society*, vol. 31, no. 7–8, 2014, p. 114.

any account that does not explicitly attempt to take account of those structures ... is *ipso facto* involved in the archival repression or suppression of what I would call the quasi-transcendental question itself, where the 'quasi-' already implies something more and more complicated than a mere apparent historicization of the transcendental.[4]

But I cannot help but wonder whether, in a justified desire to explode an all-too-common assumption that we ought to be done with Derrida and that those who grieved him should be done with their mourning, Bennington does not, by the end of this analysis, fall into the other trap, the one against which he cautions at its start. Deploying the 'lurid' image of the putting an escaped tiger back in its cage, he warns that one should not be so quick to put a text back into its (historical) context or at least, even if that is a productive way to go, not without 'accounting for its initial escape'.[5] This escape figures the necessity for ideas to exceed any given context if there is to be such a thing as reading. There must be a promise of the future (of reading, reaction, response at some point in the future) for there to be an archive in the first place. Just as the archive should not – or, more accurately, cannot – be consigned or confined to the past, the Derridean tiger will always already have been out of the cage – and not by accident. It is too late to contain the feverish mayhem. This leads Bennington to make a claim of the archive, or at least the Derridean one, the archive *of* Derrida, which is necessarily both a subjective and objective genitive, the archive of what he has said and written, and the archive that he has conceptualized. Bennington claims, then, that the archive is not a historical object since one cannot get outside it; its historicity is already folded in. When everyone is telling him to be done with mourning, he wants to insist, militantly, on his melancholia: in

---

4. Ibid., p. 118.
5. Ibid., p. 111.

other words, that one can never be done with, repress or suppress deconstruction now that it is out of the cage.

And yet it is this escape of the idea that seems to elude Bennington precisely when he most insists on it and at the same time insists on the irreducible quasi-transcendental ruin of the idea. He argues that one cannot engage the Derridean archive outside of this economy of the quasi-transcendental, according to which any reading of deconstruction will always already have been irreducibly contaminated by deconstructive reading: no reading of deconstruction (objective genitive) without the reading of deconstruction (subjective genitive). Bennington thus ends up insisting, in spite of himself, that the Derridean idea cannot in fact escape its own context. As soon as it is archived and thus taken outside itself, both what is archived and the event, the act, of archiving can only be understood by reference to the Derridean idea of the archive, on which presumably this quasi-transcendental logic operates retroactively.

What I want to do here is to read the Derridean archive according to another deconstruction – deconstruction from the point of view of the aneconomical, the unconditional, the impossible; not as the negation of the possible, of its economization, but as the infinitization of its calculus. In this way, I also hope to read Bennington in a way that takes account of the radical transformation in and effected by his own thought, in the cage with Derrida – specifically of the unconditional in whose name conditional and conditioned acts are done without ever coinciding with it, of what Bennington analyses by way of the Derridean syntagm *digne de ce nom*.[6] The irony is that Bennington raised this very question – and Derrida answered him – at the end of the lecture 'Mal d'archive'. As a footnote to the published text reveals:

6. See, for example, *Scatter 1: The Politics of Politics in Foucault, Heidegger, and Derrida*, Fordham University Press, New York, 2016, pp. 250ff.

At the end of this lecture, not without irony, I imagine, with as much depth as astonishment but, as always, with an intractable lucidity, Geoffrey Bennington remarked to me that by underlining, and first by bringing into play, such an untranslatability, I risked repeating the gesture I seemed to put into question in the hands of the other, namely, the affirmation of the unique or of the idiom. (*MA* 125n/78–9 n15)

Derrida records that he responded by clarifying that he wanted to affirm both the singularity of the idiom *and* the impurity of *différance* as irreducibly necessary.

Ironically, perhaps, in order to address these questions of the unconditional and the impossible in relation to the archive, and to reading the Derridean archive today, I want to put *Mal d'archive*, if not back its historical cage, then at least in dialogue with the context of Derrida's own thinking and intellectual activity in the 1990s. Specifically, I will explore all too briefly the entanglement of *Mal d'archive* with the two-year seminar 'Le parjure et le pardon' given at the École des hautes études en sciences sociales (EHESS) in 1997–99.[7] In this way, I believe we can say something more incisive about what Derrida's thought of the archive might mean for us today, as archives and their destruction become increasingly intense sites of political struggle, of imperialist repression, suppression, and instruments of violent oppression. What do these two intertwined strands of thought have to say to us about the silences and silencings of archives today and in the future?

In that footnote to Bennington's question in *Mal d'archive*, Derrida underscores the importance of the double affirmation of the infinite and the finite, the conditional and the unconditional,

---

7. The seminar was published as Jacques Derrida, *Le parjure et le pardon. Volume I. Séminaire (1997–1998)*, ed. Ginette Michaud, Nicholas Cotton and Rodrigo Therezo, Seuil, Paris, 2019; *Perjury and Pardon, Volume I*, trans. David Wills, Chicago University Press, Chicago IL, 2022; and *Le parjure et le pardon. Volume II. Séminaire (1997–1998)*, ed. Ginette Michaud, Nicholas Cotton, and Rodrigo Therezo, Seuil, Paris, 2019; *Perjury and Pardon, Volume II*, trans. David Wills, Chicago University Press, Chicago IL, 2022) The first volume is hereafter cited in the text as *PP1*.

the possible and the impossible: 'What one does next, both with
this affirmation, and with this impurity, is precisely where all
of politics comes in' (*MA* 125n/79 n15). In her entry 'Archive' for
A Lexicon of Political Concepts, Ariella Azoulay lets – even drives
– Derrida out of the cage. In a way arguably no less marked by
the Derridean transformation of concepts than Bennington's
reading, she at first gives Derrida credit for breaking open the
repressive constitution of the archive consigned to the past by
the powerful and instead putting it in the hands of those 'citizens' who will enter, read, engage with archives and create new
ones according to other logics not authorized by the state.

> In his book *Archive Fever*, Derrida presents the figure of the archon,
> guardian of the documents, the sentry as one of the three pylons
> upholding the archive. The other two are the place and the law.
> The discussion of sentries enables Derrida to slightly reduce the
> abstractedness of the archive idea, and speak of figures of power
> that legislate, repeat their law and enforce it. However, his look at
> the sentries from the outside, as those who set the archive borders,
> lets them fool him at times and force him to look at the threshold
> from their point of view – namely inward, at the way in which
> they uphold the law of the archive and leave him, Citizen Derrida,
> outside, beyond its conceptualization. Derrida fools them in his
> turn, writing: 'It is a question of the future [*d'avenir*], the question
> of the future itself, the question of a response, of a promise and of a
> responsibility for tomorrow.'[8]

But then she outbids Derrida:

> Archive fever crosses borders. It is manifested in the claim for access
> to that which is kept in the archive, and no less in partaking in
> the practice of the archive through founding archives of new sorts,
> such that do not enable the dominant type of archive, founded by
> the State, to go on determining what the archive is. Archive fever
> challenges traditional protocol by which official archives have
> functioned and continue to do so. It proposes new models of sharing
> the documents stored therein in ways that requires one to think

---

8. Ariella Azoulay, 'Archive', in *A Lexicon of Political Concepts* 1, www.politicalconcepts.
org/archive-ariella-azoulay. The Derrida quotation is from *MA* 60/36.

the public's right to the archive not as external to the archive but rather as an essential part of it, of its character, of its raison d'être. 'Archive Fever' is not simply a problematic translation of a book title, Derrida's *Mal d'archive*. It is a real phenomenon that Derrida ignores.

Instead of blunting the cruelty by safeguarding it in the inaccessible or not-yet accessible past, Azoulay wants to rethink the archive 'from the fever'. To be fair to Derrida, he does speak of the necessity of democratizing the archive, in a footnote (*MA* 15–16n/4 n1) and he chastises Freud for stopping short in deconstructing the archontic principle of the archive by constraining equality and liberty to the community of brothers and to patriarchal filiation.

The question of justice and the politics of the archive come to the fore in Derrida's reflections on the impossibility of forgiveness in *Le parjure et le pardon*. Let me lay out some of the entanglements and resonances: that is, how the deconstruction of forgiveness is radically transforming the deconstruction of the archive and vice versa. First, there is a historical-contextual link: in the summer of 1998, in the interval between the two years of the seminar, Derrida participated in the 'Refiguring the Archive' seminar series in Johannesburg, which was devoted to *Mal d'archive*.[9] The transcribed interventions show him engaging in exchanges about the preservation and destruction of archives in expressly political terms and with reference to the Truth and Reconciliation Commission, which would be a central focus in the first three sessions of his seminar's second year.

Second, there is a textual link when Derrida refers to *Mal d'archive* in the Ninth Session of the first year:

I one day spoke of archive fever [*mal d'archive*], that was my title, but a seminar on forgiveness is also a seminar on the archive of harm [*archive du mal*] – and moreover, in *Archive Fever* I never thought it

9. The proceedings were published as Carolyn Hamilton, Verne Harris, Jane Taylor, Michele Pickover, Graeme Reid and Razia Saleh, eds, *Refiguring the Archive*, Kluwer, Dordrecht, 2002.

was possible to separate the two, whence the title: archive 'sickness' (as desire and passion for the archive) and the archive of harm, of a harm that pertains to some crime or past suffering, of course, but also to the terrible law of the archiving machine, which selects, filters, orders and forgets, suppresses, represses, destroys as much as it keeps. (*PP1* 241–2/264–5)

Derrida was already in *Mal d'archive* anticipating the question of forgiveness and how it can, or cannot, be distinguished from other categories with which it shares a family resemblance (excuse, amnesty, indulgence, acquittal, forgetting) when he describes the archive an act of resistance to forgetting (*MA* 122 n2/76 n14), even if forgetfulness is necessarily at the heart of remembering 'by heart' (27/12). He then immediately goes on to characterize as repressive the totalizing gathering that he will starkly criticize as an obstacle to peaceful coexistence between Israelis and Palestinians in an address to the 37th Colloquium of French-Speaking Jews in Paris in December 1998, drawing on the material of the seminar on 'Le parjure et le pardon'.[10] In *Mal d'archive* parallels are already being drawn between the deconstruction of the sovereignty of the archive and the deconstruction of nation-state sovereignty.

In both cases – of archivization and of forgiveness – Derrida speaks of a theatricalization, of a scene and staging, and crucially of their limits and what is beyond them. Moreover, it is surely no coincidence that this theatre and the limits of its scene are a matter of a barely audible voice (*PP1* 220/165) or what is expressly played out as an offstage voice-off in the second year of the seminar. What Derrida calls the 'silent vocation' of *mal d'archive* (*MA* 25/10), I am suggesting, may be heard to resonate in the still,

---

10. Jacques Derrida, 'Leçon: Avouer – l'impossible', in *Comment vivre ensemble? Actes du XXXVIIe Colloque des intellectuels juifs de langue française*, ed. Jean Halpérin and Nelly Hansson, Albin Michel, Paris, 2001, pp. 181–216; 'Avowing – The Impossible: Returns, Repentance, and Reconciliation: A Lesson', trans. Gil Anidjar, in Elisabeth Weber, ed., *Living Together: Jacques Derrida's Communities of Violence and Peace*, Fordham University Press, New York, 2013, pp. 18–41.

small voice, whisper or murmur in *Le Parjure et la pardon* which points to an outside of the scene, to an experience before or long after the scene of *pardonnance*, or where there is no need to enter it or its economy. The notion of 'record' operates as a pivot between the archive and the 'accord' or 'misericordia' said to contaminate and conditionalize forgiveness with the economy of excuse, of recognition, identification and reciprocity:

> The event, if there is one, leaves its trace, it operates only in the place of interruption, of breathlessness. The best is here closest to the worst, to its opposite, *perhaps* as always, and the most alive speech is closest to immaculate silence, that of absolute muteness or automatic grammar – or the recording of a message machine – or the machinic trace – or the record of a CD. Subtitle of the seminar, perhaps: what is the heart? Record and *misericord*, memory (*recordatio*), trace of evil and evil of the trace, forgiveness of the heart and the archive machine. (*PP1* 220/165)

To the extent that this scarcely audible voice points to a harm that has irreversibly and culpably come to pass, to a scene already played and kept in memory, that is decidedly offstage, it has an affinity with the death drive, which *Mal d'archive*, at first blush, appears to distinguish from the finite, calculable limits of the archive.

> Such is the scene, at once within and beyond all staging: Freud can only justify the apparently useless expenditure of paper, ink, and typographic printing, in other words, the laborious investment in the archive, by putting forward the novelty of his discovery, the very one which provokes so much resistance, and first of all in himself, and precisely because its silent vocation is to burn the archive and to incite amnesia, thus refuting the economic principle of the archive, aiming to ruin the archive as accumulation and capitalization of memory on some substrate and in an exterior place. (*MA* 17/12)

Between forgiveness and the archive there is an economy of harm and its unconditional outbidding. In the seminar this is encapsulated in a refrain, *y a pas d'mal*, discerned at the heart of all excuse and forgiveness too, which he imagines is sung until the voice is hoarse and out of breath and which he associates with the 'stuck needle of the archive' (*PP1* 216/162). This little phrase, *y a pas d'mal*, relieves the harm, tending towards leaving nothing to forgive, even as the elision of the *ne* points to the possibility of affirming the harm. The apparent distinction in *Mal d'archive* between repression and suppression (*MA* 49–50/28), between unconscious denial and the knowingly destructive, thus seems to map onto the fragile distinction between the excusable in which fault tends to be negated and sublated, and a fault so unforgivable (precisely for being committed knowingly) that its forgiveness is unconditional, beyond all calculus of the excuse. The opposition is deconstructed, however, as Derrida shows that forgiveness is repeatedly drawn into the economy of excuse, forgetting and so on through an identificatory recognition of the fault, and there is also a feverish, hyperbolic infinitization of the latter's calculating drive that absorbs death and forgiveness without return there where they ought to remain aneconomic, unconditional.

This leads Derrida to conclude that, like the death drive, which operates in silence to efface its traces (*MA* 24/10), the impossible is anarchivic. Both efface the negation that is set in motion. In the Third Session of the first year of *Le parjure et le pardon*, Derrida deviated from his script to ask: 'What trace does [the im-possible] leave? What documents does it leave? What archive?' (*PP1* 115 n1/76 n15). His answer:

> That im-possible is characterized, precisely, by the impossibility of leaving the most minimal archive and, perhaps, pure forgiveness in the sense I am speaking of it here is a forgiveness that is bound not to leave any archive. (*PP1* 115 n2/76 n16)

Where does that leave the politics of the archive? The archive must be allowed to get away from its context, to escape its silences, to go outside the scenes of repression and suppression and touch the unheard-of. Like Azoulay, Saidiya Hartman, well known for her work on the archives of slavery, is interested in responses in the future to the constitutive impossible silence of the archive in the past – responses that, through creative practice, make, remake and abolish archives according to unauthorized logics.[11] How, asks Hartman, in a quiet voice that nonetheless lets the Derridean tiger out of its cage for our own times, 'How does one tell impossible stories?'

11. On the method of 'critical fabulation', see Saidiya Hartman, 'Venus in Two Acts', *Small Axe* 26, 2008, pp. 1–14.

Image credits

PREFACE

Kote Mikaberidze, *My Grandmother*, 1927, film, 67 mins (Georgian National Film Centre), installation still, CINEMAKEK, Bozar, Brussels, October 2023.

WORKSHOPS

Maxi Mamani (aka Bartolina Xixa), *Dry Twig, Permanent Coloniality*, 2019, video, 5 mins, still, installation shot, El Sur: Narratives of Extraction, Färgfabriken, Stockholm, April 2024.

LECTURES

Louisiana Seafood, Bergen, Norway, February 2024.

OUTTAKES

Outtake, Millennium Bridge Gateshead, March 2024.

PANEL

Ana Alenso, *Blood of the Earth*, 2019, installation with audio, in El Sur: Narratives of Extraction, Färgfabriken, Stockholm, April 2024.

All photographs by Peter Osborne.

Contributors

ANNA ARGIRÒ is a PhD candidate in Modern European Philosophy in CRMEP working on a thesis on Hannah Arendt. She holds a BA and MA from La Sapienza–University of Rome and was a visiting scholar at the Hannah Arendt Center for Politics and Humanities at Bard College, New York in 2022. She is currently co-editing a special issue of the journal *Studies in the Maternal* based on a symposium she co-organized at Kingston University on the topics of sexuality, motherhood and social reproduction.

ISABELLE ALFANDARY is Professor of American Literature and Critical Theory at Sorbonne Nouvelle University, philosopher and psychoanalyst. She was the former President of Collège international de philosophie (2016–19). She co-founded and runs the Northwestern University Sorbonne Nouvelle Institute for Psychoanalysis. Her books include *Derrida–Lacan: L'écriture entre psychanalyse et deconstruction* (2016) and *Science et fiction chez Freud: Quelle épistémomogie pour la psychanalyse?* (2021).

ÉRIC ALLIEZ is Professor of Contemporary French Philosophy in the CRMEP and a Professor in the Department of Philosophy at the University of Paris–8, Saint-Denis. His most recent books are *Duchamp with (and against) Lacan: Essay on Queer Mutology* (2022) and *Wars and Capital* (with Maurizio Lazzarato, 2018).

HOWARD CAYGILL is Professor of Modern European Philosophy in the CRMEP. His next book *The Aesthetics of Madness* will be published by Bloomsbury in spring 2025.

DANIEL GOTTLIEB is a translator and doctoral candidate in Modern European Philosophy at the CRMEP, working on a thesis on the history and politics of the concept of tradition in nineteenth-century German philosophy and law. He was the co-editor (with Cooper Francis) of Volume 5 of the CRMEP Books series, *Institution: Critical Histories of Law* (2023).

LOUIS HARTNOLL completed an AHRC-funded PhD on Theodor W. Adorno's philosophy and social theory at the CRMEP, during which he spent time as a visiting researcher at the Institute for Social Research, Frankfurt. He currently works as a lecturer in aesthetics, critical theory and philosophy at the University of Groningen and Leiden University; he is also an associate editor at the journal *Historical Materialism*. In autumn 2024 he will join the University of Amsterdam as a postdoctoral researcher supported by the Leverhulme Trust.

ORAZIO IRRERA is Maître de conférences in Philosophy at the University of Paris-8, Saint-Denis, and the director of a programme at the Collège international de philosophie. He is the co-editor of the journal *Materiali foucaultiani* and of the series of Foucault's earliest lectures courses currently appearing in French.

PETER OSBORNE is the Director of the CRMEP. His books include *The Politics of Time: Modernity and Avant-Garde* (1995, 2011), *Anywhere or Not at All: Philosophy of Contemporary Art* (2013), *The Postconceptual Condition* (2018) and *Crisis as Form* (2022).

ERIC PRENOWITZ teaches in the School of Fine Art, History of Art and Cultural Studies at the University of Leeds.

MORTEZA SAMANPOUR recently completed his PhD thesis – *Marx's 'Capital', From Colonialism to Contemporary Capitalism: Historical Ontology and Social Temporalities of the Reproduction Process* – at the CRMEP. His research focuses on the world-historical reproduction of capital and offers a political reading of social form through temporal analyses of Marx. He currently serves as the assistant editor for *Marx and Philosophy Review* and a member of the editorial board of the *Materialist Research Group*.

STELLA SANDFORD is a Professor of Modern European Philosophy in the CRMEP. Her most recent book is *Vegetal Sex: Philosophy of Plants* (2022). Her current research focuses on critically on conceptions of plant 'self' and 'agency'. She is also the author of *Plato and Sex* (2010), *How to Read Beauvoir* (2006) and *The Metaphysics of Love: Gender and Transcendence in Levinas* (2000).

NAOMI WALTHAM-SMITH is Professor of Music at the University of Oxford and Douglas Algar Tutorial Fellow at Merton College, Oxford. An interdisciplinary scholar working at the intersection of continental philosophy and sound studies, she is the author of *Music and Belonging Between Revolution and Restoration* (2017), *Shattering Biopolitics: Militant Listening and the Sound of Life* (2021), *Mapping (Post)colonial Paris by Ear* (2023), and *Free Listening* (2024).

SIMON WORTHAM is Professor of Critical Humanities at Kingston University. He is the author of books including *The Derrida Dictionary* (2010) and *Resistance and Psychoanalysis: Impossible Divisions* (2017), as well as, more recently, a trilogy of creative works published by Ma Bibliotheque: *The small*, *Early Mass*, and *Berlin W.*

Index